Civilised by beasts

CW01497430

MANCHESTER
1824
Manchester University Press

Civilised by beasts
Animals and urban change in nineteenth-century Dublin

Juliana Adelman

Manchester University Press

Published by Manchester University Press
Oxford Road, Manchester M13 9PL
www.manchesteruniversitypress.co.uk

British Library Cataloguing-in-Publication Data is available

ISBN 978 1 5261 4605 2 hardback
ISBN 978 1 5261 6070 6 paperback

First published by Manchester University Press in hardback 2020

This edition published 2021

The publisher has no responsibility for the persistence or accuracy of URLs for any external or third-party internet websites referred to in this book, and does not guarantee that any content on such websites is, or will remain, accurate or appropriate.

Typeset by Servis Filmsetting Ltd, Stockport, Cheshire

In memory of David Prifti (1961–2011)
One of the best human animals I have ever known

Contents

List of figures and tables   viii
Preface   x
Acknowledgements   xii

Introduction   1
1   Political zoology: class, religion and animal exploitation,
    1830–45   22
2   How to live on your pig: improvement and the poor during
    the Great Famine, 1845–50   62
3   The market metropolis: cattle and urban development,
    1850–65   91
4   Enforcing values and controlling animals: dogs, pigs and
    police, 1865–80   127
5   Progress or decline? Associating animals with urban
    success and failure, 1880–1900   168
Epilogue   199

Bibliography   207
Index   229

Figures and tables

Figures

0.1 Sackville Street *c.* 1820 by Samuel Brocas.   2
0.2 The former Emerald Dairy on the corner of Seville Place and Emerald Street.   12
0.3 A boy on a pony at the Smithfield Horse Fair in 2013.   13
0.4 Concentrations of animal businesses in Dublin during the nineteenth century.   15
1.1 Entrance gate to the Dublin Zoological Gardens, erected in 1831, as depicted in the *Dublin Penny Journal* (29 August 1835).   30
1.2 The elephant in the Zoological Gardens as depicted in the *Dublin Penny Journal* (29 August 1835).   31
1.3 An open pen and a cottage orné style enclosure in the Zoological Gardens as depicted in the *Dublin Penny Journal* (23 April 1836).   32
1.4 'Crinoline in Dublin', a print showing two ladies on a drive in the Phoenix Park.   43
1.5 'A car your honour—20 minutes or no money', a print showing Dublin cab drivers competing for fares.   44
1.6 'Returning from "The Brook"', a print showing overloaded cabs containing drunk passengers pulled by emaciated horses.   45
2.1 The opening of Alexis Soyer's famine soup kitchen in Dublin, 1847.   68
2.2 'A gentleman in difficulties': Daniel O'Connell is pulled in opposite directions by two pigs.   79
2.3 'Contrast the poor man's pig', drawing by Samuel Brocas.   81
3.1 Market stalls and secluded butcher shop in a Dublin lane, *c.* 1880.   97

3.2 Slaughters in Dublin slaughterhouses by month and type
of animal, 1865.   101
3.3 The new Dublin Cattle Market, opened in 1863 and
photographed *c*. 1890.   105
3.4 Map showing the relationship between Dublin city,
County Dublin and the province of Leinster.   107
3.5 Comparison of Sheet 6 of the Ordnance Survey maps of
Dublin between 1847 and 1864 showing development
around the new cattle market.   115
4.1 Prize winners at the first Dublin dog show, 1864.   131
4.2 'Put that in your pipe and smoke it': Cartoon showing a
man contemplating the new taxes on tobacco, income
and dogs.   138
4.3 'A new song on the saucy dogs of Ireland', written in
response to the new dog tax.   140
4.4 People and their animals fleeing the whiskey fire that
erupted in June of 1875 on Chamber Street in the south
inner city.   146
4.5 Numbers of pigs per one hundred persons in Dublin and
Ireland between 1865 and 1880.   152
5.1 'Dear, dirty, Dublin' as drawn by Thomas Fitzpatrick for
The Lepracaun in 1908.   169
5.2 Sackville Street *c*. 1890, showing the operation of horse
trams.   176
5.3 Trams in front of Trinity College Dublin, *c*. 1890.   177
5.4 'Registered Dairy' from the collection of cartoons drawn
by Thomas Fitzpatrick, *c*. 1905.   191

Table

3.1 Growth in Irish cattle numbers between 1855 and 1880.   108

Preface

This was supposed to be a book about zoology in Dublin. To para-phrase Gerald Durrell, once I let some of the city's ordinary animals into the book they proceeded to establish themselves and invite all their friends to share the chapters.[1] The result is, I believe, a much richer story about the nineteenth-century city.

The transformation of my research project had already begun when I received an intriguing notice from the Dublin City Council. My husband and I had applied for planning permission to convert our shed into an office and permission was granted on the condition that we did not use the shed 'for the keeping of pigs, poultry, pigeons, ponies or horses'. Here were the bye-laws that many nineteenth-century reformers fought for, still being deployed to maintain the boundary between urban and rural life in the twenty-first century. They begged the question of how and why the Council decided to prohibit keeping animals in sheds and what the city was like before it did so. This book begins to answer these questions and my hope is that the stories I tell here show how much recent urban change is about animals as well as people. Dublin provides an example of a conflict common to Western modernising cities in the nineteenth century. Urban development consumed more animals to serve human needs from food to com-panionship, just as modern ideas demanded that these animals be controlled, regulated, eliminated or concealed in the urban environ-ment. The resolution of this dilemma, and the compromises it created, had consequences for human and animal lives.

I have set the boundaries of my study by significant animal-related developments. The book opens not with the coronation of Queen Victoria but with the foundation of the Dublin Zoological Society in 1830. It closes in 1900 not because that is the end of the century but because in that year a second public health report on the city explicitly condemned the persistence of private slaughterhouses and dairy yards.

The cities that so many of us live in today reflect the accumulation of decisions made about animals more than a hundred years ago. If our forerunners had defined urban modernity differently or pursued different reform agendas, I might have a shed full of poultry, pigs or a pony. Instead, I'm here with my cats.

Note

1 Durrell was writing about how his family members invaded his intended work on the natural history of Corfu. See *The Corfu Trilogy* (London: Penguin, 2003 [1978]), p. 5.

Acknowledgements

My first debt is to my husband, Martin Fanning. While this book has been progressing (or stalling) we have been raising two children, two fish and two cats. We have lived in two houses. There has been joy and sorrow and boredom and excitement and plenty of fatigue. I can honestly say that I would not have finished this without him. We have been a team, sometimes more SpongeBob and Patrick than Batman and Robin. I am lucky, and grateful, to have him in my corner. Thank you to Aidan and Cian Fanning who made this book much more difficult but our lives much more interesting. Thanks also to my family. My mother, Lydia Rogers, has always been interested in animals and is the definition of 'life-long learner'. My father, Burt Adelman, has managed to continue to sound genuinely interested in all my pursuits no matter how arcane. My brother Ian and my sister Elizabeth have listened to me talk about this a lot without asking too often when I thought I might finish it. Thanks to the Ballymun Kickhams Mothers & Others football team and the Huffers and Puffers who have kept me sane and relatively fit, and are looking forward to the party I've promised them.

I would also like to thank many colleagues who have had the dubious privilege of reading draft chapters. Special thanks goes to the three anonymous reviewers for Manchester University Press who exemplified the best version of the peer review process. Their constructive comments helped to significantly improve this book. I also thank Kelly Adamson, Nina Bresnihan, Sean Connolly, David Dickson, Deirdre Foley, Lisa Griffith, Carole Holohan, Alice Jorgenson, Jimmy Kelly, Matthew Kelly, Leeann Lane, Sinead McNally, William Murphy, Cormac Ó Grada, Eoin O'Mahony, Ciaran O'Neill, Jennifer Redmond and Ciaran Wallace for reading all or part of the manuscript (sometimes more than once). Thanks to my writing wives, Catherine Cleary and Aoibheann Sweeney, who not only read drafts but whose encouragement and positivity made me believe this could actually get done. Mistakes and infelicitous phrasings are all my own.

Thanks to the Irish Research Council and to the Trinity Long Room Hub who funded my initial years of research on this project, as a postdoctoral fellow at Trinity College Dublin from 2008 to 2011. A semester research fellowship from St Patrick's College, Drumcondra helped to revive the flagging project and funding from the Faculty of Humanities and Social Sciences at Dublin City University helped to defray image costs.

I would like to thank the staff of the libraries and archives that have been critical to the research for this book. The National Library of Ireland became a home away from home and I have always found the library's staff helpful and professional. I hope the government gets around to funding them in the way they deserve. Thank you to the Royal College of Physicians in Ireland, the Dublin City Library and Archive, Early Printed Books and Manuscripts at Trinity College Dublin, the Royal Irish Academy, the Royal Dublin Society and the National Archives. Thanks also to the Guinness Brewery (Diageo), the Royal Society for the Prevention of Cruelty to Animals and the Dublin Society for the Prevention of Cruelty to Animals for allowing me to access their institutional records.

Thank you to Alun Richards at Manchester University Press for taking an interest in this book and shepherding it successfully through the process. He has been thorough and responsive.

Introduction

I was a little incredulous when I heard him say, that 'man had been civilized by wild beasts'.[1]

On 10 May 1830, Dr Whitley Stokes spoke to a hall packed with Dublin's 'gentlemen and noblemen'. He congratulated them on the foundation of a zoological society, a project he had been advocating for at least a year. Humans owed the beasts an education, he joked, because 'man had been civilized by wild beasts'. To convince those who were 'a little incredulous', Stokes explained that the first cities had been founded to protect humans from beasts. Ancient men and women gathered behind walls 'to guard against their inroads'.[2]

But no wall kept the beasts out of nineteenth-century Dublin. People like Stokes had brought thousands of them into the city to help create the urban civilisation that they enjoyed. Stokes had probably been hauled to his lecture by a horse, while an ox or a cow may have been killed in a city slaughterhouse to provide him with meat for his dinner. While he spoke, pigs settled down to sleep in sties and dogs wandered alleys looking for a scrap to eat. After his lecture he could have visited Madamoiselle D'Jeck, an elephant who drank champagne on the Royal Theatre's stage.[3] Yet historians of Dublin have ignored the city's beasts and in doing so they have missed much about urban life during the nineteenth century.

The city, past and present, has often appeared as a human-only space. Nineteenth-century city views, for example, often excluded

0.1. Sackville Street *c.* 1820 by Samuel Brocas. Note the emptiness
of the street and the absence of any animals other than horses.
Image courtesy of the National Library of Ireland.

urban animals. Samuel Brocas's depiction of Dublin's main thoroughfare in the 1820s (Sackville Street) shows a quiet scene where a few
well-behaved horses are the only animal presence (see Figure 0.1).
This image makes it difficult to imagine what every nineteenth-
century Dubliner knew: one street to the west lay a warren of butcher
shambles crowded with cattle, and even passengers in an elegant carriage could catch the scent of bone boilers and piggeries on the breeze.

Stokes expressed what Dorothee Brantz has called 'the fundamental
premise of modernity': that nature and culture are separate spheres.[4]
He also reminds us how important animals were, and are, to defining
what it means to be human.[5] His historical fantasy of cities created to
exclude wild beasts reflected the dominant ideas of his class about the
relationship between nature and culture, history and natural history,
urban and rural, human and animal. Such ideas did more than
provide flowery rhetoric for speakers launching new voluntary associations. Ideas about animals in particular shaped reform movements
in the city, altered its social and economic geography and affected the
daily lives of its human and animal inhabitants. This book examines
these ideas about animals, and how they changed, in Dublin between
1830 and 1900. I focus on ideas about human–animal relationships

and the role of animals in the city. The book shows that as the middle classes became increasingly engaged in urban improvement they also sought more control over animals and how they were used. Driven by concerns about order, poverty and public health, urban elites implemented new ways of dealing with urban animals, from dog licensing to slaughterhouse surveillance. In doing so they had to negotiate with Dubliners of all classes and with the physical presence of the animals themselves.[6] The chapters that follow explore this negotiation and how it is entangled with the story of urban change.

The city that Dubliners now live in is the result of attempts to resolve what Keith Thomas has called 'the human dilemma'. Thomas argued that the idea of human ascendancy over nature was gradually eroded in early modern England by the appearance of new ideas such as a duty of kindness to animals and an enthusiasm for 'wild nature'. These ideas led to the development of the human dilemma: the conflict between a desire to live in a civilisation dependent upon the exploitation of nature and a feeling that such exploitation is wrong. For Thomas, the emergence of this dilemma is a feature of modernity in England, where 'a mixture of compromise and concealment have so far prevented this conflict from having to be fully resolved'.[7] English society has invented ways to avoid the conflict by, for example, concealing the slaughter of food animals and doting on captive wild animals.[8] This book investigates the particular human dilemma that arose in Dublin and the acts of compromise and concealment it engendered.

The chapters that follow analyse Dublin from the foundation of the Zoological Society (1830) to the publication of a public health report condemning the presence of food animals (1900) in terms of ideas about human ascendancy and the emergence of the human dilemma. The idea of human ascendancy over animals persisted almost unchallenged well into the nineteenth century in Dublin. Poverty and politics made asserting distance between human and animal particularly important. The human dilemma that emerged became one of the driving forces behind urban improvement. Yet in contrast to early modern England, the most important ideas leading to 'compromise and concealment' in Victorian Dublin were not ideas of kindness towards animals or interest in nature but concerns about poverty, order and health. Certain forms of animal exploitation (private slaughter houses, home pig-rearing, uncontrolled dogs, small dairies) seemed to risk Dublin's reputation as a metropolis of Ireland

and to prevent the city from improving. To bourgeois Dubliners, such activities made Dublin seem uncivilised. Dublin could become more civilised, many thought, by introducing new ways of controlling and concealing certain types of animal exploitation. In other words, the more the city approached Stokes's idealised human-only civilisation the better it would be.

Most nineteenth-century cities housed a menagerie of domestic animals. Historians have demonstrated that new forms of transportation such as railways and trams expanded dependence on horses and did not eliminate the use of urban livestock to supply fresh meat and milk.[9] Bacon curing, rendering and tanning remained urban industries.[10] The urban fashions of pet-keeping and visiting animal spectacles expanded during the nineteenth century.[11] As a consequence, animals have begun to appear more frequently in urban history. For example, horses have been studied as symbols of social status but also urban technologies and drivers of economic systems.[12] Pets, particularly dogs, are now integrated into historical accounts of the rising urban middle classes during the nineteenth century.[13] Urban pigs and cattle feature in narratives of sanitary improvement.[14] City slaughterhouses have a wide literature of their own.[15]

Emphasising animals in the city in this narrative of Dublin provides a new perspective on familiar aspects of urban change including public health, transportation, policing and associational culture. This book reveals a Dublin integrated into the agricultural ebbs and flows of Ireland rather than insulated from them and a city where class, religion and politics affected attitudes towards pigs and cattle and dogs. Efforts to control, regulate and conceal the exploitation of animals also reflected middle-class ideas about the city's poor.

A focus on human exploitation of animals intersects with key areas of interest to urban historians. For example, animals provide another perspective on class relations because social class shapes a person's experience of the non-human world. Stephen Mosley has suggested that socio-environmental history should consider differences in 'access to nature and its resources', how social divisions might affect the way people experience their environment and how they think about environmental problems and dangers.[16] Such differences shaped experience of urban as well as rural life. The ability to exploit animals and the animals available for exploitation differed across social classes. Attempts to reform practices of animal-keeping in cities often brought the middle and lower classes into conflict and pitted immigrants against established residents.[17] Class also affects an urban resident's exposure to animal nuisances. Poor urban residents are most likely to suffer from rat infestations while wealthy suburbanites risk Lyme disease carried by deer ticks.[18] The burden of pollution, often from animal exploitation, fell (and falls) most heavily on the poor.[19] The urban lower classes often resisted efforts at reform because measures such as centralised abattoirs and laws about beating horses disproportionately affected their working lives.[20]

The expanding field of urban environmental history highlights the importance of animals to the creation and development of cities. William Cronon's ground-breaking history of Chicago, *Nature's Metropolis*, examines the impact of changes to meat processing on the city and its hinterland.[21] Clay McShane and Joel Tarr have demonstrated the degree to which reliance on horses shaped nineteenth-century American cities.[22] Yet few individual cities have been examined with a focus on the consumption, control and regulation of animals over time. Most urban histories of animals concentrate on specific categories of animals such as horses or pets.[23] Harriet Ritvo's work on animals in Victorian England has not been surpassed but its focus is not urban.[24] Peter Atkins's edited volume *Animal Cities* covers a variety of animals in multiple cities across the nineteenth century.[25] Hannah Velten's history of animals in London reveals the potential richness and variety of urban animal stories over many centuries but its episodic nature tells us less about urban change.[26] Frederick L. Brown's history of Seattle demonstrates the potential of studying animals in a single city. Brown argues that the process of sorting animals into categories, and the difficulty of agreeing on clear categories, played a crucial role in the creation of specific patterns of social and economic segregation.[27] Spatial history work on animals in other American cities shows the extent to which cities evolved in relation to ideas about where animal businesses should be.[28] More recently, Thomas Almeroth-Williams's *City of Beasts* has argued that animals contributed at least as much as humans to Georgian London's economic and social transformations.[29]

While this book is not strictly an urban environmental history, the stories within it suggest the entanglement of urban and rural worlds and the processes by which people try to separate the spheres of 'culture' and 'nature'.[30] As the following chapters will show, Dublin capitalised on the agricultural industries of Ireland, and these industries shaped the city in specific ways. New markets and networks of transportation were created to serve them and these changed the urban 'habitats' of humans.[31] Most of the regulations introduced around animals between 1830 and 1900 sought to alter the urban environment by removing animals, and their wastes, from it.

Animals provide a new perspective on the history of nineteenth-century Dublin. Despite its status as a nascent capital, historians have had much less to say about modern Dublin than other European cities. The historical narratives of nineteenth-century Dublin include the rise of the middle classes, the development of social segregation, rising nationalism in the Dublin Corporation, the growing problems of poverty and public health, and the city's modernity (or lack thereof).[32] The view of Victorian Dublin as a city in decline has lingered despite attempts to dislodge it.[33] All of these narratives have shaped this book in some way, but by using new sources and a new approach I have been able to show a different side of the city.

While evidence of Dublin's grinding poverty, high mortality rate and economic stagnation are plentiful, our understanding of the multi-layered experience of ordinary life in the city remains hazy.[34] Mary Daly's comprehensive social and economic history has not been challenged, but it begins in 1860 and is not concerned with the textures of daily life.[35] Jacinta Prunty's work on the Dublin slums is wonderfully detailed on the living conditions of Dublin's poor and the efforts to remedy them but this is only one side of the city.[36] Research on Dublin's middle classes continues to grow, balancing out the emphasis on poverty. For example, Susan Galavan's work on suburban housing development brings nuance to bourgeois home lives and demonstrates the significance of the building trade to the evolution of both the city and its middle classes.[37] Stephanie Rains's study of the city's shopping districts has given insight into ordinary lives but particularly the relationship between city and suburb.[38] A growing literature emphasises the engagement of Dublin's bourgeoisie in a vibrant scientific culture.[39]

But we are still missing the use of a wider range of sources, voices and perspectives with which to make sense of what David Dickson has called Dublin's 'hybridity' and complexity. His recent survey of Dublin since medieval times provides three chapters on the nineteenth century and introduces the idea of 'four cities', or four social layers, as a corrective to the commonplace that Dublin was divided neatly into wealth and poverty.[40] Yet in seeking to 'understand the evolution of the city', he argues, 'the focus has to remain disproportionately on those who actually wielded influence', and the definition of who wielded influence has remained narrow.[41] While a recent article setting 'an agenda' for urban history in Ireland notes the importance of learning more about class and the role of women in cities, references to the environment, to animals and to the relationship between urban and rural change are absent.[42]

This book supports the importance of the middle classes to urban change, but instead of examining them in isolation these chapters bring them into conversation with those people and places they sought to reform. Focusing on animals helps to reveal aspects of daily life and relationships between classes because, as Frederick Brown has observed, those in power often had different ideas about the role of animals than those with less power.[43] Animals help to evoke the tensions and variation that characterised nineteenth-century Dublin, a city that could be described at the *fin de siècle* as 'a hundred years behind the times—a faded capital' but also a 'bright and cheerful city'.[44] I use animals to consider nineteenth-century Dublin on its own terms, to see it as a place created by reforming ideas and resistance to them, by rich and poor, by the needs of humans and by economic and cultural reliance on animals. The city emerges not as a failure but as a reflection of a unique set of social, political, economic and environmental circumstances.

In shaping my approach to this history of nineteenth-century Dublin I have drawn on the work of many scholars who seek to include animals in history. Early work such as that by Keith Thomas and Harriet Ritvo focused on human ideas about animals, how these ideas changed over time and how they reflected other social and cultural shifts.[45] More recent work has sought to embed animals more directly into the historical narrative. Susan Nance, for example, has argued for historicising animals in the way that we do humans, rather than assuming animals never change.[46] She uses Thomas's work to propose the idea of 'animal modernity', a specific period in history where the lives, experiences and bodies of animals have been changed by human action.[47] Nance has also suggested that writers of animal history should avoid 'passive-voice or animals-as-objects prose' which reduces animals to 'raw materials of supposedly independent human action'.[48]

There are many shades of history between fully historicising animals and considering them as inanimate objects. Frederick Brown, as an environmental historian, does not really engage in the issue of animal agency but considers that 'animals constrain human actions'.[49] Thomas Almeroth-Williams uses Bruno Latour's actor–network theory to reach a similar conclusion about animals in Georgian London. He argues that the city was a hybrid created by humans and animals. The idea that humans relied on animals for industrial advancement is different than how Thomas understood animals in history but does not quite extend to re-periodising human history.[50]

My approach to looking at animals in nineteenth-century Dublin is that of a social historian, influenced by environmental history and animal studies. My actors are people and I am interested in how people think about animals. Nonetheless I have tried to be sensitive, where sources allow, to animal lives and experiences. In each chapter I have pointed to ways that human exploitation of animals affected animal lives as well as humans.[51] In Dublin, for example, demand for meat crowded more cattle into city markets, city slaughterhouses and city quays waiting for ships to England. The humane movement had some success in improving the treatment of working animals but the city also demanded more of them. The dog fancy encouraged the elimination of certain types of dogs and changed acceptable dog behaviours. The city that emerged at the end of the century was a compromise between reformers' desires for markers of urban civility and the need to accommodate continued exploitation of animals. Using an animal for food or transportation or entertainment has always required that humans make at least basic accommodation to the needs and characteristics of the animal in question. As Brown and Almeroth-Williams have shown in different cities, Dublin's animal residents often constrained the actions of its human ones.

My social history orientation has determined my choice of sources and my approach to them. To get an idea of what kinds of animals the city used, where they existed and how they were regulated, I have relied on administrative records such as the archives of city government, parliamentary papers and the archives of voluntary societies. To help establish how people thought about animals I have also examined diaries, periodicals, pamphlets, ballads, images, poems and fiction. And to further analyse the workings of the animal economy I have consulted travel guides, trade directories and business records. Animals inhabit all of these sources; you only have to look for them.

Although it may be possible to tell a story of Dublin showing how beasts actively civilised people, I interpret 'civilized by beasts' in the way Stokes intended. He argued that people created civilisation as a response to animals, to protect themselves from the predation of beasts in the wilderness. The process of civilising, he suggested, created barriers between people and animals. I am interested in this process of creating barriers, the people and the ideas that drove it. Like Erica Fudge, I see animals as being central to defining what it means to be human and thus ideas about animals have played an important role in defining what is special about the city, often considered a pinnacle of human creation.[52] Some people considered the city the only place where civilised life could occur. Samuel Haughton, for example, claimed that Ireland's rural residents 'do not live, they only vegetate', by contrast with the 'livelier people' of the city who experienced literature and culture.[53] Reformers invested in the cultural promise of the city saw the control or concealment of certain animals as a means of pushing the real city closer to an imagined ideal.

This book might also be considered a contribution to the study of governmentality in urban contexts because the human dilemma has been a driving force behind new practices of power. Michel Foucault introduced the term governmentality to explain the transition from early modern to modern forms of governance. He argued that a modern government's power lay not in the ability to take life from subjects but to shape lives by collecting data about a population and applying this data to governing them. Foucault demanded the study of power as a practice, and pointed to 'the idea that power and power relations are located in the fabric of everyday life'.[54] Efforts at 'compromise and concealment' created new ways to exercise power, from the regulation of slaughterhouses to the euthanising of stray dogs. Despite this connection, I have not explicitly focused on governmentality in these chapters because my aim here is different. Rather than show how power is exercised, I want to give readers a fuller sense of what it was like to live in nineteenth-century Dublin and who its residents were. Studies of governmentality can obscure the individuals who wielded power, while my intention is to reveal new actors who played a role in shaping Dublin.[55]

* * *

The book follows a chronological and thematic approach, with each chapter examining different ways that animals were thought about and used.

Chapters 1 and 2 focus on the idea of human ascendancy and on the ways that Dubliners' ideas about animals, and their distance from humans, shaped reform in the city between 1830 and 1850. Chapter 1 introduces the Dublin Zoological Society (f. 1830, DZS) and the Dublin Society for the Prevention of Cruelty to Animals (f. 1840, DSPCA). The comparison of these organisations shows how difficult it was to challenge the idea of human ascendancy in Dublin's specific social, religious and political context. While the politics of tolerance supported the Zoological Society, the politics of nationalism hindered the DSPCA. Urban reformers who sought to control how the poor used animals risked being accused of favouring animals over the Irish people. Chapter 2 covers the Great Famine and argues that a desire to reassert human ascendancy over animals is reflected in reform movements during and after the crisis. I focus on debates over feeding the poor and improving urban public health. In both cases the way to be human, the way for a city to be civilised, was to live *on* animals rather than *with* animals.

Chapters 3 and 4 are concerned with the human dilemma, or how Dubliners tried to reconcile their exploitation of animals with concerns about civility, health, morality and class. Chapter 3 focuses on the impact of a post-Famine shift to livestock farming on Dublin. Ireland's reliance on cattle exports coupled with increased urban meat consumption forced the Dublin Corporation to consider how to capitalise on cattle without allowing the city environment to become degraded. I argue that coping with cattle during life, slaughter and death changed the infrastructure, environment and regulation of the city. Chapter 4 shifts to the example of regulating dogs and pigs as a way of exploring how Dubliners decided which animals were wanted in the city. The chapter examines the simultaneous rise of the middle classes and the Dublin Metropolitan Police and their respective roles in changing how animals were controlled. I argue that policing animals affected social classes differently, eliminating the poor man's pig and the roving cur while allowing for the persistence of large pig slaughterhouses and expensive pedigree dogs. Both chapters show that ideas about how to regulate animals in the city were contingent on social factors specific to time and place rather than a fixed idea that all urban animals were nuisances at all times.

By the closing decades of the century, Dublin had the trappings of a modern city by bourgeois Victorian standards, including a system of trams and a system of bye-laws regulating urban life. Yet many of the problems complained of in earlier decades had not disappeared. Chapter 5 argues that Dublin in the final decades of the nineteenth century was a city created by compromised solutions to the human dilemma: still full of animals and the evidence of their exploitation but regulated and controlled in new ways. The chapter shows how different animals had come to be associated with different ideas of what a city should be. In the Epilogue I bring the story forward to consider how nineteenth-century changes affected the city in the twentieth century.

What ties these chapters and their different characters and stories together is a narrative of the growing influence of a number of groups including the middle classes, the police and the Dublin Corporation. One way in which these groups asserted their power was by attempting to implement new ideas of what a city should be like. Proliferating bye-laws to regulate animal businesses, policing cruelty to animals, building Zoological Gardens, licensing dogs, removing pigs, building a new cattle market and public abattoir: these were all acts of modernisation in the eyes of those who pursued them.[56]

* * *

Older residents of Dublin still recall a city with 'horses and cattle and pigs flying about the streets'.[57] This city slowly vanished during the twentieth century although the observant can still find traces of it today. Boot scrapers adjacent to doorways in the neighbourhoods of Smithfield and Stoneybatter attest to the dirty business of driving and selling cattle in the nearby market. Street names such as Bull Alley, Cow's Lane and Stable Lane recall former businesses. Large sheds behind derelict buildings once held dairy cattle and probably a few pigs (see, for example, the former Emerald Dairy, Figure 0.2). Horses remain sequestered in vacant lots and yards around the city; they still prance around the city's most desirable squares for €25 per ride. Twice per year, horse dealers sell them in the former market square (see, for example, Figure 0.3, Smithfield horse fair). And of course urban residents eat meat and drink milk in even larger quantities than their forebears. Thousands of cats and dogs keep them company. But these animals simply do not have the same presence in urban life, or our idea of urban life, that they once had. Dogs do not roam free. Food animals appear only as images on supermarket packaging or restaurant signs. The horse is no longer 'king of the roads'.[58]

0.2. The former Emerald Dairy on the corner of Seville Place and
Emerald Street. Photograph by the author.

The story of how we got from the animal city of the past to the
animal city of the present is a story worth telling. Even the animals
we don't see are part of the modern city: they live on in bye-laws, in
cultural habits and in social and economic geography.

0.3. A boy on a pony at the Smithfield Horse Fair in 2013. Image courtesy of Fountain Resource Group.

Setting the scene: nineteenth-century Dublin and its animals

For readers less familiar with nineteenth-century Dublin and Ireland, a little additional background may prove useful. This book begins in 1830 when the foundation of the Dublin Zoological Society and the emergent movement for the humane treatment of animals overlapped with a rising Catholic political voice. The book closes in 1900 when a public health inquiry condemning the continued presence of slaughterhouses and dairies in the city coincided with advancements in horse and mechanised transportation.

The period 1830 to 1900 encompasses significant political, economic and social changes to the city with impacts on humans and animals. Dublin, between 1830 and 1900, experienced a small population growth from about 230,000 people to around 260,000.[59] This rise masks periods of decline and is insignificant compared with many British, American and European cities. Influx from rural areas provided around 30 per cent and up to 40 per cent of the population, although many of these migrants may have continued onward to Britain.[60] The majority of the population was poor. Poverty, along with mortality, increased over the time period.[61]

Only a very small percentage of Dublin residents could vote and thus participate in local or national politics. In 1840, legislation reformed the municipal corporation of Dublin in line with other towns and cities in the United Kingdom. Before 1840 the Corporation had been considered a Protestant stronghold, and separately appointed boards performed many civic functions such as street maintenance and public health. Both Catholic Emancipation (1829) and the reforms of 1840 ensured that the city's elected government became increasingly Catholic and nationalist. Councillors included professionals and elite businessmen but also an increasing number of shopkeepers and publicans.[62]

The changing composition of civic government was accompanied by changing duties. The Dublin Improvement Act of 1849 consolidated many tasks under the Corporation including public health, paving, water and lighting. Four committees divided these duties among themselves as well as those of overseeing markets, Corporation property and taxation. The post-Famine expansion of the livestock trade meant that the Corporation held control of an economic keystone in the city's cattle market. Although bound by parliamentary legislation produced in London, the Corporation created bye-laws that shaped the day-to-day running of the city. The Dublin Metropolitan Police (founded in 1836) provided an enforcement wing for bye-laws while voluntary associations and lobby groups sought to shape them. Voluntary associations provided a significant voice for Protestant Dubliners, whose 20 per cent minority in the city declined over the time period.[63] From the middle of the century many well-to-do Dubliners retreated to the growing suburbs but they continued to influence urban change through government and voluntary associations. Expanding and diversifying transportation networks facilitated this from the first railway (1834) to the first horse tram (1872).[64] The quest for a healthful atmosphere drove suburban migration and also focused the energies of many reformers. Parliament passed several rounds of public health legislation (most significantly in 1866, 1874 and 1878) and sponsored two commissions of inquiry into the city's health (1880, 1900).[65]

As this book demonstrates, many of these changes affected animals and trades using animals. Transportation demanded an increase in horses; public health demanded a decrease in pigs and cattle. Public health initiatives also sought to control and clean up after those animals that remained and to regulate how they were housed and

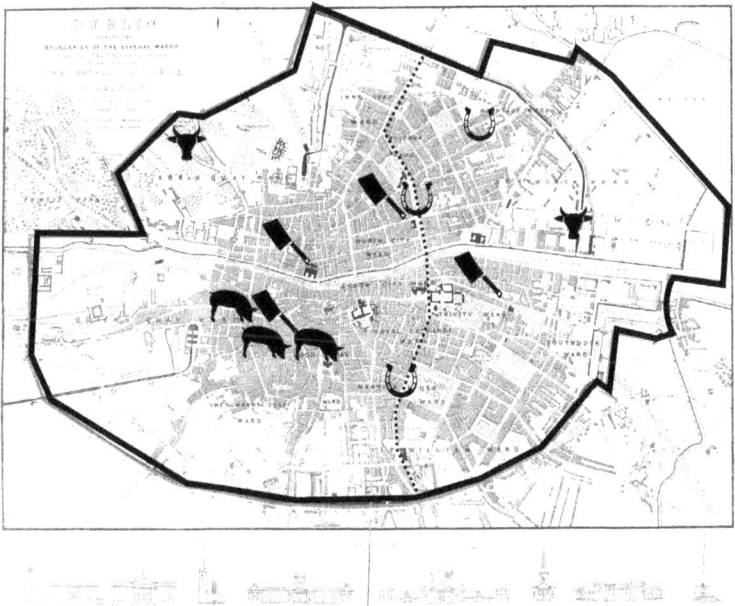

0.4. Concentrations of animal businesses in Dublin during the nineteenth century. The map is modified from *Thom's Irish Almanac and Official Directory of the United Kingdom of Great Britain and Ireland* (Dublin: Alexander Thom, 1865). This is a summary map abstracted from a more comprehensive map created with Dick Tobin using GIS to locate animal businesses extracted from directories for 1831 and 1901 and from the minutes of the Dublin Corporation between 1851 and 1861.

slaughtered. Economic changes increased the size and importance of the cattle market. Policemen rounded up stray dogs and arrested drovers who beat cattle.

Until 1901, when Dublin absorbed several suburbs, the city was very compact and ringed by two canals and the Circular Road. The map in Figure 0.4 was printed in 1865 for Thom's street directory.[66] The city's boundaries are indicated on the map by a thick black line. The River Liffey divides the city into north and south while the dashed line from Sackville Street (now O'Connell Street) in the north down Westmoreland Street in the south provides an east–west division. The four quarters of the city created by these divisions are related to concentrations of particular animals and to social and economic gradients.

What cannot be seen on the map is gradients of social and economic status that Dubliners would have known and experienced. The western and northern areas of the city were poorer than the southern and eastern portions. Areas of particular deprivation were scattered throughout the city, but foci included Inn's Quay Ward in the north-eastern inner city and South City Ward in the south-western district. In the eighteenth century the north-east of the city had held the prosperous and elegant squares, but fashion later moved to the south-east and its adjacent suburbs.

Not only people but animals had specific urban distributions. While butcher shops and livery stables could be found just about everywhere, large concentrations of particular businesses characterised certain areas. For example, the tanning business was conducted almost exclusively in the area around Watling Street along the south side of the River Liffey. Large numbers of slaughterhouses dominated several districts including the areas around Thomas Street, Townsend Street, Ormond Market and Moore Street (indicated by butcher cleavers). Animals were penned and exported from the quays on the north side (indicated by a cow's head in the north-east quadrant). Livery stables and veterinary surgeons took advantage of the Georgian houses that fashion had abandoned. Horses, carriages, cabs, omnibuses and later trams thronged Sackville Street, in contrast to Brocas's sedate depiction. Three horseshoes on the map indicate areas with substantial numbers of horse businesses. The cattle market (1863) and the public abattoir (1882) hugged the north-western edge of the city (indicated by a cow's head). In 1830 grazing fields had dominated the area around the market but by 1900 housing had encroached on most of the open space. Pigs were widely distributed but concentrated near bacon-curing businesses and the provision markets of the south-western edge (indicated by pig silhouettes).

Notes

1 'Zoological Society'; Richard Lalor Sheil is paraphrasing the speech of Whitley Stokes, *Freeman's Journal* (11 May 1830).
2 *ibid.*
3 'Theatre Royal', *Freeman's Journal* (5 May 1830).

4 Dorothee Brantz, 'Introduction', in Dorothee Brantz (ed.), *Beastly Natures: Animals, Humans and the Study of History* (Charlottesville: University of Virginia Press, 2010), p. 3.
5 Erica Fudge, 'A left-handed blow: writing the history of animals', in Nigel Rothfels (ed.), *Representing Animals* (Bloomington: Indiana University Press, 2002), pp. 3–18.
6 Susan Nance, *Animal Modernity: Jumbo the Elephant and the Human Dilemma* (Basingstoke: Palgrave Macmillan, 2015), p. 4.
7 Keith Thomas, *Man and the Natural World: Changing Attitudes in England, 1500–1800* (London: Penguin, 1983), p. 303.
8 Nance, *Animal Modernity*, p. 3.
9 P. J. Atkins, 'London's intra-urban milk supply, circa 1790–1914', *Transactions of the Institute of British Geographers*, 2:3 (1977), 383–99; Richard Scola, *Feeding the Victorian City: The Food Supply of Manchester, 1770–1870* (Manchester: Manchester University Press, 1992); F. M. L. Thompson, 'Nineteenth-century horse sense', *Economic History Review*, 29:1 (1976), 60–81; Clay McShane and Joel Tarr, *The Horse in the City: Living Machines in the Nineteenth Century* (Baltimore, MD: Johns Hopkins University Press, 2007).
10 See, for example, Peter Atkins, 'Animal wastes and nuisances in nineteenth-century London', and Sabine Barles, 'Undesirable nature: animals, resources, and urban nuisance in nineteenth-century Paris', in Peter Atkins (ed.), *Animal Cities: Beastly Urban Histories* (London: Routledge, 2016), pp. 19–52, 173–88.
11 On the dog fancy see, for example, Harriet Ritvo, 'Pride and pedigree: the evolution of the Victorian dog fancy', *Victorian Studies*, 29:2 (1986), 227–53; Philip Howell, *At Home and Astray: The Domestic Dog in Victorian Britain* (Charlottesville: University of Virginia Press, 2015), pp. 150–74. On urban zoos see Kay Anderson, 'Culture and nature at the Adelaide Zoo: at the frontiers of "human" geography', *Transactions of the Institute of British Geographers*, 20:3 (1995), 275–94; Harriet Ritvo, *The Animal Estate: The English and Other Creatures in the Victorian Age* (Cambridge, MA: Harvard University Press, 1987), pp. 205–42; Eric Baratay and Elisabeth Hardouin-Fugier, *Zoo: A History of Zoological Gardens in the West* (London: Reaktion, 2004), esp. chapter 2; Kathleen Kete, 'Animals and human empire', in Kathleen Kete (ed.), *A Cultural History of Animals in the Age of Empire* (London: Bloomsbury, 2007), pp. 1–24.
12 McShane and Tarr, *The Horse in the City*, pp. 14–17; Diana Donald, '"Beastly sights": the treatment of animals as a moral theme in representations of London *c.* 1820–1850', *Art History*, 22:4 (1999), 514–44; Kathryn Miele, 'Horse-sense: understanding the working horse in Victorian London', *Victorian Literature and Culture*, 37 (2009), 129–40.

13 Kathleen Kete, *The Beast in the Boudoir: Pet Keeping in Nineteenth-Century Paris* (Berkeley: University of California Press, 1998); Ritvo, 'Pride and pedigree'; Howell, *At Home and Astray*; Ingrid Tague, *Animal Companions: Pets and Social Change in Eighteenth-Century Britain* (State College: Pennsylvania State University Press, 2015).

14 Many essays in Atkins (ed.), *Animal Cities* cover this topic. See also Ian MacLachlan, 'A bloody offal nuisance: the persistence of private slaughter-houses in nineteenth-century London', *Urban History*, 34:2 (2007), 227–54; Chris Otter, 'The vital city: public analysis, dairies and slaughterhouses in nineteenth-century Britain', *Cultural Geographies*, 13:4 (2006), 517–37; Catherine McNeur, 'The "swinish multitude": conflicts over hogs in ante-bellum New York City', *Journal of Urban History*, 37:5 (2011), 639–60.

15 For a useful introduction see Paula Young Lee, 'The slaughterhouse and the city', *Food & History*, 3:2 (2005), 7–25; and Paula Young Lee (ed.), *Meat, Modernity and the Rise of the Slaughterhouse* (Durham: University of New Hampshire Press, 2008).

16 Stephen Mosley, 'Common ground: integrating social and environmental history', *Journal of Social History* (2006), 915–33: 921. Two books on animals that use this approach are Virginia De John Anderson, *Creatures of Empire: How Domestic Animals Transformed Early America* (Oxford: Oxford University Press, 2004); and Sandra Swart, *Riding High: Horses, Humans and History in South Africa* (Johannesburg: Wits University Press, 2010).

17 See, for example, McNeur, 'The "swinish multitude"'; and Bettina Bradbury, 'Pigs, cows, and borders: non-wage forms of survival among Montreal families', *Labour/Le Travail*, 14 (1984), 9–48. The same conflict occurred in colonial cities; see Antonio Santoyo, 'De cerdos y de civilidad urbana. La descalificación de las actividaded de explotación porcina en la ciudad de México durante el ultimo tercio del siglo XIX', *Historia Mexicana*, 47:1 (1997), 69–102.

18 Dawn Biehler, 'Embodied wildlife histories and the urban landscape', *Environmental History*, 16 (2011), 445–50.

19 See, for example, Ken Cruikshank and Nancy B. Bouchier, 'Blighted areas and obnoxious industries: constructing environmental inequality on an industrial waterfront, Hamilton, Ontario, 1890–1960', *Environmental History*, 9:3 (2004), 464–96. See also Angela Gugliotti, 'Review essay: nature and policy in the city: environmental history and urban history', *Journal of Urban History*, 35:4 (2009), 561–70; and Bruce Stephenson, 'Review essay: urban environmental history: the essence of a contradiction', *Journal of Urban History*, 31:6 (2005), 887–98.

20 On the humane movement's class elements see, for example, Ritvo, *The Animal Estate*, pp. 31–4; and Hilda Kean, *Animal Rights: Political and Social Change in Britain Since 1800* (London: Reaktion, 1998), p. 36.

21 William Cronon, *Nature's Metropolis: Chicago and the Great West* (New York: W. W. Norton & Co., 1992); animals are the central focus of chapter 5, 'Annihilating Space'.

22 McShane and Tarr, *The Horse in the City*.

23 See, for example, Kete, *The Beast in the Boudoir*; Tague, *Animal Companions*.

24 Ritvo, *The Animal Estate*; but also Harriet Ritvo, *Noble Cows and Hybrid Zebras: Essays on Animals & History* (Charlottesville: University of Virginia Press, 2010).

25 Atkins (ed.), *Animal Cities*.

26 Hannah Velten, *Beastly London: A History of Animals in the City* (London: Reaktion, 2013).

27 Frederick L. Brown, *The City is More than Human: An Animal History of Seattle* (Seattle: University of Washington Press, 2016).

28 See, for example, Andrew Robichaud's work on San Francisco slaughterhouses and butcher shops: 'Trail of blood', Stanford University Spatial History Project (visualisations co-created with Erik Steiner) (2010), http://www.stanford.edu/group/spatialhistory/cgi-bin/site/pub.php?id=31 (accessed 7 May 2020).

29 Thomas Almeroth-Williams, *City of Beasts: How Animals Shaped Georgian London* (Manchester: Manchester University Press, 2019).

30 Martin Melosi, 'Humans, cities and nature: how do cities fit in the material world?', *Journal of Urban History*, 36:1 (2010), 3–21.

31 One of the best examples in the literature of the relationship between city and country is still Cronon, *Nature's Metropolis*.

32 On the middle classes and social segregation see Susan Galavan, *Dublin's Bourgeois Homes: Building the Victorian Suburbs, 1850–1901* (London: Routledge, 2017); and Mary E. Daly, *Dublin, the Deposed Capital: A Social and Economic History, 1860–1914* (Cork: Cork University Press, 1984). For an excellent overview of national politics and the Corporation see Ciaran Wallace, 'Civil society in search of a state: Dublin 1898–1912', *Urban History*, 45:3 (2018), 426–52; on poverty and public health see Jacinta Prunty, *Dublin Slums 1800–1925: A Study in Urban Geography* (Dublin: Irish Academic Press, 1998); and Prunty, 'Improving the urban environment: public health and housing in nineteenth-century Dublin', in Joseph Brady and Anngret Simms (eds), *Dublin Through Space and Time (c.900–1900)* (Dublin: Four Courts Press), pp. 166–220; on modernity see Hugh Campbell, 'The emergence of modern Dublin: reality and representation', *Architectural Review Quarterly*, 2 (1997), 44–53; Yvonne Whelan, *Reinventing Modern Dublin: Streetscape, Iconography and the Politics of Identity* (Dublin: University College Dublin Press, 2003); and Erika Hanna, *Modern Dublin: Urban Change and the Irish Past, 1957–1973* (Oxford: Oxford University Press, 2013).

33 Campbell, 'The emergence of modern Dublin'; Joseph V. O'Brien, *Dear, Dirty Dublin: A City in Distress* (Berkeley: University of California Press, 1982), p. 5.

34 David Dickson, 'The state of Dublin's history', *Éire-Ireland*, 45:1&2 (2010), 198–212; O'Brien, *Dear Dirty Dublin*; Daly, *Dublin, the Deposed Capital*; Prunty, *Dublin Slums*; Ciara Breathnach and Brian Gurrin, 'A tale of two cities: infant mortality and cause of infant death in Dublin, 1864–1910', *Urban History*, 44:4 (2017), 647–77.

35 Daly, *Dublin, the Deposed Capital*.

36 Prunty, *Dublin Slums*.

37 Galavan, *Dublin's Bourgeois Homes*.

38 Stephanie Rains, *Commodity Culture and Social Class in Dublin 1850–1916* (Dublin: Irish Academic Press, 2010).

39 Juliana Adelman, *Communities of Science in Nineteenth-Century Ireland* (London: Pickering and Chatto, 2009); Adelman, 'Evolution on display: promoting Irish natural history and Darwinism at the Dublin Science and Art Museum', *British Journal for the History of Science*, 38:4 (2005), 411–36; Tanya O'Sullivan, 'The perception of place and the "origins of handedness" debate: towards a cognitive cartography of science in nineteenth-century Dublin', *Endeavour*, 39:3–4 (2015), 139–46; O'Sullivan, *Geographies of City Science: Urban Lives and Origin Debates in Late Victorian Dublin* (Pittsburgh, PA: University of Pittsburgh Press, 2019); Clara Cullen, 'The Museum of Irish Industry, Robert Kane and education for all in the Dublin of the 1850s and 1860s', *History of Education* (2007), 1–14.

40 David Dickson, *Dublin: The Making of a Capital City* (London: Profile Books, 2014), p. 307.

41 Dickson, *Dublin*, p. xiv.

42 Richard Butler and Erika Hanna, 'Irish urban history: an agenda', *Urban History*, 46:1 (2019), 2–9.

43 Brown, *The City is More Than Human*, pp. 8–9.

44 O'Brien, *Dear, Dirty Dublin*, p. 39; and Joseph Brady, 'Dublin at the turn of the century', in Joseph Brady and Anngret Simms (eds), *Dublin Through Space and Time* (Dublin: Four Courts Press, 2001), p. 221.

45 Thomas, *Man and the Natural World*; Ritvo, *The Animal Estate*, pp. 5–6.

46 Susan Nance, 'Introduction', in Susan Nance (ed.), *The Historical Animal* (Syracuse, NY: Syracuse University Press), p. 6.

47 Nance, *Animal Modernity*.

48 Nance, 'Introduction', p. 3.

49 Brown, *The City is More Than Human*, p. 13.

50 Almeroth-Williams, *City of Beasts*, pp. 8–9.

51 See Nance, *Animal Modernity*.

52 Fudge, 'A left-handed blow'.

53 Samuel Haughton, 'Address in public medicine', *British Medical Journal* (6 August 1887), 294–95: 295.

54 Simon Gunn, 'From hegemony to governmentality: changing conceptions of power in social history', *Journal of Social History*, 39:3 (2006), 705–20.

55 Gunn, 'From hegemony to governmentality'. Yes, this paragraph is here because a reader requested it.

56 I refer to the views of the actors themselves that a better and more modern city resulted from these changes. The debate on modernisation and history continues although historians of the city frequently use the term 'modernity'. For two useful discussions relevant to social history see Raymond Grew, 'More on modernization', *Journal of Social History*, 14:2 (1980), 179–87; and Peter N. Stearns, 'Modernization and social history: some suggestions and a muted cheer', *Journal of Social History*, 14:2 (1980), 189–209. For the idea of multiple modernities see, for example, Dorothy Ross's explanation in 'AHR roundtable: American modernities, past and present', *American Historical Review*, 116:3 (2011), 702–14.

57 Horse dealer Antoinette Healy, as quoted in Kevin C. Kearns, *Dublin Street Life and Lore* (Dun Laoghaire: Glendale, 1991), p. 187.

58 Paddy Crosbie, *'Your Dinner's Poured Out!'* (Dublin: O'Brien Press, 1981), p. 72.

59 Daly, *Dublin, the Deposed Capital*, p. 3.

60 Daly, *Dublin, the Deposed Capital*, p. 4.

61 Prunty, *Dublin Slums*, p. 75.

62 Daly, *Dublin, the Deposed Capital*, pp. 203–5.

63 Daly, *Dublin, the Deposed Capital*, p. 122.

64 Michael Corcoran, *Through Streets Broad and Narrow: A History of Dublin Trams* (Hersham: Ian Allan, 2008), pp. 8–10.

65 See Prunty, *Dublin Slums*, pp. 69–88.

66 For an enlarged discussion of animal geographies in Dublin see Juliana Adelman, 'Towards an environmental history of nineteenth-century Dublin', in Matthew Kelly (ed.), *Nature and Environment in Nineteenth-Century Ireland* (Liverpool: Liverpool University Press, 2019), pp. 139–58.

1

Political zoology: class, religion and animal exploitation, 1830–45

The elephant, which has been for some time expected at these grounds, arrived in town, and will be immediately placed in the gardens for the gratification of the curious in natural history.[1]

Mr Calder stated that on Friday afternoon, passing through College-Green, he perceived a horse after falling down in the street beneath a load on a dray. A crowd was collected about the animal; several persons were beating him cruelly in order to force him to rise, but he could not do so from his exhausted state.[2]

An elephant in the Dublin Zoological Gardens and a dying cart horse in College Green could both attract a crowd of onlookers in early nineteenth-century Dublin. Groups intent on reforming Dublin tried to turn the horse and the elephant into different types of lessons. The elephant helped the Zoological Society to teach natural history, boost Dublin's scientific reputation, improve class relations and soothe political tensions. The horse and its injuries became examples of a form of ignorance that the DSPCA wished to eradicate through policing and punishment. Between 1830 and 1845, horses and elephants became part of very different approaches to the reform and improvement of Dublin, especially its working classes. By comparing the DSPCA and the Zoological Society this chapter shows how ideas about human–animal relationships were entwined with ideas about class, religion, politics and urban improvement.

Mr Calder's views on the treatment of horses differed significantly from those of both the owner of the dray and the other workers who helped the owner beat the horse 'in order to force him to rise'. Likewise, visitors to the elephant in the Zoological Gardens ranged from the Lord Lieutenant to 'ragged boys', from those interested in amusement and socialising to those 'curious in natural history'.[3] The peculiarities of class, religion and politics in Dublin helped to make the Zoological Gardens a popular success while the DSPCA languished. The caged animals in the Dublin Zoological Gardens presented a clear view of human ascendancy over nature and did not often provoke tensions between Catholic and Protestant, nationalist and unionist, rich and poor. Almost no one cried foul at the manner in which animals lived and died to amuse the visiting public. By contrast, the DSPCA's detection of animal cruelty amongst poor workers in Dublin's streets prevented the Society from gaining a public following. 'Poor' was too easily interchanged with 'Catholic' or 'Irish', thereby suggesting that policing cruelty to animals might represent a form of Protestant English oppression.

This chapter is divided into three parts. The first part uses a horse-powered trip to the Zoological Gardens to tease out some of the ways class affected human–animal relationships in early nineteenth-century Dublin. The second part then looks closely at the development of the Zoological Gardens and how animals were useful to a reforming project intended to unite all classes and creeds. The third section examines the DSPCA and its divisive impact, including detractors who considered it a threat to the idea of human ascendancy with political consequences for Ireland.

Between 1830 and 1845 the city consumed animals in the thousands. Attitudes towards these animals, from exotic big cats to ordinary cab horses, reveal ideas about class and identity that made nineteenth-century Dublin unique: a city of Catholics ruled mostly by Protestants, a metropolis of Ireland but a second city of the United Kingdom, a city of middle-class professionals that recalled aristocratic times. We can read the Zoological Society and the DSPCA for signs of the city's prejudices and pretensions just as Dubliners might have read the high-stepping gait of a horse or an open sore on its back for signs of the owner's character.

Social class, political reform and human–animal relationships

One Monday in May 1837 a young woman 'out driving' arrived at the Dublin Zoological Gardens. Being wealthy, she travelled in her family's carriage, the same one that her father used to visit his patients.[4] Families such as hers kept the streets crowded with carriages and the coachmakers 'in such full employment that no contract could be obtained for building coaches on the Dublin and Kingstown railroad'.[5] The horses drawing the carriage may not have matched the 'near to perfect' bay mares owned by the president of the Zoological Society but they were probably glossy, healthy animals around six years old. Horses drawing private carriages stood out from the city's 7000 working horses, most of which had not been selected for their beauty.[6] The young lady's carriage may have been similar to that constructed for a doctor in 1822 by John Hutton and Sons. At a cost of £205 the carriage included a leather roof, mahogany panelling, leather seats, curtains, lamps and harness for a pair of horses.[7] Arriving in dry comfort, she would have paid 1s at the gatehouse to enter the Zoological Gardens on foot while the driver minded the horses. Once inside, she 'staid [sic] some time & did not hear even one tune from the band'. She recorded nothing of the animals within the gates, although she mentioned meeting a friend. Elite Dubliners used the gardens to socialise, paying extra on fete days for a glimpse of the Lord Lieutenant and other 'bipeds to be seen'.[8] She returned a week later for one such fete where she stayed until midnight but, due to rain, did not even leave the shelter of the marquee to stroll the grounds. The exotic animals did not merit description, unlike Toby the Sapient Pig, whom she visited twice in a shopping arcade to see him tell the hour and spell his name.[9]

Perhaps other classes of visitors found the zoological spectacle in the gardens more compelling. Over 20,000 made their way to the gardens on a single day in 1838 when the Zoological Society opened them for free to mark Queen Victoria's coronation.[10] Dubliners lacking a carriage could have queued at a jaunting car stand, perhaps on Sackville Street, and paid to be jolted along to the gardens by the combination of 'vociferous' driver and malnourished nag.[11] While the wealthy young lady passed through the muddy streets in sheltered comfort, the passenger on the open jaunting car felt the rain, smelled the perfume of wastes that passed under the car's wheels and heard the driver lash the horse. Occasionally an exhausted horse collapsed in the road and would not rise, no matter what sort of beating the driver delivered. Most cab horses were old (about ten to twelve years) and approaching inevitable consignment to the knacker's yard. Yet from the 1830s, a cab driver who cruelly beat his horse was committing a crime and may have attracted the attention of a police officer or a member of the Society for the Prevention of Cruelty to Animals. A trip to the magistrate would have resulted in a fine he could ill afford to pay from wages that may have been as low as 1s 6d per week, or barely more than the standard entry fee at the gardens.[12] But by 1838 even the cab driver could afford to visit the Zoological Gardens. In that year the Zoological Society began to offer one-penny admission on Sundays to attract 'the lower orders'. The cab driver, like most other Sunday visitors, probably arrived on foot.[13]

The carriage horse might toss his head and prance but his days of glory were numbered: he would soon find himself under a cab driver's whip. Perhaps he (as they were nearly all geldings) had recently been 'young, fresh and engaged perfectly sound' at a house auction or brought from England 'just out of breeders hands' at one of the city's many horse repositories.[14] City work wore him down: as his physical body declined, he moved through jobs of diminishing prestige.[15] Most horses were at their peak at the age of five or six; a twelve-year-old horse was close to the end of its usefulness. As the *Irish Sportsman* described, a rural-bred hunter was 'only going through his probationary course to fit him' for being a roadster, a cart horse or entering 'into the services of "Larry Doolin," ... [who] whirls us across the city for sixpence a "set-down"'.[16] A horse at its peak might be used as an elite family's carriage horse but, once it declined, be sold off for use as a cab or cart horse.

The young lady in her carriage had the privilege to think little of the horse that pulled her: the family's groom and driver took care of that. When he was worn out he would be replaced. The cab driver, by contrast, thought of his horse all the time, from how fast it was moving to how much food it would need and when it would need re-shoeing. Class determined whether you used your animals to display economic fortune or depended upon them to prevent economic misfortune.

Social class shaped human–animal relationships in city streets as well as in special places such as zoological gardens. Historians have argued that the middle- and upper-class supporters of zoological societies and humane societies were often more concerned with working-class behaviour than they were with the animals that ostensibly motivated their efforts. Western zoos imposed a particular view of animals, and of human–animal relationships, in an effort to 'overcome all other local cultural interpretations'.[17] In Australia the ruling classes of the nineteenth and twentieth centuries used zoos to control the behaviour of those 'whose difference was in some way threatening'.[18] The zoo controlled nature (in the form of the animals) and people (in the form of the visitors). Likewise the middle classes in the Western world promoted humane treatment of animals as a way to control working-class behaviours that they disapproved of or to 'suppress dangerous elements of human society'. Teaching kindness to animals, some believed, could teach self-control to children and to the poor.[19] Kindness to animals became a mark of civilisation; the British parliament enacted measures against animal cruelty before prohibiting child labour or abolishing slavery.[20] Ideas about class influenced the choice of which acts of cruelty to pursue. Our wealthy young lady's brother and father may have participated in hunting free from scrutiny while the Royal Society for the Prevention of Cruelty to Animals (RSPCA) focused attention on cab drivers, cattle drovers and butchers.[21]

In Britain the period from 1830 to 1845 has been called the 'age of reform'. Successive Whig governments expanded the franchise, increased religious liberty and opened opportunity in government service beyond a self-selected few. In Ireland Catholic Emancipation was introduced, and municipal Corporations, the Poor Law and the police were all reformed. The Zoological Society and the DSPCA each reflected this period's enthusiasm for reform.

The physicians, politicians and urban elites who founded the Zoological Society in 1830 were responding directly to political reform. In 1829 parliament granted Catholic Emancipation and thus opened the doors of government office to Catholics. The legal changes, which had been debated since the eighteenth century and in truth affected few, were seen as a broader victory for Irish Catholics.[22] Daniel O'Connell's advocacy of Emancipation cemented his role as a leading political figure in London and Dublin. He used his power to pursue a campaign for repeal of the Act of Union, through which he exacted other concessions for Ireland.[23] The effects of these changes were felt in Dublin as Catholics were, for example, accepted gradually into the judiciary and the police force.[24] Yet the political campaign to introduce Emancipation had been a 'subject of animosity', bringing Sheil and 'those who differ from him on a question that is now gone by' together to found a zoological society as an act of political and social reconciliation.[25] The Society's founding members included Catholics and Protestants, liberals and conservatives, nationalists and unionists. Few of the founders had a reputation in zoological science. What they shared was social and economic status and a desire to make their city great. Together they could use the Dublin Zoological Society as an avenue to civic and national improvement.

The Dublin Society for the Prevention of Cruelty to Animals also responded to political change and saw its aims as reforming. The humane treatment of animals in Ireland, as Helen O'Connell has demonstrated, was linked to the literature of improvement.[26] The foremost advocate of the humane movement in Ireland, Richard 'Humanity Dick' Martin, was a politician and supporter of Catholic Emancipation.[27] Yet Martin had also been in favour of the dissolution of the Irish parliament, and many advocates of the cause of animal rights appeared to see it as an extension of efforts to civilise and assimilate the Irish poor (especially the rural poor) into the United Kingdom.[28]

Both the DSPCA and the Zoological Society copied London examples. Our doctor's daughter may have read in a Dublin newspaper about the London Zoological Gardens, opened in 1828, which 'become every day more and more an object of attraction'.[29] The founders of the Dublin Zoological Society envisioned 'a collection of living animals on the plan of the Zoological Society of London'.[30] Our Dublin cab driver may have been unaware of growing scrutiny of his London counterparts after the 1822 and 1835 acts against cruelty to animals, but he soon faced notices and placards demanding that he comply with the new laws. By 1836, Dublin-based advocates for the Society for the Prevention of Cruelty to Animals (SPCA) had begun to watch him in the streets and test the magistrates' willingness to fine him for beating horses, skinning cats or enjoying certain types of blood sport.[31]

Yet the specific context of nineteenth-century Dublin meant that societies such as the Zoological Society and the DSPCA would be received very differently than they were in London. Class had different connotations in Dublin where it was entangled with religion and politics. Our doctor's daughter was part of Dublin's growing Catholic middle class whose allegiances defy easy classification. Her family socialised at the Lord Mayor's Mansion (a Protestant-dominated space before municipal reforms), complained about 'papists' and attended Mass each week.[32] Many elite Catholics such as her participated in British fashions from clothing to pets to amateur zoology. They bought British magazines, followed the lives of the Royal family and sought social advancement through service to the British Empire.[33] Even nationalist politicians such as Daniel O'Connell balanced loyalty to the Queen with demands for Irish legislative independence.[34] These elite Catholics moved in social circles that included Protestants, even if each sect sometimes viewed the other with suspicion. What Dublin's Catholic elite shared most strongly with its Protestant elite was a combination of class identity and civic pride, both of which could be celebrated in the Zoological Gardens. The Zoological Society gave this elite a way to participate in international zoological science, a place to socialise with their peers and an opportunity to support a cheap leisure activity for working men.

Our cab driver was part of the city's vast Catholic lower class. While Dublin contained some working-class Protestants, they were by far the minority.[35] Cab drivers and others like them served as a target for the reforming zeal of the middle and upper classes regardless of whether elites were Catholic or Protestant, national-ist or unionist. Advocates of Irish independence used the poor man's plight to demonstrate the effects of English oppression. Supporters of maintaining the union between Britain and Ireland argued that only tighter adherence to British laws and norms would save the Irish poor. Most could agree on improving the cab driver by provid-ing him with rational recreation in the Zoological Gardens. By con-trast, many contested the importance of applying English humane legislation to Ireland. Nationalists scoffed at a British parliament that would legislate to protect dogs before it would do justice to the Irish poor.[36] If a cab driver cruelly beat his horse he was often arrested and fined. Yet popular support for eliminating cruelty to animals did not bloom in Dublin: the DSPCA failed to attract the enthusiastic patron-age of almost any Dubliners of note.

In both the Zoological Gardens and the street, most Dubliners expressed an interest in animals and a certainty about their differ-ence from humans. The idea of human ascendancy over animals was a commonplace in most of the Western world during the nineteenth century.[37] Zoological gardens celebrated human mastery of nature as the ability to collect, display and therefore 'tame' large numbers of wild animals. Yet just as the Dublin Zoological Gardens were being built, reformers and voluntary societies began to challenge human ascendancy through, for example, laws that outlawed the beating of a weak or injured horse.

The Zoological Gardens

Anyone who visited the Zoological Gardens had to travel some distance to the western edge of the city and the Phoenix Park. Situated about one mile from Sackville Street (Dublin's major shopping street, now called O'Connell Street), the park in the nineteenth century housed a miscellany of buildings as well as areas of green space. The park contained, for example, a hospital, the home of the Lord Lieutenant of Dublin, a half-completed monument to the Duke of Wellington, military barracks, pastures for grazing animals and avenues used by wealthy citizens to parade in horse and carriage.[38]

The Dublin Zoological Society's gardens encompassed four and a half acres in a hollow about half a mile from the park's gate nearest to the city.[39] Upon reaching the gatehouse, a visitor paid their fee or signed in as a member (for an image of the gate see Figure 1.1).

All visitors entered the same zoological park where they could view the same animals. If they had visited in the summer of 1835 they may have seen the elephant, hired at £100 per month and cared for by its own attendant who received 15s per week from the Zoological Society (see Figure 1.2).[40] Visitors could tip the attendant for a chance to ride the elephant or purchase biscuits to feed it. Others may have been drawn to the harbour seal, captured in Dublin Bay and expected to live only a few weeks in captivity.[41] In 1838, they may have watched the carnivores in the newly built 'deambulatorium' as they lunched on diseased butcher's meat seized by the Lord Mayor or a horse's leg purchased from one of the city's knacker yards.[42]

The visitors could follow paths through the landscaped gardens and stop at the scattered displays of different animals. Like many other zoological gardens opened at the same time, the Society had confined the animals in either outdoor pens or small buildings. Figure 1.3 shows visitors to the gardens viewing a llama in an iron-barred enclosure, a common style. Newspaper descriptions of the crowds in the gardens suggested that visitors strolled at ease in the pleasant surrounds, paying more or less attention to the animals depending on their level of interest. In the gardens,

THE
DUBLIN   PENNY   JOURNAL
CONDUCTED BY P. DIXON HARDY, M.R.I.A.

| Vol. IV. | AUGUST 29, 1835. | No. 165. |

GATE-HOUSE OF THE ZOOLOGICAL GARDENS, PHŒNIX PARK.

1.1. Entrance gate to the Zoological Gardens, erected in 1831, as depicted in the *Dublin Penny Journal* (29 August 1835). Image courtesy of the board of Trinity College Dublin.

> The man of science may study, the man of pleasure lounge—the youth of both sexes be instructed in geography, history, and literature—for beholding the beasts and birds of foreign climes and distant regions naturally leads to the contemplation of each—the ordinary man of business be amused, and the soul of the serious Christian be lifted up.[43]

Quiet contemplation and polite conversation may indeed have been the experience of many visitors. We know that artists visited to draw the animals.[44] Other visitors responded to the 'number, fashion and beauty of the numerous visitors'.[45] Yet other visitors arrived drunk and imagined the gardens as a particularly attractive spot for picnicking and merry making.[46] The genius of the gardens was that they somehow accommodated all of these types of visitors.

Nelson, del.

THE ELEPHANT.

1.2. The elephant in the Zoological Gardens as depicted in the
Dublin Penny Journal (29 August 1835). An elephant was initially
hired in 1835 and provided rides to visitors for a fee paid to the keeper.
Image courtesy of the Board of Trinity College Dublin.

Visitors and the Zoological Society saw the gardens as a place of
retreat from the city that promised a kind of superior nature created
by human ingenuity. The *Dublin University Magazine* praised the
gardens for the 'appearance of rurality and nature', superior to
the 'artificial—and "menagerie" like appearance of the gardens at
London and Liverpool'.[47] The *Dublin Penny Journal* enthused over 'this
delightful spot, possessing natural advantages which the wealth of
London, or the munificence of the French government could not purchase for their Gardens'.[48] A member of the Zoological Society who
produced a guide to the gardens noted the 'natural and artificial
beauty of the grounds'.[49] To enhance the gardens' 'artificial beauty',
the Society hired architect Decimus Burton. Burton (also architect
to the London Zoological Society) suggested building variety into the
landscape through ponds, plantings and cultivated views. Visitors

LAMAS.—VIEW IN THE ZOOLOGICAL GARDENS.

1.3. An open pen and a cottage orné style enclosure in the Zoological Gardens as depicted in the *Dublin Penny Journal* (23 April 1836). Note the man appears to reach his hand into the cage, which holds both peacocks and a llama. In the background a house that holds a monkey and some other quadruped is visible. Image courtesy of the Board of Trinity College Dublin.

would experience 'a succession of objects to please by variety and concealed from each other by plantations'.[50] By 1846 many of his plans had been implemented and a guidebook to Dublin described the gardens as 'a large space of undulating uneven ground ... well laid out in walks, ornamented with a great variety of trees, shrubs, and flowers'. Scattered amongst the plantings were 'cages for birds, and rustic buildings for the larger animals'.[51] The overall effect was not natural so much as a kind of man-made Eden. As the *Dublin Penny Journal* asked, 'as we enter, can we not fancy ourselves in Paradise, and removing the idea of cages and barriers, think we see Adam and Eve walking in innocence amongst the creatures?'[52]

Making the gardens appear like Eden, with the animals arranged in an ornamental landscape, was important for distinguishing the

Zoological Gardens from the myriad of public spectacles on offer in Dublin. Humans made different meanings for animals depending upon the circumstance in which they encountered them. A lion exhibited in a cage of Batty's menagerie was a curiosity while the lion in the Zoological Gardens was a zoological specimen. Batty's lion offered the working man a moment's amusement; the zoological lion offered him self-improvement.[53] The Zoological Society made animals a junior partner in their campaign of social reform.

As a scientific space, the gardens could champion a kind of limited social equality. The universal appeal of looking at animals facilitated the transformation of the gardens from 'a most fashionable lounge' to a place filled with 'immense crowds of the lower orders'.[54] By 1837, Philip Crampton, seven times president of the Zoological Society, claimed that in the gardens 'persons of every rank and condition of life, meet on terms of perfect equality'.[55]

Persons of varied social ranks met in many other urban locations (the theatre, the streets) but not 'on terms of perfect equality'. It was the animals that enabled this equality, both by their universal appeal to humans from all walks of life and by their animal-ness. All the animals in the gardens, despite representing hundreds of different species, shared one thing: they were not human. All the humans in the gardens, despite their variety of clothing and occupations, shared one thing: they were not animals. The comparison of the gardens to Eden was significant: what separated diverse visitors from the animals they visited was their immortal souls. The gardens reinforced the idea of a Christian hierarchy in which humans held a special position while every other organism had its place. As a guidebook by a Zoological Society member described, 'each species is, in all its parts, perfectly designed for a particular purpose, just as it was originally ordained'.[56]

The gardens and their public message continued to interest politicians, even after the initial enthusiasm had waned. It is significant that the gardens appealed to periodicals such as the *Dublin University Magazine* and *Saunder's Newsletter*, with a conservative and unionist audience, as well as the *Freeman's Journal*, which had a more liberal (and later nationalist) orientation.[57] Daniel O'Connell joined the Zoological Society but not the Dublin Society for the Prevention of Cruelty to Animals. Isaac Butt, a conservative Protestant who would become an advocate of Home Rule for Ireland, delivered a lecture to the Zoological Society in 1847. He suggested that the gardens were a more potent symbol of the advance of civilisation than 'the mightiest building of which imperial Rome could boast'.[58] For Butt, the gardens demonstrated the superiority of Christian civilisation: looking at animals made 'harmless and unharmed' reminded the visitor that 'the Almighty knows all the cattle on a thousand hills' and has made each creature suited for its place.[59]

The gardens did not always live up to their promise of social integration or zoological education. Members paid an annual subscription of £1, or £1 10s with the privilege of bringing guests.[60] During the week the gardens often held fewer than one hundred visitors, all of them middle or upper class, either members or visitors paying the highest 1s entrance fee.[61] Working men and their families dominated the crowds of over 2000 that visited the gardens on Sundays (penny days from 1837), when members visited in small numbers.[62] Some Dublin elites enjoyed the spectacle of working-class visitors and chose to visit on Sundays in the same way as they chose to attend Donnybrook Fair, a notorious lower-class entertainment.[63] The Zoological Society believed that the example of respectable people helped to improve the behaviour of the working classes and its visiting inspectors often remarked on their good behaviour as though expecting the opposite.[64]

The Society declared itself devoted to zoological education while its methods remained vague. A catalogue of the gardens suggested that its use would 'render the collection, as far as possible, subservient to the useful purpose of diffusing knowledge', but few could afford or understand such a catalogue.[65] The *Dublin University Magazine* imagined that visitors would 'learn, at least something [...] while we are thinking only of amusement'.[66] The Society claimed that its collection contained 'a number of highly instructive and beautiful specimens' and argued that the gardens had the benefit of helping 'the casual and thoughtless visitor to the inquiries that lead to knowledge'.[67]

Yet the Zoological Society provided little guidance to visitors to assist them in understanding the natural order. Visitors may have purchased a guidebook by William Tighe Hamilton, a member of the Society, and tried to match its numbered entries with the numbers of the animals' cages.[68] Or they may have purchased a cheaper and more amusing illustrated guide produced by Philip Dixon Hardy, the editor of the *Dublin Penny Journal*. Neither book precisely corresponded with the animals resident in the gardens. Both Hamilton and Hardy included descriptions, and even illustrations, of animals that 'have not yet been procured for the Society'.[69] The Society provided few labels and had arranged the animals in groups according to their physical needs rather than their scientific classification.[70] A visitor calling himself 'Homo' complained to the *Freeman's Journal* in 1843 that 'the total omission of anything like either classification or science made the whole appear to me as if forming rather a collection for the mere gaze of the idly curious'.[71] Homo bemoaned the few labels on the cages, which lacked information about 'the class or order of the inhabitant' and made it impossible for even the educated to make scientific sense of the animals on display.

One explanation for this lackadaisical approach to zoological education is that the most important message for the public was the inclusion of all Dubliners in a universal and shared humanity in contrast with nature or animals. Yes, the visitors might learn the 'manners and habits of the different animals, and a geographical description of the countries from which they came'. But they might also use the animals to prompt fantastical stories of jungle savagery which clearly demarcated the human realm from the animal one.[72] Visiting the gardens led people to compare. They compared animals to one another, animals to people and people to other people. The *Dublin Penny Journal* noted that the ostrich resembled a man 'who stalks through life thrusting his long Paul Pry neck into every body's business but his own' and that a bird of prey was a 'fit type of the hypocrite' who 'amidst the shades of night was abroad pursuing things vile and atrocious.'[73] Yet comparison might lead to more disturbing conclusions about the relationship between the city's poor and animals. *Paddy Kelly's Budget* rhymed about the superior conditions in the gardens compared with those of Dublin's working men: 'confined in iron cages,/Beasts and birds—all sorts and ages,/Russian bears, and wolves from Siam,/Are much better fed than I am'.[74] The gardens could emphasise social inequalities while claiming to ignore them.

Despite *Paddy Kelly's* observations, the distance between human spectators and animal spectacle was emphasised by the animals' captivity and mortality. Visitors commented on the poor conditions that animals endured in the gardens. In 1832, for example, a visitor from Belfast complained to the *Dublin Penny Journal* that he or she 'was surprised at the very confined space in which so many were crowded'. In a room about twenty-five by twelve feet the visitor noticed 'a leopard and leopardess, a hyena, several monkeys, a squirrel, an ichneumon, a pelican, several macaws and parrots, a Kestrel hawk, and two fine herons, birds, tortoises and others'. The visitor felt sorry for the animals who 'must feel their strict confinement anything but pleasant' but also for the visitors who could not see them very well.[75] The Society had chained the birds of prey in small spaces where they could not perch and confined sea birds far from any water. Similar complaints emanated from *Paddy Kelly's Budget*. Through the fictional character of Darby Dunn the magazine commented on the 'dark, filthy house' that held a leopardess but also 'a sloth bear, a badger, and two or three monkeys'.[76] The more sober *Dublin University Magazine* remarked in 1833 on 'the air of desolation which is presented by the gardens, and the appearance of total neglect which reigns throughout the whole establishment; and in corroboration of what is here asserted hardly a month elapses without the death of some valuable animal'.[77]

The Society always sought new specimens and accepted high mortality rates as routine. As the council remarked in 1835, they were 'extremely anxious [to] increase their collection by purchase or otherwise'.[78] In the early years, supporters donated animals: the king provided a leopard, wolf and hyena, while citizens such as Mr Egan of Dorset Street gifted the more mundane monkeys and foreign birds.[79] By 1833 the Society had gathered a collection of 139 animals.[80] The Society relied on purchases to fill in the gaps or to provide animals of extra interest. Animals were short-lived. The Zoological Society placed newspaper advertisements urging visitors to view the seal captured in 1835 soon because 'the life of such an animal in confinement is precarious'.[81] Despite this, animals often commanded higher prices than workers in the gardens. They paid the first keeper £30 per year, although this quickly rose to £100.[82] Other labourers received much less while the Society paid £14 for a pelican, £77 for a camel and £150 per month to rent a rhinoceros.[83]

As the Society built more enclosures, acquired more animals and continued to develop the grounds, public complaints about poor conditions tended to lessen. By 1837 the *Dublin University Magazine* had altered its view of the gardens and saw them as an important national project. Better cages, including an ornamental elephant house built in 1836 and a giraffe house built in 1845, improved the appearance of the gardens.[84] Aesthetic changes made the gardens more pleasant for human visitors but did not change the reality of confinement for animals. Indeed, the Society's idea of how to improve conditions for animals was often misguided. In 1838 the Society built a 'deambulatorium' for the carnivores. The large wire cage would place a tigress 'in a situation where she can display her powers'.[85] A celebratory song composed for the opening ceremony suggested that the captive animals who had been 'in narrow dens confined ... our savage wildness changed for a sullen sad chagrin' would now 'frisk with joy and glee'.[86] Unfortunately neither the tigress nor any of the other carnivores liked the cage and it was eventually broken up to make bear cages.[87]

The Society offered few animals a space as large as the 'deambulatorium'. Crowded, dirty conditions caused injury, illness and death. Post-mortem examinations on animals that died in the zoo suggest the difficulties of life in confinement. Dr Houston claimed that, having examined 'a great number' of dead monkeys, he could not recall any 'in which the animal had not died either of consumption, or, having lost its life from some other cause, did not present marks of incipient phthisis in its lungs'. Consumption, now known as tuberculosis, spread easily among residents of the crowded, damp cages much as it did among the poor in Dublin's tenements. Houston also dissected, in a single year, a deer that had been gored, a golden eagle that had refused food and wasted away and a macaw with a tumour and several broken bones.[88] In 1836, for example, the elephant hurt herself by trying to break down the door of her cage and an eagle died while fighting with another eagle.[89] The Society, acutely aware of accusations of mistreatment, announced in its 1837 report that 'in health, longevity and prolific powers its animals very greatly excel those in the Gardens of London and Paris, and any report to the contrary should be contradicted'.[90] Despite such claims, death and illness continued to be frequent occurrences. In 1840 the Society ordered special food and regular baths in an attempt to prolong the life of the dying elephant.[91] In 1841, rats killed several birds.[92]

Visitors interacted with the animals, sometimes violently. Normal interactions included feeding and petting the animals. The concerned visitor from Belfast, for example, fed the red grouse and petted the Wapiti deer.[93] The Society permitted H. D. Richardson, a natural history writer and dog breeder, to tame the tigress in the gardens and he 'got so far as to be able to stroke the creature on the head and back'.[94] Other visitors behaved less gently. The Society placed a notice declaring 'that any person who may be detected in the act of tormenting the animals will be prevented from again visiting the garden'.[95] In 1839, thieves stole four jackals from the gardens and succeeded in selling one to Bernard Finn of the Kilruddery Hounds Club, who advertised it as 'an extraordinary foreign fox' for the next hunt.[96] Patrick Devitt, a visitor from the country, pulled feathers from a bird to make fishing flies because, he later claimed in police court, 'I began to think, as it was moulting season, and as the ould feathers must be very troublesome to the poor things, that it would be a charity to draw them'.[97]

In 1840, Caesar Otway delivered a lecture on 'The Intellectuality of Domestic Animals' for the Zoological Society. Otway was an evangelical Protestant clergyman as well as an author and magazine editor.[98] Otway concluded with the assertion that a combination of zoological knowledge and Christian humanity 'may teach us to treat kindly, considerately, inferior animals' and lead to a 'happy millennial period ... when the inferior animals may stand in the same relation to man as they did to Adam before the fall'.[99] Responses to Otway's lecture suggest the depth of social divisions that the Zoological Society often succeeded in papering over. Otway had described the views of a number of religious thinkers on whether animals had souls or not. He claimed that a French Jesuit had tried to reconcile his belief that animals had reason with the views of his Church that they did not have souls and wound up concluding that all animals were devils. Two audience members walked out because they felt that he had mocked Catholic ideas about animals. Ideas about human–animal relationships always had the potential to bring social, religious and political divisions to the surface. Such divisions would prevent the success of the Dublin Society for the Prevention of Cruelty to Animals.

Dublin Society for the Prevention of Cruelty to Animals

The animals in the Zoological Gardens experienced far from perfect conditions yet they mostly had enough food and people rarely beat or killed them. They endured tedium rather than exertion or danger; the Society and its visitors treated them more like pets than like working animals or food.[100] Outside the private carriage that conveyed our doctor's daughter to and from the Zoological Gardens, working animals and food animals lived very different lives. If she had parted her curtains to glance into the street she might have witnessed many acts that would have shocked the sensibilities of a young woman who grieved when her dog died, recording in her diary, 'it would seem ridiculous to add how sorry I am' and that she 'never could care about another dog'.[101] Drovers beat cattle until they bled and butchers slaughtered them without regard for swiftness, draymen prodded asses with sharpened metal points and cab drivers whipped exhausted horses until they collapsed, young boys skinned cats and young men watched dogs tear one another apart. If the Zoological Gardens imitated Paradise then the streets better resembled hell.[102]

While the Zoological Society carved out its 'pleasing retreat from the din of the city', other Dubliners turned their attention to civilising that din by policing how people treated animals.[103] If they failed to bring about Otway's imagined 'happy millennial period' they sought at least to reduce the daily acts of cruelty that appeared part and parcel of city life dependent on the consumption of tens of thousands of animals. Our doctor's daughter was not among the advocates who eventually established the DSPCA in 1840 but her sympathies with some 'inferior animals' echoed those of a growing number of her class.[104] Perhaps the prevalence of pets in the nineteenth century indicates increased care for non-human animals, but arguments for treating animals kindly have a lengthy pedigree.[105] The nineteenth century saw new anti-cruelty legislation in much of the Western world and a rise in associations charged with enforcing humane treatment of animals.[106]

In Dublin the movement for humane treatment of animals took on a specific local flavour and reflected the tensions between, and the pretensions of, its citizens. While many middle-class Dubliners agreed that cruelty was wrong, few were willing to pursue a cab driver in the streets and send him to jail for lashing his horse. The same divisions that made the Zoological Gardens welcome made the DSPCA less so. Some with nationalist sympathies believed that the criminalisation of poor Irish Catholics for mistreating dumb animals represented an absurd excess of English, Protestant rule. Perhaps fearing controversy, few prominent Dubliners openly supported the DSPCA.

The humane movement in Dublin, like the foundation of the Dublin Zoological Society, followed developments in London. The first 'act to prevent the cruel and improper treatment of cattle' of 1822 became known as 'Martin's Act' because of the advocacy of an Irish Member of Parliament from Galway, Richard 'Humanity Dick' Martin. A London Society for the Prevention of Cruelty to Animals was founded in 1824 in order to enforce the Act in the metropolis and advocate for further legislation.[107] By 1826, Mrs Frances Maria Thompson, or 'Dick Martin in petticoats', had begun bringing acts of cruelty before the Dublin magistrates. A wealthy lady, Thompson put her own money into several humane societies in England and on-the-ground efforts in Dublin. At least one newspaper poked fun at Thompson, claiming that she 'could not place her head upon her pillow without being humbled by the spectre of a lacerated donkey'. But the Dublin magistrates took her testimony seriously enough.[108]

The passage of revised legislation in 1835 encouraged Thompson and her supporters to expand their activities. The Act to Consolidate and Amend the Several Laws Relating to Cruel and Improper Treatment of Animals extended protection to pets and prohibited certain types of animal sports including bull baiting and cock fighting.[109] Thompson hired a man to pace the streets wearing a sandwich board with text that prevailed upon the public to treat animals kindly.[110] The London SPCA sent Mr Rothe, 'an active and highly efficient agent', to police the Dublin streets and took out advertisements in the newspapers to threaten animal abusers that 'the most prompt and rigorous measures will be put in force' to punish them.[111] Thompson found a supporter in Sir John de Beauvoir (an MP with Irish connections) who wrote to the SPCA in London about founding a Dublin society.[112] Between 1837 and 1839, Mrs Thompson corresponded with the London SPCA, attended a meeting in London and extracted £60 to support a Dublin society.[113] She also supported the London-based Association for Promoting Rational Humanity Towards the Animal Creation, a rival to the London SPCA, and contributed letters to its publication *Voice of Humanity*.[114] From 1839, Thompson gained the active support of Major William Moore with an address in the prosperous suburb of Rathmines.[115]

In 1836 and 1837 Mr Rothe walked the streets of Dublin in search of acts of cruelty. He found a starving horse in a knacker's yard eating the mane of another horse, two groups of boys engaged in worrying a cat with dogs, a man organising a badger baiting with stolen dogs, a car driver beating a horse, a thousand people watching a dog fight in the Phoenix Park and a man keeping two starved donkeys in his house.[116] In almost all cases a sympathetic magistrate convicted in Rothe's favour.

From 1838 Major Moore and Thomas Carman detected acts of cruelty on behalf of the nascent Dublin Society for the Prevention of Cruelty to Animals. They found car drivers beating injured horses in Ship Street, Annesley Bridge, the Drumcondra Road, the Cabra Road and the Finglas Road; men beating injured asses as they entered the city from Glasnevin, Finglas and Drumcondra; a ten-year-old boy prodding a donkey with an iron point in Jervis Street; a cock fight in Hammond Lane; twenty-three drivers overloading their horses at

Donnybrook Fair; a knacker selling an exhausted and starved horse in Red Cow Lane; men throwing lambs into a steamer; a man beating cattle in the Dublin cattle market; a man hunting a cat with two dogs in Prospect Street; and a man beating a donkey in Thomas Street.[117] Police officers also took cases to the magistrates, including a man flogging his horse in North Frederick Street; two men conveying a sick and injured cow in a cart with a dead cow in Cross-Guns Road; a man working an injured horse in Dolphin's Barn; a car driver beating his horse in Upper Sackville Street; a man beating a horse hauling an omnibus; many car drivers overloading their horses on the way to Donnybrook Fair and a group of three beating an exhausted cow in Nicholas Street.[118] Concerned citizens occasionally brought cases based on witnessing cruelty in the street or because an employee, such as a stable hand, had treated their animal badly.[119] As with the period covered by Mr Rothe, almost all cases resulted in convictions.

In London, the public nature of the acts of cruelty was significant as was the social class of the abusers.[120] Despite incomplete records of either the DSPCA or the Petty Sessions courts, the Dublin cases show a similar pattern.[121] Only rarely did officers of the DSPCA or police officers enter private buildings: they detected crimes in the public streets. In most cases the accused was poor, and many went to prison because they could not afford the fine imposed. Reporting of the cases indicated broad agreement that cruelty to animals was a bad thing, that it was associated with ignorance and that it should be detected and punished. Different to London, support for the idea of humane treatment of animals did not extend to public support for the DSPCA.

Cruelty to animals in the public streets concerned people who read the streets as an indication of the city's progress. Visitors to Dublin, for example, surveyed the city for signs of its health and future. Almost all remarked on the social disparities: 'Everywhere one looks, poverty stands at the door of wealth', wrote one visitor. Another claimed that the streets presented 'contrasts between the greatest imaginable luxury and the utmost state of human destitution'.[122] One indication of these two sides of the city was a row of 'splendid equipages followed by a long row of hackneys'.[123] The contrast between the private carriage with its shiny horses and the cheap car for hire with its skinny nag served as a constant public reminder of the gulf between rich and poor. Such a gulf struck visitors as demonstrating that Ireland and Dublin were uncivilised. Places such as the Zoological Gardens hid these gaps by admitting only the respectable: they projected a potential city of the future free from visible reminders of destitution.

In Dublin as in London, the working horse embodied a contrast between the welcome bustle of a prosperous city and the consequences of this prosperity for human and animal lives. An abused cab horse, its driver bent on speed, suggested both economic progress and moral decline.[124]

A beautiful horse could demonstrate wealth and taste. The city's better-off residents used horses and carriages to project their status in the streets. One English visitor to the city claimed that even 'a Dublin tradesman who has realised 10,000 L, or perhaps a greatly less sum, [...] sets up his jaunting-car, becomes the possessor of a villa, and entertains company'.[125] Isaac Butt insisted that 'the love of display is so great that many persons, who live very badly in all other respects, still manage to keep carriages and horses'.[126] Philip Crampton, the Surgeon General for Ireland, was well known for his expensive and beautiful horses.[127] Driving could display both horses and passengers. Open spaces such as the Phoenix Park provided a horse-drawn promenade (see Figure 1.4).

By contrast with these wealthy passengers, the appearance of cab drivers and their horses projected not just poverty but ignorance, intemperance and inhumanity. Travellers often had their first encounter with a native Dubliner as a passenger in his cab. Henry Inglis recalled arriving into Dublin harbour to meet 'a new race, the drivers of the jaunting-cars, vociferous in their recommendations of the superior advantages of their vehicles, in convenience and cheapness, over all rival and more ambitious conveyances'.[128] Such convenience and cheapness was bought at the expense of the horses. Figure 1.5, from an 1840 collection of prints of Dublin street life, is entitled 'A car your honour—20 minutes or no money'. In the foreground the driver attempts to engage a fare while the rest of the image bristles with raised whips urging half-starved horses to speed. The drivers' pursuit of a fare at all costs is depicted with terrible consequences. A baby falls beneath a horse's hooves, presumably trampled. The ragged humans in the foreground (including one picking the prospective fare's pocket) suggest that the driver does not provide for his family. Even the passengers evince a callous disregard for life: a man looks the other way as his wife almost drops the baby and registers no alarm. A second picture from the same series of prints is shown in Figure 1.6. 'Returning from the "Brook"' brings out the association

1.4. 'Crinoline in Dublin', a print showing two ladies on a drive in the Phoenix Park. What cannot be seen in the black and white reproduction is that the horse's trimmings have been tinted to match the ladies' skirts. Image courtesy of the National Library of Ireland.

between violence towards animals, poverty and vice even more strongly. 'The Brook' refers to Donnybrook, the popular Dublin fair of which the Zoological Society also disapproved. While a crossroads/ crucifix looms in the background, the drivers whip miserable animals dragging overloaded carts. The passengers are drunk, the women are immodest. Inhumane and poor, drivers are made to resemble animals in picture and word. Mrs Frederick West would have recognised the cab drivers in the images as similar to the one she described: 'To the protruding jaw of the ape, he added a pair of cheeks so oddly puffed out, as to resemble a monkey pouching his nuts against a future occasion.'[129]

It was not clear that animals always benefitted from efforts to eradicate cruelty. As Mrs Thompson sought to establish the DSPCA, she persuaded the Commissioners of Police to round up and inspect all the horses used by hackney drivers. John de Beauvoir bragged to the RSPCA that

1.5. 'A car your honour—20 minutes or no money'. The print shows Dublin cab drivers competing for fares and raising their whips to speed up their horses. Note the combination of poverty, theft and cruelty depicted. Image courtesy of the National Library of Ireland.

the Commissioners of Police called in fourteen hundred cars, when every disabled and defective horse was discharged, and the *proprietor deprived of his license.*

As no licenses are now granted till the horses are inspected, the result is, that the entire number of the cars are furnished with excellent animals, and all the carriages are in the best order.[130]

For elite reformers such as de Beauvoir and Thompson, such an act made the public streets a better place and insured that travellers such as Mrs West and Mr Inglis might have fewer complaints about their transportation. The inspection of horses improved conditions for people. No mention was made of the 'discharged' horses, presumably sent for slaughter. Cab drivers certainly perceived the laws to be more about them than about their animals. They claimed that 'more laws had been made for their use than for many other trades'.[131]

A diverse group of workers, not just cab drivers, appeared before magistrates to answer for acts of cruelty. They were united by poverty and religion. The records of the Dublin Metropolitan Police show that the vast majority of those convicted in every year were poor Catholic men between the ages of fifteen and thirty. Some could read, but most

1.6. 'Returning from "The Brook"', a print showing overloaded cabs containing drunk passengers pulled by emaciated horses. Image courtesy of the National Library of Ireland.

could not write. They were predominantly classed as 'labourers' or having 'no trade'. In contrast to London, coachmen were only about one third of all those arrested.[132] Between 1838 and 1845 only one woman was arrested for cruelty to animals.[133] Although the statistics collected do not include religion, we can make some deductions from census data. In 1861, the first year that information about religious denomination was collected in association with occupation, the vast majority of workers in any aspect of the urban animal economy were Catholic. In the census returns for Leinster (the province of which Dublin is the principal city), there were 8000 people occupied as herders and drovers. Of these, 7444 were Catholic men. Owners and drivers of cars comprised 5546 persons, of whom 5226 were Catholic men.[134]

Catholic workers dominated Dublin's streets while those who detected and prosecuted abuses were generally Protestant. Circumstantial evidence suggests that the DSPCA's early enforcers, Major Moore and Mr Rothe, were Protestant. Further, the Dublin police court was a predominantly Protestant space. Only nineteen of ninety-one magistrates, six of twenty judges and 530 of 1644 lawyers of all kinds were Catholic in 1861. The proportion had probably been lower during the 1840s. Thus if a cab driver appeared before the magistrate or judge in one of the city's courts he might reasonably presume that his case would be heard by a Protestant, in the same way that a judge sitting in the court might reasonably presume that the cab driver was Catholic. No one mentioned religion in these proceedings, but it lurked beneath the surface as an understood distance between accused and accuser.

The newspaper reports often depicted the poor labourer as ignorant and brutish, his crimes described as evidence for his inferior state of civility. While no one mentioned religion, social class was always clear. A cab driver committed 'brutal maltreatment' of his horse.[135] Boys who worried a cat showed 'brutality' and 'wanton and unfeeling cruelty'.[136] A driver of a donkey car was 'a rough, savage looking fellow'.[137] Reports often noted the social gulf between accuser and accused. For example, in 1839, 'a gentleman' brought the driver of a dray to the magistrates after he witnessed him beating a fallen horse in College Green. The driver was one of 'several persons' but not a gentleman.[138] Masters reported on servants to punish them for poor treatment of the animals they had been hired to care for. In 1842 a Mr Knox, owner of a stables, brought his stable hand before the magistrate and charged him with cruelty to a horse in his care. After taking a horse for treatment at the veterinary surgeon the boy had ridden the horse until it died.[139] A surgeon named O'Reilly brought his groom to the magistrate for cruelly driving his horse at a furious pace and making him lame.[140]

Many of the accused pled poverty but the magistrates never accepted this as an excuse. An organiser of a badger fight said he had done it 'for the purpose of procuring subsistence for a large family'.[141] A man who beat his horse 'complained that through the sluggishness of his horse he had lost two or three jobs in the last few days'.[142] Another driver claimed that if he had to wait for his horse's back to heal before using the horse 'it would be better for him to send him at once to the tan-yard'.[143] Two keepers of starving donkeys argued that they fed the animals whenever they could afford to buy food.[144]

The association between poverty and cruelty is underscored by the relationship between the Poor Law (which provided relief through workhouses) and the Acts against animal cruelty. The 1835 humane legislation specified that a proportion of money collected from violations of the Act was to be given to the poor of the parish. Before the 1838 reform of Ireland's Poor Law, legal opinion was that the humane legislation did not apply either.[145] This link between the reformed Poor Law (overseen by appointed Boards of Guardians) and punishment for cruelty to animals suggests a system of taking from the 'undeserving' poor to give to the 'deserving' poor.

The mass arrests of cab drivers during Donnybrook Fair allowed magistrates, police officers and members of the public to express disapproval of poverty, cruelty and intemperance all at once. The fair took place on the outskirts of Dublin in August, ostensibly for the purpose of buying and selling livestock. The Catholic and Protestant churches and many urban reformers agreed that the notoriously licentious, intemperate event ought to be supressed. Failing that, the fair provided an opportunity to punish those who participated in its excesses. Large groups of individuals appeared before the police court charged with a variety of crimes, including cruelty to animals.[146] In 1842 the DSPCA hired extra constables to prosecute acts of cruelty at the fair.[147]

Despite evidence of a system to punish acts of cruelty, the DSPCA attracted little public support. Absence of support may reflect the political and religious divisions of Dublin during the 1840s. The reform of local government and the municipal franchise in 1841 created a Dublin Corporation that reflected the Catholic and liberal majority of the city. Politicians in favour of an independent Irish parliament (Repealers) gained over half of the council seats and Daniel O'Connell was elected Lord Mayor. He was the first Catholic to hold the post in centuries.[148] The city's substantial Protestant, conservative minority retained control of a number of government-appointed boards that collectively represented considerable political and economic power. Tensions ran high. In this charged atmosphere, the DSPCA failed to gain a foothold.

Moore and Thompson might have reasonably hoped for more support. As we have already seen, the Dublin Metropolitan Police arrested Dubliners for acts of cruelty and city magistrates imposed fines and prison sentences. The city was full of pets, as Chapter 4 will discuss. Moore and Thompson could have looked to Philip Crampton— eight-time president of the Zoological Society of Dublin, Surgeon General for Ireland, owner of a stable of horses and a pack of hunting dogs.[149] Crampton's letters to his son were full of dogs and horses. Crampton took in John's dog when he departed for Russia and wrote to tell him that the dog was 'the best little boy in the world perfectly gentle & obedient'. In another letter he recounted taking his grandson and a pet cat into his bed where 'we three lay together for ½ an hour the cat purring all the time'.[150] In a lecture in 1838 to the Royal College of Surgeons he publicly condemned the practice of vivisection.[151] Yet Crampton never joined nor became a patron of the Dublin SPCA.

Major Moore's early correspondence to the London SPCA contained a litany of complaints about the indifference of the Dublin citizenry. In October 1840 he asked for advice on how to encourage donations and subscriptions, having so far collected only about 30s. There was money in Dublin to support societies: the Zoological Society collected enough in its first few months to permit it to pay £75 for landscaping plans and hire a full-time keeper.[152] While touting his rate of prosecution and conviction in January of 1841, Moore again remarked on 'the indifference manifested by the inhabitants of Dublin to the objects of the Auxiliary Society and the want of funds'.[153] In February he was cheered by the support from the pulpits of Reverend Dr William Urwick and another unnamed minister, but he still needed funds from London. In 1843, Moore gave up on his fellow citizens and proposed to 'come to London to solicit subscriptions in and out of the Society' to aid the cause in Dublin.[154] In the same year the Queen became the Society's patron. All three vice-patrons were also English. The expanded committee held only one name of local renown: Robert Guinness, a barrister and lesser-known member of the great Protestant family of brewers and businessmen.[155]

Political support for the DSPCA was conspicuous in its absence, although a few Irish parliamentary politicians other than 'Humanity Dick' engaged in issues around the humane treatment of animals. Maurice J. O'Connell, son of Daniel O'Connell and MP for Dublin, debated and approved several bills relating to the treatment of dogs. The O'Connells, like the Cramptons, kept a pack of hunting dogs. In 1843, Maurice O'Connell backed a bill to ban the use of dogs to pull carts in cities and in 1844 he voted in favour of a bill to make dog stealing a felony.[156] Yet no Irish MPs engaged with the bills of 1822 and 1835. Two Irish MPs (a Liberal and a Repeal politician) voted against the latter, suggesting some antipathy. However, these were only two MPs out of one hundred.[157] The biggest obstacle may have been indifference.

The DSPCA's failure is surprising as societies flourished in other provincial cities of similar size including Belfast and Bristol.[158] As historian Kathleen Kete has suggested, the issue of animal protection has been entangled with defining 'us' and 'them'. Kindness to animals suggested a separation between 'we' who behave civilly and 'you' who do not. In London and England, the middle classes increasingly asserted themselves as a collective 'we' in matters of public behaviour and social order. But Dublin's middle class was conscious of divisions along religious and political lines and these prevented unity in some areas of reform.

Religious differences contributed to the troubles faced by the Dublin SPCA. In Belfast, religious support from the city's dissenting Protestant community had proved crucial to the establishment of the SPCA there.[159] In Catholic Dublin, early humane activists sought the support of Dr Daniel Murray, the moderate Catholic Archbishop of Dublin. In 1835, Sir John de Beauvoir MP approached Murray and reported to the RSPCA that he was favourable to the Society.[160] Politicians viewed Murray as liberal and tolerant: he had cooperated with government to support the establishment of the controversial non-denominational national schools. He opposed political activity by the clergy and did not participate in the Repeal movement.[161] Nonetheless Murray did not become involved and Moore sought out dissenting Protestants. He delayed the foundational meeting in 1840 until the city's Quaker leaders had returned from their provincial meeting and recruited the support of Reverend Dr Urwick.[162] Yet Urwick failed to raise a significant following among his flock for the humane cause and his collected sermons have much to say on the abolition of slavery but nothing to say on humane treatment of animals.[163] The support of other Dublin Quakers, such as Joshua Abell, had little effect.[164]

The rise of the movement for the Repeal of the Union, led by Catholic politician Daniel O'Connell, hindered the formation of the DSPCA. The Repeal movement included Protestants, but its core support came from middle- and lower-class Catholics.[165] These same lower-class Catholics were the butchers, cab drivers and cattle drovers that the DSPCA targeted in its efforts to eliminate cruelty to animals. The city's rising Catholic middle class may have been shy of targeting those who paid the 'Repeal rent' and supported nationalist political causes. Moore delayed the foundational meeting in 1840 multiple times, probably because of the excitement caused by the foundation of the Loyal National Repeal Association and the subsequent speeches by O'Connell. The first public DSPCA meeting in September in the Lord Mayor's mansion was 'anything but numerous'.[166] Moore might have feared that Repealers would mock any public figure who embraced his cause. Instead, no such public figure emerged.

Enthusiasm for Repeal threatened the potential support base of the DSPCA because Repealers used the language of cruelty to refer to the actions of the British government against the Irish people. Messages about cruelty to animals could be seen as trivial by comparison. In the Repeal Catechism, a farmer and an 'agitator' discussed their political ambitions for Ireland. The agitator explained to the farmer what had been lost through the Union with Britain and what could be gained by its repeal. The farmer understood that England had tried to enrich and strengthen Ireland for its own gain 'precisely as I fatten my horse—not for love of the animals, but in order that they may be strong enough to carry greater burdens for me'. The catechism alleged English cruelty towards the Irish to support its claims for Repeal. For example, the agitator claimed that England used physical torture and beatings that had 'by the common abhorrence of mankind, been for centuries abolished from civilized states' to force the passage of the Union. He made the baseless allegation that men were 'flogged nearly to death' or 'actually flogged to death' in order to extract confessions. Witnesses 'heard the lash resound'. The streets rang with the 'hideous shrieks of the victims and the more hideous exultation of the fiends who tortured them and carried the Union'. The 'cruelty and treachery of the English government toward Ireland' was assessed as even worse than the excesses of revolutionary France.[167] In further chapters the farmer declared that the lack of an Irish parliament was 'cruelly absurd'.[168]

If the English parliament had been cruel to Ireland, the promotion of legislation to prevent cruelty to animals in Ireland could be construed as mockery. Referring to the anti-cruelty acts became a useful device, allowing the speaker to emphasise the contradiction between English attitudes towards beasts and their attitudes towards Irish people. As one supporter of Repeal wrote,

> nothing good could be expected for Ireland from a Saxon legislature, which has more care for the dogs and asses of England (as is evident from its acts to prevent cruelty to these animals), than it has for the starving peasantry and tenantry of Ireland. The dogs of England have excited the commiseration and obtained the protection of the parliament—the human beings of Ireland, made after the image of God, have been left to die, without having a word spoken in their favor.[169]

The idea that animal protection might slide into excessive sympathy for beasts over men was not an exclusive concern of Catholics or Repealers. The idea featured in debates over humane legislation in

England and appeared in the popular press in Ireland as well. In an article advocating the keeping of pets as a way of developing kindness in children, the author cautioned that excessive fondness would weaken the bond with other humans: 'In childhood, therefore, the disposition to love even the domestic animals born for our use should be sedulously fostered, but not to such excess as to weaken the affection for parents, brothers, sisters, or friends.'[170] In a critique of a much earlier bill to prevent cruelty to animals (supported by Lord Erskine in 1809), the *Irish Magazine, and Monthly Asylum for Neglected Biography* offered a number of examples of this balance gone wrong. A false humanity was at work when a poor blind man was imprisoned for beating his dog or a hungry child chastised for trying to retrieve gingerbread stolen by a goat. Further evidence of the absurdity of the bill was the fact that 'Connacht is covered with fat sleek cattle and ragged and hungry men'.[171] These examples were found in conservative, Protestant journals rather than liberal, nationalist or Catholic ones. However, in the context of the Repeal movement such arguments took on a specific political tone. Patronising the cause of humane treatment of animals could be seen as callous disregard for Irish humans, a position that would not win supporters in 1840s Dublin.

Thus the Irish political and social context favoured some types of human–animal relationships and not others. The animal as zoological spectacle provoked little protest and considerable support among the city's reforming elites. Middle-class Dubliners could pass their leisure time as consumers of a wholesome animal spectacle or they could join the Zoological Society and become benefactors of science and popular education. A great swathe of the city's population willingly paid to visit the spectacle. In this arrangement politics were pushed to the side, class and religion were declared irrelevant and the consequences for animals of captivity was ignored. The DSPCA could not so easily dismiss politics, class and religion in its mission to defend animals against cruelty. Defence of animals required prosecution of people and these people were overwhelmingly poor Catholics. The treatment of poor Irish Catholics, rather than the treatment of animals, was at the centre of Irish political debates during the turbulent 1840s. The DSPCA's mission could easily be identified as political.

Although ostensibly concerned with animals, both the DSPCA and the Zoological Society sought to improve the habits of human Dubliners, especially poor human Dubliners. They encouraged cab drivers to behave more like doctor's daughters, following the mores and habits of a middle class whose influence was growing across the British Isles.

Visiting Paris in 1840, a writer in the *Irish Penny Journal* claimed, one would be 'forcibly struck' by the sight of 'persons of inferior degree, who with the greatest attention, and in the most decorous and orderly manner, inspect the various objects presented to their notice' at museums, menageries and other places of public education.[172] 'A most decided improvement in the habits and feelings of the humbler classes of the community has really taken place.'[173] The writer rejoiced that while in the past the ordinary people of Dublin had often mistreated 'the property of the few liberal individuals who offered to share their pleasures with their less fortunate fellows', now a new spirit of 'improved education and temperate habits' prevailed. The people could now be trusted to behave themselves even at exhibitions 'of objects of great intrinsic value'.[174] 'Improper conduct in public places', the writer opined, would soon be a distant memory and Dublin would be a city as civilised as Paris.

Unbeknownst to Dubliners, a crisis of vast proportions would soon draw attention to Ireland's poor and make kindness to animals and zoological science seem of little practical value. Touring Dublin after the devastation of the Great Famine, the writer Thomas Carlyle reluctantly visited the Zoological Gardens on the invitation of the council of the Zoological Society. He recorded only 'Animals &c.,—Public subscription scanty—Government helps:—adieu to it.'[175] He had no patience for such dilettante efforts at civilising the demonstrably backward Irish. He was much more interested in the model farm and agricultural school in Glasnevin, on the city's northern edge. Ireland's rescuers, according to Carlyle, would be 'practical missionaries of good order and wise husbandry', rather than metropolitan intellectuals.[176] He noticed no improvement in the habits of the Irish poor, now reduced to starvation, disease and emigration by their reliance on the potato, a food many thought better suited to animals.

Notes

1 'Zoological Gardens—Yesterday', *Freeman's Journal* (31 July 1835).
2 'Dublin Police Court. College-Street. Cruelty to Animals', *Freeman's Journal* (17 September 1839).
3 Visitor books make the social class mixing particularly clear but are only available from 1859. On 'ragged boys' see, for example, Royal Zoological

Society of Ireland, Visitor Books, MS 10608/8/1, Trinity College Dublin, entry for 23 June 1861 [Hereafter RZSI Visitor Books].

4 Anonymous diary of a young woman from 1836–1837, Ms 32,633/2, National Library of Ireland; see entries for 22 and 23 January 1837 and 22 May 1837 [Hereafter Diary of a young woman in Dublin]. Despite many efforts I have not been able to identify the diarists with sufficient certainty to give them names.

5 Henry D. Inglis, *A Journey Throughout Ireland: During the Spring, Summer and Autumn of 1834* (London: Whittaker and Co., 1835, 3rd edn, 2 vols), vol. 1, pp. 8–9.

6 *Returns of Agricultural Produce in Ireland, in the Year 1850* [1404], HC 1851, l, 1. See table on pages 256 and 257.

7 John Hutton and Sons, 'Estimate of a new chariot for ___ Baker Esq', 17 May 1822, MS 21,017, National Library of Ireland.

8 'The Vice-Regal Visit to the Zoological Gardens', *Paddy Kelly's Budget*, 10 June 1835, 154.

9 Diary of a young woman in Dublin, entries for 1 April 1837, 22 May 1837 and 29 May 1837.

10 Royal Zoological Society of Ireland, rough minutes 1830 to 1840, MS 10608/2, 23 June 1838, Trinity College Dublin [Hereafter RZSI Rough Minutes].

11 Inglis, *A Journey Throughout Ireland*, pp. 7–8.

12 'Dublin Police—Yesterday', *Freeman's Journal* (22 February 1839).

13 Darby Dunn, 'A visit to the Zoological Gardens', *Paddy Kelly's Budget*, 1 (1833), 143–4.

14 See, for example, 'Sale of the late Judge Vandeleur's property at Furry Park near Raheny', *Freeman's Journal* (30 June 1835); 'Carriage horses of the pure Yorkshire Breed', *Freeman's Journal* (7 April 1840).

15 Clay McShane and Joel A. Tarr, *The Horse in the City: Living Machines in the Nineteenth Century* (Baltimore, MD: Johns Hopkins University Press, 2007), p. 25; Kathryn Miele, 'Horse-sense: understanding the working horse in Victorian London', *Victorian Literature and Culture*, 37:1 (2009), 129–40; Ralph Turvey, 'Horse traction in Victorian London', *Journal of Transport History*, 26:2 (2005), 38–59.

16 'The Chase', *Irish Sportsman* (5 November 1870), 5.

17 Bob Mullan and Garry Marvin, *Zoo Culture: The Book About Watching People Watch Animals* (Urbana: University of Illinois Press, 1987), p. 3.

18 Kay Anderson, 'Culture and nature at the Adelaide Zoo: at the frontiers of human geography', *Transactions of the Institute of British Geographers* 20 (1995), 275–94: 292.

19 Harriet Ritvo, *The Animal Estate: The English and Other Creatures in the Victorian Age* (Cambridge, MA: Harvard University Press, 1984), pp. 131, 132.

20 Kathleen Kete, 'Introduction', in Kathleen Kete (ed.), *A Cultural History of Animals in the Age of Empire* (Oxford: Berg Publishers, 2011), p. 3.
21 Ritvo, *The Animal Estate*, pp. 134–7.
22 Alvin Jackson, *Ireland, 1798–1998: War, Peace and Beyond* (Oxford: Wiley-Blackwell, 2010), pp. 35–6.
23 Jackson, *Ireland*, p. 39.
24 Jackson, *Ireland*, p. 45.
25 'Zoological Society', *Freeman's Journal* (11 May 1830).
26 Helen O'Connell, 'Animal welfare in post-Union Ireland', *New Hibernia Review* 19:1 (2015), 34–52.
27 Patrick M. Geoghan, 'Martin, Richard', in James McGuire and James Quinn (eds), *Dictionary of Irish Biography* (Cambridge: Cambridge University Press, 2012), https://dib-cambridge-org.dcu.idm.oclc.org/viewReadPage.do?articleId=a5487 (accessed 12 May 2020).
28 See O'Connell, 'Animal welfare in post-Union Ireland'.
29 'The Fashionable World', *Freeman's Journal* (25 September 1828).
30 D. J. Cunningham, *The Origin and Early History of the Royal Zoological Society of Ireland* (Dublin: The Council of the Society, 1901), p. 4.
31 'Cruelty to animals', *Freeman's Journal* (14 December 1836); 'Society for the Prevention of Cruelty to Animals', *Freeman's Journal* (11 January 1837).
32 See diary of her brother NLI MS 32,633 entry for 18 January 1837, and her NLI MS 32,633/2 entries for December 1836 and January 1837.
33 See Keith Jeffrey, 'Introduction', in Keith Jeffrey (ed.), *'An Irish Empire'? Aspects of Ireland and the British Empire* (Manchester: Manchester University Press, 1996), pp. 1–24: 16–17.
34 See, for example, James Murphy, *Abject Loyalty: Monarchy and Nationalism in Ireland During the Reign of Queen Victoria* (Cork: Cork University Press, 2001), pp. 8–9, 35.
35 Mary E. Daly, *Dublin, The Deposed Capital: a Social and Economic History, 1860–1914* (Cork: Cork University Press, 1984), pp. 124–8.
36 P. Morgan to Charles Gavan Duffy, 'Letters', *Nation* (27 May 1843).
37 See, for example, Hilda Kean, *Animal Rights: Political and Social Change in Britain Since 1800* (London: Reaktion, 1998); Keith Thomas, *Man and the Natural World: Changing Attitudes in England 1500–1800* (London: Penguin, 1984); Ritvo, *The Animal Estate*.
38 John McCullen, *An Illustrated History of the Phoenix Park* (Dublin, 2009).
39 Catherine De Courcy, *Dublin Zoo: An Illustrated History* (Cork: The Collins Press, 2009), p. 4.
40 RZSI Rough Minutes, 31 July 1835 and 24 July 1835.
41 'Zoological Gardens' (advert), *Saunder's Newsletter* (21 July 1835).
42 RZSI Rough Minutes, 4 August 1838, 1 October 1831 and 27 July 1839.
43 'The Zoological Gardens', *Freeman's Journal* (28 November 1832).

44 Royal Zoological Society of Ireland Transaction Books, MS 10608/9/1, entry for 24 November 1836, Trinity College Dublin department of manuscripts [Hereafter RZSI Transaction Books].

45 'The Zoological Gardens', *Saunder's Newsletter* (22 July 1835).

46 RZSI Transaction Books, entry for 11 August 1826.

47 'Zoology in Dublin', *Dublin University Magazine*, 10 (1837), 666–71: 671.

48 Philip Dixon Hardy, *A Visit to the Zoological Gardens, Phoenix Park, Dublin* (Dublin: P. D. Hardy, 1838), p. 4.

49 William Tighe Hamilton, *A Descriptive Catalogue of the Animals in the Collections of the Zoological Society of Dublin* (Dublin: Hodges and Smith, 1833), p. v.

50 RZSI Rough Minutes, 19 November 1832.

51 Nathaniel Whittock, *A Picturesque Guide Through Dublin* (London: J. Cornish, 1846), p. 101.

52 Hardy, *A Visit*, p. 4.

53 The London Zoological Gardens, as in Dublin, argued that it exhibited scientific specimens while also using more commercial attractions to lure visitors. This fact caused it to become entangled in issues around local taxation. See Takashi Ito, *London Zoo and the Victorians, 1828–1859* (Woodbridge: Boydell and Brewer for the Royal Historical Society, 2014), pp. 132–6.

54 'The Zoological Gardens', *Saunder's Newsletter* (22 August 1832); 'The Coronation—Rejoicings', *Freeman's Journal* (27 August 1838).

55 'Zoology in Dublin', *Dublin University Magazine*, 10 (1837), 669.

56 Hamilton, *A Descriptive Catalogue*, p. 2.

57 The *Freeman's Journal* had a Catholic editor in 1831 and was later edited by the liberal and nationalist Gray family. See Felix Larkin, '"A great daily organ": the *Freeman's Journal* 1763–1924', *History Ireland*, 14:3 (2006), 44–9.

58 Isaac Butt, *Zoology and Civilization* (Dublin, 1847), p. 24. Butt later became a liberal politician and one of a small group of elite Protestants who embraced the idea of Home Rule. See Philip Bull, 'Butt, Isaac', in McGuire and Quinn (eds), *Dictionary of Irish Biography*, https://dib-cambridge-org.dcu.idm.oclc.org/ (accessed 12 May 2020).

59 Butt, *Zoology and Civilization*, p. 31.

60 RZSI Rough Minutes, 15 May 1833.

61 RZSI Weekly Returns, entries for 6 and 13 May 1847 and 4 May 1848.

62 The earliest weekly returns book is from 1847. See RZSI Weekly Returns book, MS 10609/16/1, for example entries 6 May 1847 and 13 May 1837, Trinity College Dublin [Hereafter RZSI Weekly Returns].

63 Séamus Ó Maitiú, *The Humours of Donnybrook* (Dublin: Four Courts Press, 1993).

64 Royal Zoological Society of Ireland, *Proceedings of the Society*, p. 14;
    Cunningham, *The Origin and Early History*, pp. 8 and 13.
65 Hamilton, *A Descriptive Catalogue*, p. vi.
66 'Zoology in Dublin', *Dublin University Magazine*, 10 (1837), 668, 671.
67 Royal Zoological Society of Ireland, *Proceedings of the Society*, pp. 15, 40.
68 Hamilton, *A Descriptive Catalogue*; RZSI Rough Minutes, 2 August 1833.
69 Hardy, *A Visit*, p. 4.
70 'Royal Zoological Society', *Freeman's Journal* (7 December 1843).
71 'To the editor of the Freeman', *Freeman's Journal* (30 November 1843).
72 Darby Dunn, 'A visit to the Zoological Gardens', *Paddy Kelly's Budget*,
    1 (1833), 143–4: 144; see also Juliana Adelman, 'Animal knowl-
    edge: zoology and classification in nineteenth-century Dublin', *Field Day
    Review*, 5 (2009), 109–22.
73 Anon. [Philip Hardy], 'A visit to the gardens of the Zoological Society of
    Dublin', *Dublin Penny Journal* 30 June 1832), 4–5.
74 *Paddy Kelly's Budget* (10 June 1835), 154.
75 I. D. M., 'The Dublin Zoological Gardens', *Dublin Penny Journal* (23
    December 1832), 181.
76 Dunn, 'A visit to the Zoological Gardens'.
77 'Zoological Society', *Dublin University Magazine* (March 1833), 334–5:
    335.
78 RZSI Rough Minutes, 19 June 1835.
79 RZSI Rough Minutes, 19 November 1832.
80 RZSI Rough Minutes, 15 May 1833.
81 'Zoological Gardens', *Saunder's Newsletter* (21 July 1835).
82 RZSI Rough Minutes, 28 May 1831 and 8 April 1833; see also
    Cunningham, *The Origin and Early History*.
83 RZSI Rough Minutes, 21 September 1832, 2 May 1833 and 12 June
    1835.
84 RZSI Rough Minutes, 13 May 1836; RZSI, MS 10608/24/128, ephem-
    era collection, plan for giraffe house, Trinity College Dublin.
85 'Enlargement of the tigress at the Royal Zoological Gardens', *Freeman's
    Journal* (27 August 1838).
86 'Deambulatorium', MS 10608/24/1, Trinity College Dublin.
87 Arthur Wynne Foot, *Guide to the Royal Zoological Gardens, Phoenix Park*
    (Dublin, n.d. [1865], 2nd edn), p. 17.
88 'Extract from a paper read by Dr. Houston at a meeting of the Zoological
    Society of Dublin, on the diseases of animals which died in their collec-
    tion', *Dublin Journal of Medical and Chemical Science*, 1 May 1834, 285.
89 RZSI Transaction Books, 11 August 1836.
90 Philip Crampton, *An Appeal to the Public, on Behalf of the Zoological Society
    of Ireland. Published by the Order of the Council* (Dublin: Joshua Porter,
    1837), p. 4.

91 RZSI Rough Minutes, 27 June 1840.

92 RZSI Transaction Books, 10 June 1841.

93 I. D. M., *'The Dublin Zoological Gardens'*.

94 H. D. R. [H. D. Richardson], 'On Animal Taming', *Irish Penny Journal*, 1:25, 19 December 1840, 208.

95 RZSI Rough Minutes, 20 April 1832.

96 'Dublin Police Court', *Freeman's Journal* (16 October 1838).

97 'Dublin Police—Saturday', *Freeman's Journal* (25 February 1839).

98 Otway was one of a group of diverse Protestants interested in humane treatment of animals in early nineteenth-century Ireland. See O'Connell, 'Animal welfare in Post-Union Ireland'. See also C. J. Woods, 'Otway, Caesar', in James McGuire and James Quinn (eds), *Dictionary of Irish Biography* (Cambridge: Cambridge University Press, 2009), https:// dib-cambridge-org.dcu.idm.oclc.org/viewReadPage.do?articleId=a7143 (accessed 20 May 2020).

99 Caesar Otway, 'The intellectuality of domestic animals', *Dublin University Magazine* (May 1840), 515.

100 There are some noteworthy exceptions. The Society kept horses for labour in the gardens, compelled elephants to provide rides for visitors, sold the privilege of having female donkeys 'covered' by their stallion zebra and bred Zebu calves to sell on to landlords.

101 Diary of a young woman in Dublin, entry for 18 and 19 December 1836, 9 June 1837.

102 See Diana Donald on the visual imagery of London's Smithfield as hell-like: Diana Donald, '"Beastly sights": the treatment of animals as a moral theme in representations of London, c. 1820–1850', *Art History*, 22:4 (1999), 514–44.

103 'Zoological Gardens', *Freeman's Journal* (5 May 1838).

104 See, for example, Ritvo, *The Animal Estate*, pp. 134–7. See also Kean, *Animal Rights*; Kathleen Kete, 'Animals and ideology: the politics of animal protection in Europe', in Nigel Rothfels (ed.), *Representing Animals* (Bloomington: Indiana University Press, 2002), pp. 19–34.

105 O'Connell, 'Animal welfare in Post-Union Ireland'; Thomas, *Man and the Natural World*; Ingrid Tague, *Animal Companions: Pets and Social Change in Eighteenth-Century Britain* (State College: Pennsylvania State University Press, 2005).

106 'Dick Martin in petticoats', *Freeman's Journal* (26 January 1826).

107 Kean, *Animal Rights*, p. 35; Geoghan, 'Martin, Richard'.

108 'Dick Martin in petticoats', *Freeman's Journal* (26 January 1826).

109 Ritvo, *The Animal Estate*, p. 128.

110 The sandwich boards are referred to in 1840 when a replacement for Mrs Thompson's board was sought. See Minutes of the RSPCA Council, vol. 3, minutes of 3 February 1840.

111 'Cruelty to animals', *Freeman's Journal* (14 December 1836).
112 Minutes of the RSPCA Council, vol. 1, minutes of 2 March 1835.
113 Minutes of the RSPCA Council, vol. 2, minutes of 10 April 1837 and 7 May 1838.
114 Kean, *Animal Rights*, p. 60; see also *Voice of Humanity*, 2 (1832), 17.
115 Unfortunately neither Thompson nor Moore has left enough of a trace to round out their biographies further.
116 All of the following reported from the Dublin Police Court: 'Cruelty to animals', *Freeman's Journal* (8 October 1836); 'Cruelty to animals', *Freeman's Journal* (12 October 1836); 'Prevention of cruelty to animals', *Freeman's Journal* (16 November 1836); 'Cruelty to animals', *Freeman's Journal* (14 December 1836); 'Cruelty to animals', *Freeman's Journal* (6 April 1837); 'Cruelty to animals', *Freeman's Journal* (19 April 1837); 'Brutal treatment of a horse', *Freeman's Journal* (29 April 1837); 'Cruelty to animals', *Freeman's Journal* (31 July 1837).
117 'Cruelty to animals', *Freeman's Journal* (26 August 1839) (horse); 'Cruelty to animals', *Freeman's Journal* (5 December 1840) (donkey); 'Cruelty to animals', *Freeman's Journal* (8 December 1840) (donkey); 'Cockfighting', *Freeman's Journal* (12 May 1842); 'Cruelty to animals: caution to knackers', *Freeman's Journal* (14 August 1841) (horse); 'Cruelty to animals', *Freeman's Journal* (27 May 1840) (lambs); 'Cruelty to animals', *Freeman's Journal* (11 December 1840) (cattle). See also Petty Sessions Order Books, CSPS/3/037, National Archives of Ireland, for example, entries on 6, 12, 13, 14, 15, 21, 23 and 24 December 1842.
118 'Horrible cruelty to animals', *Freeman's Journal* (5 October 1842) (cow); 'Cruelty to animals', *Freeman's Journal* (16 July 1842) (horse); 'Cruelty to animals—caution to car drivers', *Freeman's Journal* (26 June 1841) (horse); 'Cruelty to animals', *Freeman's Journal* (30 May 1840) (cow); 'Cruelty to animals—the Duke of Newcastle's Law', *Freeman's Journal* (4 June 1842) (horse).
119 'Cruelty to animals', *Freeman's Journal* (30 March 1842).
120 Ritvo, *The Animal Estate*.
121 For example, the annual police reports listed eighteen cases in 1838 but not all could be found in newspaper reports. Of the sixty-nine cases listed in 1840 and 113 listed in 1845, only a small proportion appeared in print. *Number of Persons Taken into Custody by the Dublin Metropolitan Police, and the Results in the Year 1838* (Dublin: Alexander Thom, January 1839); *Number of Persons Taken into Custody by the Dublin Metropolitan Police, and the Results in the Year 1839* (Dublin: Alexander Thom, 1840); *Number of Persons Taken into Custody by the Dublin Metropolitan Police, and the Results in the Year 1840* (Dublin: Alexander Thom, January 1841); *Number of Persons Taken into Custody by the Dublin Metropolitan Police, and the Results in the Year 1841* (Dublin: Alexander Thom, 1842); *Number of*

Persons Taken into Custody by the Dublin Metropolitan Police, and the Results in the Year 1842 (Dublin: Alexander Thom, 1843); *Number of Persons Taken into Custody by the Dublin Metropolitan Police, and the Results in the Year 1843* (Dublin: Alexander Thom, 1844); *Number of Persons Taken into Custody by the Dublin Metropolitan Police, and the Results in the Year 1844* (Dublin: Alexander Thom, 1845); *Number of Persons Taken into Custody by the Dublin Metropolitan Police, and the Results in the Year 1845* (Dublin: Alexander Thom, January 1846). These are available in the National Library of Ireland as printed reports.

122 Eoin Bourke (ed., trans.), *'Poor Green Erin': German Travel Writers' Narratives on Ireland from Before the 1798 Rising to After the Great Famine* (Oxford: Peter Lang, 2012), words of Jakob Venedy visiting in 1843, p. 426 and words of Karl von Hailbronner *c*. 1836, p. 261.

123 From Bourke, *'Poor Green Erin'*, words of Jakob Venedy 1843, p. 426.

124 Donald, '"Beastly sights"'.

125 Inglis, *A Journey Throughout Ireland*, p. 13.

126 Isaac Butt, *Irish Life: In the Castle, the Courts, and the Country* (London: How and Parsons, 3 vols, 1840), vol. 1, p. 251.

127 William Gibson, *Rambles in Europe in 1839: With Sketches of Prominent Surgeons, Physicians, Medical Schools, Hospitals, Literary Personages, Scenery &c.* (Philadelphia, PA: Lea and Blanchard, 1841). Gibson visited Crampton and viewed his horses; see pp. 226–8.

128 Inglis, *A Journey Throughout Ireland*, pp. 7–8.

129 Mrs Frederick West, *A Summer Visit to Ireland in 1846* (London: Richard Bentley, 1847), p. 7. On the appearance of the Irish ape in English caricature, see L. Perry Curtis, Jr, *Apes and Angels: The Irishman in Victorian Caricature* (Washington, DC: Smithsonian Institution Press, 1971).

130 *Royal Society for the Prevention of Cruelty to Animals, 11th Annual Report, with the Proceedings of the Annual General Meeting* (London: The Philanthropic Society, 1837), pp. 37–8, emphasis in original.

131 'Important meeting of the car-owners of Dublin', *Freeman's Journal* (12 May 1838).

132 There may be another reason for this. The Dublin Metropolitan Police also enforced the Carriage Acts and perhaps a local interpretation of the laws may have been to convict coachmen under the Carriage Acts rather than the anti-cruelty legislation. 'Furious driving', for example, could be construed as both a cruelty to the horse and a danger to human lives. As the latter, convicted under the Carriage Acts, it carried a heavier fine.

133 Information gleaned from the annual printed reports of police statistics, these are bound together and found in the National Library of Ireland. See footnote 122 for the full list of reports consulted.

134 *Census Ireland for the Year 1861. Part IV. Reports and Tables Relating to the Religious Professions, Occupations and Ages of the People. Vol. 1.* [C 3204] HC 1863, lix, 1.

135 'Dublin Police—yesterday', *Freeman's Journal* (26 June 1841).

136 'Dublin Police—yesterday', *Freeman's Journal* (19 April 1837).

137 'Dublin Police', *Freeman's Journal* (5 December 1840).

138 'Dublin Police', *Freeman's Journal* (17 September 1839).

139 'Dublin Police—yesterday', *Freeman's Journal* (3 March 1842).

140 'Dublin Police—yesterday', *Freeman's Journal* (17 September 1842).

141 'Dublin Police', *Freeman's Journal* (14 December 1836).

142 'Dublin Police—yesterday', *Freeman's Journal* (26 June 1841).

143 'Dublin Police—yesterday', *Freeman's Journal* (16 July 1842).

144 'Dublin Police', *Freeman's Journal* (8 October 1836).

145 *Royal Society for the Prevention of Cruelty to Animals, 11th Annual Report*, p. 34.

146 For example, over twenty were tried together in 1841. See 'Dublin Police—yesterday', *Freeman's Journal* (4 September 1841).

147 'Cruelty to animals', *Freeman's Journal* (24 August 1842).

148 David Dickson, *Dublin: The Making of a Capital City* (London: Profile Books, 2014), p. 339.

149 Gibson, *Rambles in Europe in 1839*, p. 226.

150 See Philip Crampton Papers, Letters from Philip Crampton to John Crampton, 6 September 1851, MS 5176–84/452 and Letter 24 July 1857, MS 5176–84/665A, Trinity College Dublin.

151 'College of Surgeons—Mr Crampton', *Freeman's Journal* (1 December 1838).

152 RZSI Rough Minutes, 30 July 1830 and 30 August 1830.

153 Minutes of the RSPCA Council, vol. 4, 4 January 1841, 75–6.

154 Minutes of the RSPCA Council, vol. 5, 7 August 1843, 129.

155 *Dublin Almanac and General Register of Ireland for the Year of Our Lord 1843* (Dublin: Pettigrew and Oulton, 1843), p. 169. The members were Matthias J. O Kelly (an activist for Catholic emancipation), Dominic J. Corrigan (doctor and later physician to the Queen in Ireland) and Robert Kane (chemist and later director of the Museum of Irish Industry).

156 See debate on a bill to ban dog carts, *Hansard's Parliamentary Debates*, Victoria Year 4, 3rd series, vol. 58, columns 1352–1400, division 9 June 1841.

157 Neal Garnham, 'The survival of popular blood sports in Victorian Ulster', *Proceedings of the Royal Irish Academy, Section C*, 107C (2007), 107–26.

158 Garnham, 'The survival'.

159 See Garnham, 'The survival', but also O'Connell, 'Animal welfare in post-Union Ireland'.

160 Minutes of the RSPCA Council, vol. 1, 2 March 1835, 212.

161 Thomas O'Connor, 'Murray, Daniel', in McGuire and Quinn (eds), *Dictionary of Irish Biography*, https://dib-cambridge-org.dcu.idm.oclc. org/viewReadPage.do?articleId=a6110 (accessed 20 May 2020).

162 Minutes of the RSPCA Council, vol. 3, 6 July 1840, 278.

163 William Urwick, *Life and Letters of William Urwick, D.D. of Dublin, Edited by His Son* (London: Hodder and Stoughton, 1870).

164 Joshua Abell was editor of the *Dublin Literary Gazette* and council member for the Dublin SPCA. See Helen Andrews, 'Abell, Joshua', in McGuire and Quinn (eds), *Dictionary of Irish Biography*, https://dib-cambridge-org. dcu.idm.oclc.org/viewReadPage.do?articleId=a0007 (accessed 20 May 2020).

165 Oliver MacDonagh, 'The age of O'Connell, 1830–45', in W. E. Vaughan (ed.), *A New History of Ireland V. Ireland Under the Union 1801–1870* (Oxford: Oxford University Press, 2010), pp. 158–68.

166 Minutes of the RSPCA Council, vol. 3, 5 October 1840, 17–18.

167 'Repeal Catechism', *Freeman's Journal* (3 January 1843).

168 'Repeal Catechism', *Freeman's Journal* (16 February 1843).

169 P. Morgan to Charles Gavan Duffy, printed in 'Letters', *Nation* (27 May 1843).

170 Martin Doyle, 'On benevolence of character', *Irish Penny Journal*, 1:2 (1840), 10–11: 11.

171 'On humanity to animals', *Irish Magazine, and Monthly Asylum for Neglected Biography* (July 1809), 291–2: 292.

172 B., 'Improper conduct in public places', *Irish Penny Journal*, 1:12 (1840), 95–6.

173 B., 'Improper conduct', 95.

174 B., 'Improper conduct', 95.

175 Thomas Carlyle, *Reminiscences of My Irish Journey in 1849* (New York, 1882), p. 10.

176 Carlyle, *Reminiscences*, p. 10.

2

How to live on your pig: improvement and the poor during the Great Famine, 1845–50

Are not all manly appeals lost upon a scoundrel who lives with his pig, like his pig; and every way but the way he should live—ON his pig.[1]

Dublin slowly became aware of a crisis developing during the autumn of 1845. The *Dublin Mercantile Advertiser*, which reported on Irish markets, noted the presence of diseased potatoes in September of 1845 but there was little suggestion of panic: the editors paid more attention to the prospects for the valuable wheat harvest.[2] Even by October, when the paper admitted that up to one fifth of the crop might have failed, in Dublin it was 'difficult to find a citizen who has seen diseased potatoes in his house or at his table'.[3] By the end of 1846 the scale of the crisis had become clearer and its impact on the city more immediate as voluntary groups began to meet not just to send relief to the countryside but to consider how to deal with Dublin's destitute.[4] In 1847 *The Advertiser* feared an influx of the poor sent back from Liverpool to a city 'already overwhelmed by pauperism'.[5] Desperate migrants calculated that conditions were better in the city: they arrived by the tens of thousands to seek food, work or a ship's passage. Many found final resting places in the Dublin workhouses where they arrived in a condition beyond relief.[6]

As the crisis of the Great Famine (1845–50) unfolded, almost every educated person in the British Isles formed an opinion of why it had happened and how it could be prevented from happening again. Newspapers, pamphlets, public halls and public houses filled with the talk of reform. From this cacophony emerged a strand of discourse that focused on separating the lives of the poor from the lives of animals. The Famine had exposed the Irish 'scoundrel' who lived with and like his pig. To live *on* a pig, or indeed any other animal, was to live a civilised, fully human existence no matter one's poverty. To live *with* and *like* a pig was beastly. Consuming animals in specific ways maintained the boundary between human and animal. By contrast, living amidst dirt brought humans down to the level of beasts. This chapter considers how the Famine affected ideas about human–animal relationships in Dublin and asks what consequences these ideas had for how people lived and how the consumption of animals was controlled and regulated.

The scale of the Famine's impact ensured its historical legacy: Ireland lost around one half of its population through death and migration between 1841 and 1901. Historical analysis has justifiably focused on how the Famine affected demographics, communities and agriculture or asked who was to blame for the starvation, disease, evictions and migration.[7] More recent perspectives have also considered the cultural legacy of the Famine years including contemporary imagery and later memorials.[8] Studies of Dublin have tended to focus on economic effects, although recent work has also looked at the spread of disease, the activities of workhouses and the distribution of poor relief.[9] These are all important aspects of the Great Famine, but this chapter takes a different perspective by examining how the crisis affected ideas about human–animal relationships and how these ideas shaped efforts to improve the lives of the poor in Dublin. While acknowledging that the most important impact of the Famine was as a human tragedy, this chapter expands our understanding of its cultural impact. The Famine encouraged different political factions to propose solutions for fixing (supposedly) broken Ireland. A surprisingly wide consensus appeared on the problem of the poor. Across the political spectrum, educated observers recoiled from the Famine's 'beastly' victims who were described as 'struggling, screaming, *shrieking*, for their prey, like some unclean and monstrous animals'.[10]

The poor have long been considered more animal-like than their socio-economic betters. As Keith Thomas describes for early modern England, 'polite education, "civility" and refinement were also intended to raise men above the animals'.[11] Opportunities for such elevation did not always extend down the social ladder. Reformers' desire to raise the poor above animals began with the assumption that they were too close to them in the first place.[12] This chapter demonstrates the importance of the Great Famine for highlighting a concern that the Irish poor needed to be raised 'above the animals'. The chapter further shows how this idea affected poor relief and public health initiatives in the city.

To separate the lives of humans from the lives of animals required one to define how humans should live. The Great Famine provided many examples of how humans should *not* live. The first part of the chapter analyses the portrayal of the 'beastly' poor during the Famine. The remainder of the chapter analyses three reforms that attempted to make the poor less animal-like. I first consider the debate over the provision of food relief to Famine victims, which identified consuming certain foods with being human. Next I look at public health and efforts to reform urban waste recycling by envisioning the city as a barn and the country as a farm. Finally, I examine attitudes towards urban pigs. In each case, middle-class reformers used animals to help them identify what it was to be truly human and applied these ideas to efforts to reform the lives of the urban poor. They revealed a tacit belief that the poor were, by definition, less human than themselves.

Reports and writings on the Famine flooded into Dublin from all directions. Many writers depicted the rural Famine victim as animal-like. The scale of the Famine as calamity suggested that the beastly Irish poor threatened the future of civilisation in Ireland if reformers could not improve their habits and reassert human ascendancy over animals.

Observers expressed horror at the poor or at their living conditions by comparing them to animals. Describing people as 'swarms' or undifferentiated mobs suggested a lack of humanity. For example, Catherine Maberly, an Irish author married to a prominent English civil servant, wrote in 1847 that 'the landlord sees himself compelled to endure the swarm daily gnawing away his subsistence' as he might endure a swarm of rats eating his grain stores.[13] Instead of poisoning the rats, she proposed assisted emigration. The writer Thomas Carlyle described the 'harpy-swarm of clamorous mendicants' that greeted him on his tour of Ireland in 1849.[14] Other writers described the desperate Irish living in underground dens or scalps that looked like 'burrowing holes' or sharing 'the ditches and the bogs with otters and snipes'.[15] Finally, episodes of cannibalism, such as those in the work of novelist William Carleton, suggested a total loss of human dignity engendered by desperation and dearth. Few cases were reported, but it was certainly feared as evidence of social collapse.[16]

In Dublin newspapers and Dublin meeting halls, observers across the political spectrum claimed that the Irish peasant had sunken to the state of a beast. The liberal *Freeman's Journal*, for example, described a group of men who robbed a bread cart as 'devouring the bread with evident voracity' and related rumours that 'the peasants in vast numbers are approaching the city'.[17] Recounting the conditions of peasants in areas where famine combined with eviction had forced people into deeper misery, *The Nation* asked 'what kind of creatures men and women become living in this dung-heap, what kind of children are reared there to grow up into a new generation'.[18] A reporter in the nationalist newspaper provided the latter account as a preface to demanding renewal of the struggle for 'Irish liberty' in the wake of a disastrous rebellion in 1848. Other sympathetic observers focused on the treatment of Irish people like beasts. James Nugent, speaking at a meeting of the Dublin General Relief Committee, claimed that landlord evictions proved 'some men thought they might treat their fellow creatures like beasts of the field, and that they could do what they pleased with that property which Providence had bestowed upon them'.[19] Another speaker complained that the bodies of the dead were being consumed as carrion: 'the kite and the ravenous dog that have feasted upon their unburied corpses,—these bear witness to the immensity of that calamity which no tongue but that of an angel's could adequately describe'.[20] To become food for dogs and wild animals was to be robbed of humanity.

Reformers also suggested that the failure of the potato crop proved that the Irish poor had been living like animals even before they began to starve. Content to raise sufficient potatoes to feed his family and his pig, the Irish peasant 'only asks to *exist*'.[21] The peasant's attachment to his pig, with whom he shared his home and food, proved he had no ambition for higher states of civilisation. The potato subsistence had lowered humans to the status of pigs, according to another Famine pamphleteer:

> man and swine feed alike on it; both meet on equal terms—not that the pig is elevated to the rank of man,—but that man has been sunk to the level of the brute. He is quite content if he can raise a stock of potatoes sufficient to support his family and fatten his pigs.[22]

Potatoes and pigs were the causes, not the symptoms, of poverty. If the Irish would only give up 'potatoes, pigs, and politics' they would experience 'industry and wealth, instead of idleness and famine—peace and contentment, in place of excitement and clamour'.[23] The idea that to be human involved eating different foods to animals and performing certain kinds of work would also impact ideas about food relief.

Even as the poor fled from the Famine they were compared to, and associated with, animals. The steam shipping business had been built up in the early nineteenth century through the demand for livestock exports. By the outbreak of the Famine the leading steamship company, the City of Dublin Steam Packet, offered cargo routes between Dublin's North Wall and Liverpool six days per week, with less frequent routes to Falmouth and Plymouth.[24] Passenger traffic ran between Kingstown, in the south Dublin suburbs, and Liverpool. Once the Great Famine began, however, the demand for passenger traffic meant that people departed from the port previously reserved for animals. Before the Famine one traveller to Dublin observed:

> there, a miscellaneous collection of pigs, sheep, oxen, and ragged but merry *spalpecns* [sic] are hurrying aboard in an undistinguished throng; the only marked difference between the brute and the man is, that the former seems reluctant to quit land in which he had enjoyed a share of nature's common bounty, while the latter evidently parts with little regret from a country where starvation is tine lot of the poor.[25]

This situation only worsened throughout the crisis. At the North Wall the poor now mixed with livestock boarding ships to England, temporarily edging out a portion of the usual cargo.[26] *The Nation* claimed the Midland Railway company had repurposed a number of cattle cars in order to 'transmit the "surplus" Connaught population to the emigrant ship or the English harvest'.[27]

Within the city, reformers tried to sort this 'undistinguished throng' so that human lives appeared distinct and separate from animal lives. They looked to diet and public health to improve Dublin's poor and bring them within middle-class understandings of civilisation.

One way to demonstrate one's ascendancy over animals is to eat them. Increased meat consumption often accompanies increased wealth and social status. Over the nineteenth century, meat consumption in the British Isles rose in quantity across all classes.[28] Meat's desirability stemmed from a combination of culture and taste and was reinforced by dietary science that celebrated it as 'the best of all foods'.[29] So important was meat to a proper diet that even the notoriously parsimonious workhouse provided inmates with a minimum weekly quantity. Some would-be reformers of the Poor Law even argued for the importance of serving festive roast beef.[30] The reformed Irish prison diet contained mostly milk, bread and grains but male prisoners in Dublin's Smithfield prison received one pound of beef each week even during the Famine.[31]

The importance of meat as a component of a good diet emerged in debates surrounding food relief during the Famine in Dublin. In these debates meat was not just nutrition; meat was a cultural necessity. Meat served to separate the feeding of humans from the feeding of animals.

Dietary reform predates the Great Famine, but the crisis focused attention on the potato as a staple and on the amount of animal matter required for a healthy human diet. Pre-Famine dietary reformers used digestive physiology to support the idea that reliance on potatoes had halted the advance of civilisation in Ireland.[32] Aside from its nutritional content, reliance on the potato was perceived as lazy. Commentators described the poor who subsisted on potatoes as existing like animals, taking what the land would offer without improving it. The *Irish Farmer's Gazette* urged the Irish peasant (unlikely to feature among its readers) to abandon the potato in favour of oats, claiming that 'potatoes are a lottery in which the prizes, when you win them, are not worth having'.[33] According to the *Gazette*, the potato had inferior nutritional value to oats. Other writers also suggested that the potato was not a fit food for humans. The Reverend George Stoddart, author of a pamphlet addressed to the Prime Minister, argued that post-Famine recovery would involve dietary change so the Irish could 'share in what the English regard as one of the simple necessaries of life—pure wheaten bread, and occasionally partake of animal food, which is found so useful in sustaining the vigour of the human frame'.[34] A diet of bread and meat represented not only improved nutrition but also a higher level of civilisation and implied a greater distance from animals. A diet made up of only vegetables, even outside of times of crisis, was considered insufficient for humans.

Opponents of the potato diet argued that its similarity to a diet for animals (especially pigs) was its chief drawback. The potato diet's critics claimed that potatoes reduced the humanity of the Irish. 'Where's the use of talking of liberty to a wretch that luxuriates in lumpers [a type of potato]?' asked *The Nation*. Luxuriating in lumpers, as the rest of the article made clear, was living like a pig.[35] Other nations who subsisted on vegetable matter, the writer claimed, had also succumbed to oppressors. While the Maori resisted the British on a meat diet, the 'Hindoos ... are kicked by the beef-eating British, like a foot-ball, from one end of India to the other'.[36] What distinguished the human diet from that of his domestic beasts, according to *The Nation*, was 'the natural animal nutriment proper to man'.[37] Only by eating other creatures (or the products of other creatures) did people become truly human.

Famine food relief also provoked debate over which foods were 'proper to man'. In Dublin, the French chef Alexis Soyer opened his first Famine soup kitchen, embraced by liberal Prime Minister Lord John Russell as a means of preventing mass starvation. Figure 2.1 provides an image of the soup kitchen. The public outcry against Soyer's model Dublin kitchen initially focused on the aesthetics of how the kitchen treated Famine victims. At the celebratory opening of the kitchen an audience paid to watch the food being dispensed, an arrangement that many felt had reduced the pauper to the status

2.1. The opening of Alexis Soyer's famine soup kitchen in Dublin, from the *Illustrated London News* (17 April 1847). Note the barrel labelled 'meat' in the upper left corner. Image courtesy of the Board of Trinity College Dublin.

of an animal. The Dublin newspapers expressed the sentiment well: 'Five shillings each to see the paupers feed!—five shillings each to watch the burning blush of shame chasing pallidness from poverty's wan cheek!—five shillings each! When the animals at the Zoological Gardens may be inspected at feeding time for sixpence!'[38]

The press and the medical profession also criticised the contents of Soyer's soup, focusing on the extremely low quantity of animal matter. Traditional recipes for pauper soup called for the boiling of cheap cuts of meat, such as an animal head. The Association for the Suppression of Mendicity in Dublin dispensed a soup made from boiled ox heads.[39] Quaker relief efforts dispensed a soup produced with boiled bones.[40] The broths were bulked out with vegetables and starches, but the meat component was considered nutritionally indispensable. Soyer's soup, by contrast, contained just eighteen pounds of meat in 100 gallons of broth intended to feed 400 to 600 people. The remaining ingredients were three and a half pounds of fat, twelve pounds of onions, twenty-four pounds of vegetables, twenty-five pounds of flour, thirty pounds of barley and a staggering nine pounds of salt and three pounds of sugar. The meat component was less than one ounce per serving. Critics denounced Soyer's soup as a fraud.[41] Even those who favoured the soup felt the need to explain how a soup 'entirely deprived of animal substance' and filled with 'farinaceous ingredients' was particularly suited to 'a stomach which has suffered from want of food'.[42] The small quantity of meat in the soup recipe, as the chef-proprietor of 'Johnson's a-la-mode Beef House' suggested, could not produce a soup that would provide 'strength, warmth and comfort'. Instead the soup was 'an innutritious compound that would only tend to weaken and destroy the constitution'.[43] The *Freeman's Journal* placed a poem mocking the ingredients of Soyer's soup ('Shin of beef from skinny cow/In the boiler then you'll throw/Onion sliced and turnip top/Crumb of bread and cabbage chop') above an account of the feeding of paupers in the North Dublin Union Workhouse.[44] At Easter the workhouse inmates received 'a plentiful dinner of prime beef, with soup of the most nutritious kind'. The writer emphasised that Poor Law officials had allocated each adult a generous serving of one pound of beef. Eating meat, and lots of meat, made the poor more human and signified humane generosity.

Other writers were even more explicit about how a vegetarian soup might reduce the humanity of the paupers to whom it was fed. Urban reformers such as John Aldridge advocated the use of meat in poor

relief. Aldridge, a doctor and scientist, was active in Dublin during
the 1840s where he was a professor of chemistry to Apothecaries Hall
and also a regular pamphleteer and speaker on issues of sanitation.[45]
In a paper to the Royal Dublin Society during one of the worst years
of the Famine ('Black '47'), Aldridge made a chemical comparison
of the soups on offer to the poor in the city. He was scornful of the
nutrition available from a vegetarian soup, claiming that a balance
had to be struck between animal, vegetable and grain components.
The vegetarian soup, Aldridge claimed, would fail to feed the people
while reducing their energy and bringing them dangerously close
to the state of animals: 'If the population of a country be fed in the
same manner as cows and sheep, manifestations of industrial exertion could not be expected ...'[46] According to Aldridge, the potato was
an even worse food than the hay provided as animal fodder because
it had a lower concentration of nutrition. He considered soup to be
a temporary measure, to be used twice a week, and to be combined
with a diet of solid foods including meat.

Of course not all dietary reformers thought meat was a necessary
component of civilised human life. Arguing in favour of the potato
diet, another Famine pamphleteer claimed that vegetable eaters could
become just as strong as meat eaters. Dr Hayden, a medical lecturer
and general practitioner who also edited *The Philanthropist*, suggested
the Irish poor who ate almost no animal matter were 'muscular but
not fat'. His claim to have rescued his horse from ill health with a
potato diet, however, did little to dispel the idea that potatoes should
feed animals rather than people.[47] Further, the fact that Hayden had to
argue that potatoes could make a man strong reflects the prevalence
of the idea that they did the opposite. A few more radical thinkers saw
meat, not potatoes, as the obstacle to the advance of Irish civilisation
and the relief of poverty. James Haughton, a dissenter and abolition-
ist who counted Daniel O'Connell as a friend, was active in Famine
relief and also the Young Ireland political movement.[48] Haughton
converted to vegetarianism during the Famine. According to his
son, 'he was influenced both by dislike to the torture and slaughter
of animals, and also on grounds of health'. He was also convinced
that the adoption of vegetarianism would improve the Irish economy,
'as the earth would supply vegetable and farinaceous food to support
a much greater population at less cost'.[49] During meetings in Dublin
where he attempted to found a vegetarian society, he emphasised
the potential of vegetarianism to reduce Irish dependence on cattle

farming and thereby increase employment in tillage.[50] Haughton was still concerned with separating the poor from animals, but in this case he viewed a vegetarian diet as a way of escaping dependence on animals for food and on cattle farming for the economy.

Few followed Haughton's example of eschewing meat to link personal reform to national improvement. The commitment to the cattle economy only strengthened during the Famine and few showed concern for the continued feeding of livestock while people starved. The Zoological Society, whose animals were only for education and entertainment, reassured its members that they fed the animals on foods unfit for human consumption. The carnivores received horse-flesh or meat that had been condemned as diseased or decayed by the Lord Mayor. Other animals received rough barley in place of bread or oats.[51] By contrast, owners of animals with an economic value saw no need to stop feeding or even fattening them for display at shows. The fattened animals appearing at the Royal Dublin Society's annual cattle show had diets that included turnips and oats, which might have fed poor humans. The presence of fattened cattle in a city potentially full of hungry people generated surprisingly little comment in the local press.

The number of cattle displayed at the Royal Dublin Society's annual show increased throughout the Famine years. In 1847, exhibitors entered 211 cattle for display including sixty fattened animals.[52] The *Freeman's Journal* remarked in 1848 that the show was 'far and away superior to any that has ever taken place on the premises of this very ancient and highly useful society'.[53] By 1849, the numbers had jumped to 305 cattle on display of which seventy-nine were fat.[54] The press praised 'Ireland's great capabilities to produce the highest luxuries' despite the 'wretchedness and poverty that overspreads the land'. The contrast between luxury and poverty proved 'there is something radically wrong in our social system', but it did not lead the *Freeman's Journal* to condemn the show or the farmers.[55] Owners described fattening their cattle on animal foods (hay, straw, oil cake) but also on foods consumed by poor humans (oats, carrots, turnips and swedes). In a tour of 1834, Henry Inglis had seen children scavenge uneaten food from the animal pens at the Royal Dublin Society's show: 'After the cattle had been fed, half-eaten turnips became the perquisite [sic] of the crowd of ragged boys and girls without.'[56] He praised the children for sharing their scraps, but condemned the 'improvidence' that it suggested.[57] Even if such direct competition between poor humans and livestock for food did not occur on the streets of Dublin during the Famine, the cattle shows displayed the indirect competition of humans and livestock for resources across the country. Farmers continued to fatten cattle while humans starved, and few saw any reason to indict them for it.

Nationalists did criticise the government for exporting food during the Famine. *The Nation*, for example, kept track of the quantities of provisions, including animals, leaving Irish ports for England.[58] Yet the newspaper continued to report on activity at the markets and to cover the Royal Dublin Society cattle show, albeit with less enthusiasm than the *Freeman's Journal*. *The Nation* viewed the 1847 show as 'tame and meagre' compared with previous years, but printed no criticism of the fact that the show was held. In recognition of the circumstances, John Aldridge delivered a lecture on the nutrient qualities of different soups.[59]

Those who protested against the fattening of animals on foods that might have fed humans tended to focus on the feeding of pigs. Cattle, as Ireland's most lucrative export product, often remained exempt from scrutiny. This emphasis also harkened back to the idea posed by Sandham Elly and others that in the potato–pig agricultural system, humans and pigs competed with one another for the same foods. For example, a writer to the *Irish Farmer's Gazette* claimed that 'to feed pigs on corn, or any other of our cultivated crops, at a time when so many millions of human beings must inevitably become consumers, or starve, would appear to be an egregious misapplication of food'.[60] The *Gazette* suggested an experiment of feeding them on wild thistle found in hedgerows.

Debates about Famine food relief and post-Famine dietary reform thus contrast with silence about livestock feeding. On the one hand, many reformers believed that poor people must eat animal products to be healthy and productive. On the other hand, few suggested that feeding humans should always take priority over feeding animals.

Food was only one area in which middle-class reformers anticipated an opportunity to use the Famine to change the habits of the poor. The Great Famine had a direct effect on sanitary reform in the city, increasing concern about urban animal-keeping and the accumulation of wastes close to human habitations. Sanitarians criticised the poorly regulated relationship between the city and the countryside, one that generated waste but also risked human health by exposure to filth.

The Great Famine combined with the public health movement in England and municipal reforms in Dublin to shape the city's approach to sanitary reform. Dublin's early public health reformers focused on personal and civic filth, in close alignment to the sanitarian ideas of Edwin Chadwick. Chadwick's report on the sanitary condition of the English poor in 1842 and his governmental influence brought public health to the fore in the United Kingdom.[61] Chadwick argued that 'filth and bad ventilation' killed more people than 'deaths or wounds in any wars in which the country has been engaged in modern times'.[62] Chadwick also blamed filth for creating 'an adult population short-lived, improvident, reckless, and intemperate, and with habitual avidity for sensual gratification'. 'Sound morality and refinement in manners', the hallmarks of a bourgeois conception of civilised life, could not exist in populations mired in filth.[63]

The idea of sanitation as a fundamental component of civic improvement took hold in Dublin during the 1840s.[64] The Dublin Corporation pushed for a greater extension of its powers to encompass bodies with a public health remit including the Paving Board and the Wide Streets Commissioners.[65] The cholera crisis of 1848 (heightened by the conditions of the Famine) inspired the foundation of a new 'Health of the City Preservation Committee' to oversee preventative measures.[66] In parallel, a group of professionals and religious leaders founded the Dublin Sanatory Association (DSA) in 1848, a voluntary body dedicated to urban reform.[67] Like the Zoological Society, the founding members and patrons represented a wide range of religious and political views.[68] They supplemented the Dublin Statistical and Social Inquiry Society (1847), a society that also made regular contributions to debates about poverty and sanitation.[69] The DSA drew inspiration from a series of sanitary reports produced by individual reformers.

The Great Famine energised the sanitary movement in the city. Poverty and filth were no longer, as John Aldridge wrote, 'evils inseparable from town life'. Aldridge, secretary of the DSA, believed these problems could be solved, like agriculture, in which he anticipated that 'a great reform is at hand, and that better times are approaching'.[70]

The Corporation developed a new infrastructure to enforce sanitary improvement in 1848. The 'Health of the City Preservation Committee' implemented a special sanitary court in two locations in the city (William Street and the Royal Barracks) for prosecuting sanitary offenders. The Association's chairman (Sir Edward Borough) acted as the magistrate for the city sanitary court and a variety of people, including police officers, Poor Law guardians, medical men and parish inspectors, were empowered to act as nuisance inspectors under the Nuisances Removal and Disease Prevention Act of 1848.[71] Encouraged by fear of cholera, the committee directed the Dublin Metropolitan Police to inquire into the sanitary state of households and seek out nuisances that might endanger the city. Magistrates tried almost 1800 offenders before the courts in nine months. Fewer than half of the offenders abated the nuisance themselves. In the remaining cases, the Corporation entered the premises and abated the nuisance. They then added the costs to the court's fine.[72] Very little detail has been recorded about these offences but newspaper reports tell us that they involved the removal of 'nuisances and noxious deposits injurious to public health'.[73] One common nuisance, addressed below, was the collection of a mixture of human and animal wastes by 'nightmen' who then sold on the waste as fertiliser.[74] Another was the keeping of animals, especially pigs.[75] These concerns of the sanitary courts can also be understood as issues of imposing order on human–animal relationships.

One way to make the city cleaner and healthier was to remove animal wastes such as manure. Reformers sought to link up city and country into an integrated system of manure collection and recycling that would both sanitise the city and improve agriculture.[76] Yet these ideas also seemed to elide the urban poor and livestock. Middle-class reformers viewed the poor as producers of unhealthy wastes, victims of poor sanitation and dependents reliant on middle-class management.

Dublin's early sanitarians saw filth as a link between the problems of city and country. Perhaps because many of them were chemists, they were inclined to view Ireland as a kind of chemical system for cycling nutrients between animals, people, soil and plants.[77] As Aldridge put it:

> A nation may be regarded as a large farm, in which every means should be taken advantage of whereby the produce of the arable and pasture land may be made sufficient for the food of the live stock; and in which the offal of the latter should be saved and economised for the nourishment of the soil.[78]

It is not at first clear if Aldridge is talking about animal livestock or metaphorically using livestock to suggest people. In his system, the city's filth was not only a danger to human lives; it was a waste of a precious resource to the detriment of rural farming. Wastes from the urban animal economy and from humans themselves should be collected and sold to farmers to 'regenerate the food of the population'.[79] Thus urban reform was linked to rural reform, where the failure of the Irish peasant farmer to improve the land through manuring was much criticised by Famine pamphleteers. Aldridge's metaphor implied that the poor were the livestock of the city. Middle-class sanitary reformers acted as improving landlords: removing wastes from the livestock and using them to replenish the countryside and grow more food.

Thomas Antisell disagreed with Aldridge in a number of particulars, but he too saw the problem of urban filth as a waste of precious human and animal manure. Like Aldridge, Antisell argued that the city's wasteful habits were detrimental to agriculture and interrupted the efficient cycling of nutrients between producers and consumers. 'Every day', he wrote, 'we madly pour into the sea that manure, which afterwards we send long voyages across the ocean to bring back from Peru and Ichaboe.'[80] Farmers bought fertiliser from abroad when they could simply look to the city to supply it. In another elision between humans and domesticated animals, Antisell estimated the annual human waste production per person in quantity (twenty tons of liquid, one ton of solid) and value (12s). He probably would have agreed with Aldridge's analogy that just 'as the livestock of a well-arranged farm are collected into a square of stalls, so the inhabitants of all civilised countries are congregated into towns and cities'. Just as the good farmer manured his fields with the animal wastes collected from his stalls, so should the nation on a larger scale manure its fields with human and animal wastes collected from the streets, alleys, drains and privies of Dublin.

During the Famine, Antisell insisted that the recycling of urban night soil was a means of improving both country and city. Speaking to the newly formed 'Practical Agricultural Association' in 1847, Antisell made a chemical comparison of human night soil to a variety of animal manures. According to Antisell, human wastes were the most efficient for returning exhausted nutrients to the soil: 'as the mineral substances of excrement were at one time those of the soil, and they ought, by being returned, restore it to the fertile state, and ought to do so better than any artificial manure'.[81] City manure was more valuable than country waste because the people in cities ate a more varied diet. Dublin drew produce from across the country and, by consuming this, its residents created wastes that were best suited to restore the fertility of the country. Antisell also warned that such wastes should be kept separate from farm manure because night soil was 'always a more rapid fermenter than the farm dung'.[82]

The analogy of the city as the stalls of a national farm was not without sinister connotations. Like the animals of a farm, sanitary reformers viewed the urban poor as pliant domesticates in their scheme to improve the city. Sanitarians, including Aldridge and Antisell, had excellent intentions to improve the public's health and make the city cleaner. Like the would-be reformers of Irish agriculture, they sought to teach new habits to the poor. The state of poverty had reduced men to beasts who did not eschew filth. As William Hogan wrote, 'physical wretchedness has done its worst on the human sufferer, for it has destroyed his mind; his wretchedness being more than humanity can bear, has annihilated those mental faculties which are distinctive of the human being, and has left him the wants and appetites of a mere animal, without its instincts'.[83]

The sanitary reformers sought to rescue the urban poor from this beastly state. Yet they started from the premise that as they were animal-like, the poor abdicated any human rights to privacy. Members of the middle classes with sanitary intentions could, and should, enter private homes on a quest for the fount of filth. Members of the middle classes could, and should, muck out the stalls of the poor. Or, as Aldridge put it, if Ireland was to become the farm to feed England's manufacturing cities, then 'it is, at least, worth while to feed, clothe, and house the labourers well and to work the farm in a scientific and efficient manner'.[84] Sanitary improvement represented good farm management in the city, but now the livestock were the human poor.

Discussions of manure recycling also raised concerns about the line between human and animal in other ways. For example, the Corporation's new sanitary courts viewed manure heaps that mixed human and animal wastes as egregious nuisances to be stamped out. In December of 1848 a group of people were fined for 'collecting manure, &c, of every description in different parts of the city, which they deposit in yards'.[85] Such manure yards, collecting human *and* animal filth, were deemed by the court as nuisances injurious to health and could not be kept or created in the borough. During the course of the trial, the division between an acceptable manure heap and an unhealthy one became clear. Manure should contain only the waste from particular animals and not human waste. Manure collection should be limited to stables and dairies, rather than a house-to-house trawl for wastes of all kinds. 'Cow or horse dung, *unmixed* with other matter, was not injurious to the health of the city', but 'the yards complained of do not come under the denomination of dairy or stable yards'. Thus the only way to properly accumulate manure was to be the owner of cattle or horses, a barrier to most poor people. Again it was the poor who were most likely to commit the offence of failing to keep human and animal separate by collecting an assortment of wastes for sale.

The Corporation and the public health movement's interest in the sanitary problem of human and animal wastes was matched by an interest in removing pigs. The Great Famine made urban pig-keeping undesirable for both cultural and medical reasons. The subject of the pig's too-close relationship with the Irish peasantry was not new, but the Famine tipped the balance from humour to horror. Criticism of subsistence agriculture based on potatoes and pig-rearing spilled over into criticism of pig-keeping in any context. Dublin's emergent public health movement identified the pig as a nuisance to be regulated or removed. Public health advocates and the Corporation removed few pigs during the Famine period, but new bye-laws on pig-keeping and changing public attitudes towards the pig shaped urban pig-keeping into the future.

Campaigns against urban pigs were common during the nineteenth century. In New York City, for example, a campaign against pigs began early in the century. 'Anti-hogites' blamed pigs for besmirching the city's streets and reputation, while 'hogites' argued for the pigs' importance as an economic form of waste removal. The cholera epidemics of the 1830s and 1840s, when sanitation fears outweighed all other arguments, helped to sweep New York City of pigs.[86] Like similar campaigns from Europe to Mexico, the pig's association with the urban poor did additional damage to its reputation.[87] The removal of pigs had reputed benefits beyond the elimination of bad smells. As 'pig' became interchangeable with 'filth' among Dublin's sanitary improvers, the removal of pigs became evidence of urban improvement.

An interest in pig removal reflected a prejudice across Western societies against the character of the pig.[88] The idea of the pig as an immoral creature was widespread in Ireland; even scientific and agricultural writers had scant praise for the animal. For example, a lecturer to the Royal Dublin Society claimed that pigs 'sometimes eat their own young ... & take infants in the cradle'.[89] Even piglets were not exempt from condemnation: 'These animals have no distinct feeling. The young ones scarce know their dams and are apt to suck the sows that come first in their way.'[90] Finally, a pig was viewed as a greedy animal: 'its great voracity exposes it nevertheless to be at the point of vomiting the good it has eat [sic]'.[91] Less strident authors still placed the pig lower in the scale of domesticated animals in terms of temperament. One writer, while recommending pig farming as profitable, acknowledged that 'the hog is a hurtful and spoiling beast; stout, hard, and troublesome to rule'.[92] Even writers who praised the pig acknowledged a persistent anti-porcine prejudice. A good way to ridicule a public figure was to depict them as a pig or associate them with the management of pigs (see Figure 2.2).

Campaigns against urban pigs often met resistance because pig-keeping was widespread and profitable. The pig was known to have clean habits (pigs defecate away from the area in which they sleep), but it would also tolerate filth, poor ventilation and minimal space.[93] If a city dweller wished to provide optimum conditions, a pigsty of seven square feet would fit in even the meagre backyard of a labourer's dwelling.[94] There were few diseases to which the pig was vulnerable.[95] A wide range of foods available in the city could be used to fatten a pig including wastes from brewing, distilling, candle-making and dairying. More gruesome was the feeding of pigs on slaughterhouse offal (including that from other pigs) and horse carcasses from the knacker's yard.[96]

Despite the rational economic reasons for keeping them, association with pigs could be an indictment of a person's moral and intellectual character. In a country teetering at the edge of civility, pigs signified lower levels of intelligence. In a lecture 'On instinct', the Church of Ireland Archbishop, Richard Whately, suggested a division between human and animal intelligence. The lecture was delivered to the Zoological Society in 1842 but reprinted in 1847, one of the worst years of the Great Famine. The timing suggests perhaps that a reminder of the differences between humans and animals was deemed necessary. According to Whately, some people 'have much of a certain practical sagacity' and can even be described as 'knowing, clever, and ingenious'. This type of intelligence, claimed Whately, was only an extension of animal abilities. These same persons would

2.2. 'A gentleman in difficulties': Daniel O'Connell is pulled in opposite directions by two pigs. Associating a person with pigs was an easy way to deliver an insult. Here the nationalist politician O'Connell is depicted as a pig driver with his pigs representing two ways of conducting his political campaign (moral force and physical force). From *Punch* (August 1846). Image courtesy of the Board of Trinity College Dublin.

be found to be lower in 'that particular kind of intelligence, which is altogether peculiar to Man'.[97] Excessively close association with animals, especially the pig, would not help to develop man's higher faculties. For this reason, writers such as Sandham Elly went so far as to suggest that porcine company lowered man to the state of an animal.[98] Fictional portrayals of the Irish often included pigs as a proxy for the bad character of their keepers. William Carleton's tale of Phil Purcell the pig-driver (first published in 1832 but appearing in subsequent editions during and after the Great Famine) described the ingenuity of Phil, who successfully swindled numerous English businessmen. He sold each man his pig then persuaded him to allow him to sleep in the barn, and quietly absconded with the pig before morning. In this way he sold his pig seven times before returning to Ireland, still in possession of the same pig.[99] Phil's intelligence was presented as more animal than human, drawing unflattering parallels between himself and his companion in fraud.

In Famine-era Dublin the influx of pigs alongside that of the rural poor may have encouraged sanitarians to act. Pigs, like cattle, provide a barometer of Dublin's connection to the rest of Ireland and to the wider Irish economy. Pig numbers dropped dramatically across Ireland in the early Famine as peasants ate or sold their only cash asset. However, pig numbers began to recover by 1849 as the situation for those remaining in Ireland slowly improved. The numbers of pigs in the metropolitan borough of Dublin, the vast majority of which were on holdings of less than one acre, increased between 1848 and 1850. So, too, did the proportion of the city's population comprised of persons born outside of Dublin. We cannot say for sure that these people had brought their pigs or their pig-keeping habits with them, but the correlation is suggestive. By 1850, there were over 6000 pigs recorded in the agricultural statistics as residing within the municipal borough.[100] Sanitary reformers may well have noted the growing numbers of pigs with alarm.

The value of the pig in Dublin, just as in rural Ireland, was as a cash asset. The individual pig reared in the home or in a small yard could be sold to one of the many bacon factors in the city when money was needed. This small economy was badly affected by the Famine, as H. D. Richardson recognised. Although pig numbers had rebounded in Dublin by 1850, in 1852 Richardson still claimed that 'pigs are not now so generally kept in Dublin as formerly, for the people do not well know what to feed them upon'.[101] Unlike the sanitary reformers, Richardson regretted this loss. The pig was a particularly useful animal in 'some states of a country, or at least of particular districts', where for a variety of reasons it might be more suitable than keeping cattle or sheep. Richardson implied that poverty and underdevelopment demanded the presence of the pig because 'twice the same weight of food may be obtained from hogs than can be obtained, from the same cost of food, by means of any other animals'.[102]

In Dublin, as elsewhere, the pig was particularly important to the economically vulnerable. The poor even kept different breeds of pigs than commercial pig breeders; their 'Irish Greyhound' pigs may have been an older and leaner breed than the new improved (and fatter) breeds of pig (Figure 2.3 shows how a greyhound pig may have looked). Songs such as the nineteenth-century ballad 'Peg Briggs and Her Pigs' give a sense of the value of a pig to women. Peg 'had a parcel of very fine pigs' which, to her misfortune, attracted the attentions of a barber. After marrying Peg, he immediately sold the pigs at market 'and lump'd into the bargain Peg Briggs'. The writer admonished women pig-keepers to be cautious 'and when lovers sigh/have an to the stye; and don't let 'em marry your pigs'; Peg's pigs were effectively her dowry.[103] The song reflects the fact that keeping pigs, like keeping poultry, was a suitable commercial activity for women. In 1846, a Dublin woman was so distressed at the killing of her piglet that she

2.3. 'Contrast the poor man's pig', drawing by Samuel Brocas. The pig depicted may have been a 'greyhound', so named because they apparently resembled dogs in their agility and did not fatten as well as 'improved' breeds. The breed is now extinct. Image courtesy of the National Library of Ireland.

refused the offer of compensation from the men who killed it and took them to court.[104]

Possibly a combination of health and moral concerns about the urban pig influenced the attitude of sanitary writers who saw the benefits of urban manure recycling but not of the urban pig. Even the pig's ability to turn waste into meat could not save it from its association with filth, laziness and immorality. The DSA used the pig as an index of poor sanitation. When conducting a survey of the area of Townsend Street (north of Trinity College), the presence of pigs was particularly damning. An inspection of 192 houses revealed a population of almost 3000 inhabitants living alongside seventy pigs. Although the number seems relatively small, the pigs symbolised the degraded state of the dwellings. Along with overcrowding and an absence of privies, the pig indicated a set of unhealthy conditions associated with poverty and leading to disease.[105]

Some sanitary reformers defined the urban pig, no matter how it was kept, as a public health nuisance. When a public health bill for Ireland was proposed, the DSA produced a pamphlet with suggested amendments. Their principal concern was to streamline the process of abating nuisances. Their designated list of nuisances included accumulations of foul matter (human or animal) as well as offensive receptacles for the same. Swine were listed individually as a self-evident nuisance; no other animals made the list.[106]

The Dublin Metropolitan Police and the Dublin Corporation sought to reduce urban pig-keeping, especially the keeping of pigs in the home. Travel writers had frequently commented on the porcine companions of the rural poor, remarking that the pig received superior treatment to human family members.[107] Fanny Hall, for example, claimed that she was told in her travels 'if there is a *better* mouthful, the pig gets it, for he has to pay the rent'.[108] Although Hall was critical, she and most other travel writers recognised that keeping a pig inside reflected its high value to the family. The Dublin Corporation and the Dublin Metropolitan Police (DMP) had begun to view indoor pig-keeping as a serious nuisance. In 1847, for example, a family were brought to the sanitary court because they had been found with seven pigs in their apartment. 'The odour from the place was of the most offensive nature, and disease was likely to follow', the magistrate ruled. The potential fine was 40s, an enormous sum for a poor family, and it was deferred to allow the defendants time to eliminate the nuisance. The magistrate emphasised the urgency of removing the pigs, calling their presence 'very dangerous' because of the potential to 'cause fever in the neighborhood'.[109] The expansion of the sanitary policing of pigs will be considered in Chapter 4.

Eating meat, cleaning up manure and removing pigs all highlight the importance of animals to defining 'human' in Famine Dublin.[110] When observers sought to emphasise the desperation and degradation of the Famine's victims, they claimed that they lived and died like animals. When reformers sought to help or improve the poor, they tried to introduce habits that drew sharp distinctions between human life and animal life. Even feeding the poor might be fraught with concerns about how to maintain the human dignity of people dependent on charity. In each case, the desire to make life in poverty less beastly revealed an assumption that the poor were, if not animals, at least lesser humans.

Social class played a central role in human–animal relationships in nineteenth-century Dublin. Poor people interacted with different animals and perhaps viewed their interactions with those animals differently. They saw no harm, for example, in keeping a pig in the house or mixing human and animal wastes together. Their behaviours were most likely shaped by economic concerns and presumably did not threaten their sense of their own humanity. Yet reformers increasingly sought to impose middle-class ideas of how to enact human ascendancy over animals. The brunt of these reforms fell upon the poor, determining, for example, which animals they could keep and how they could keep them.

As we have seen in this chapter, attitudes towards animals and animal wastes were inconsistent. Creating and prosecuting a system of public health involved defining how animals might become nuisances. Stable manure (from cattle or horses) might be considered 'not injurious to the health of the city' while human wastes or mixed wastes were thought to contribute to the spread of disease.[111] Pigs were often identified as a nuisance, but the much more numerous urban cattle and horses were not. Reformers increasingly made distinctions between living animals, dead meat and animals soon to slaughtered. Living cattle did not register as an urgent public health problem until the final quarter of the century (see Chapter 5). As the next chapter shows, the influx of cattle into the city after the Great Famine raised concerns about how to accommodate them without risking human health and welfare.

The Famine has long been recognised as an important factor in pushing Ireland towards greater reliance on livestock and reducing the amount of land devoted to tillage. The consequences of this change for rural Ireland have been recognised while very little consideration has been given to how these changes affected the capital city. As the Famine drew to a close, rising numbers of cattle were accommodated and welcomed into the city as a sign of economic progress. Dublin became ever more entangled with the export of cattle to Britain. At the same time, dead cattle and the men who killed them began to vex both the Corporation and public health advocates.

Notes

1 'A panegyric of potatoes', *Nation* (11 April 1846).
2 'The harvest', *Dublin Mercantile Advertiser* (5 September 1845).
3 'The potato blight', *Dublin Mercantile Advertiser* (24 October 1845).
4 'Distress in the city of Dublin', *Dublin Mercantile Advertiser* (18 December 1846).
5 'Removal of Irish paupers', *Dublin Mercantile Advertiser* (9 July 1847).
6 Cormac Ó Grada and Timothy Guinnane, 'Mortality in the North Dublin Union during the Great Famine', in Cormac Ó Grada (ed.), *Ireland's Great Famine: Interdisciplinary Perspectives* (Dublin: University College Dublin Press, 2006), pp. 86–105; Cormac Ó Grada, *Black '47 and Beyond: The Great Irish Famine in History, Economy, and Memory* (Princeton, NJ: Princeton University Press, 2000), chapter 5.
7 The Famine literature is too vast to summarise here. A good introduction to geographical approaches is found in John Crowley, Mike Murphy and William J. Smyth (eds), *Atlas of the Great Irish Famine, 1845–1852* (Cork: Cork University Press, 2012). A classic on the social and economic impact is Cormac Ó Grada, *Ireland Before and After the Famine: Explorations in Economic History, 1800–1925* (Manchester: Manchester University Press, 1988); see also Ó Grada, *Black '47 and Beyond*. For a range of views on the issue of responsibility see Cecil Woodham-Smith, *The Great Hunger: Ireland 1845–1849* (London: Hamish Hamilton, 1962); Joel Mokyr, *Why Ireland Starved: A Quantitative and Analytical History of the Irish Economy, 1800–1850* (London: Allen & Unwin, 1985); Christine Kinealy, *This Great Calamity: The Irish Famine, 1845–52* (Dublin: Gill and Macmillan, 1994); and Enda Delaney, *The Great Irish Famine: A History in Four Lives* (Dublin: Gill and Macmillan, 2014).
8 See, for example, Luke Gibbons, *Limits of the Visible: Representing the Great Hunger* (Hamden, CT: Quinnipiac University Press, 2014); and

Catherine Marshall, *Monuments and Memorials of the Great Famine* (Hamden, CT: Quinnipiac University Press, 2014).

9 See, for example, William J. Smyth, 'The province of Leinster and the Great Famine', in John Crowley, William J. Smyth and Mike Cronin (eds), *Atlas of the Great Irish Famine* (Cork: Cork University Press, 2012), pp. 325–33; and Smyth, 'The role of cities and towns during the Great Famine' in the same volume, pp. 240–54; Raymond J. Raymond, 'Dublin: the Great Famine, 1845–1860', *Dublin Historical Record*, 33:3 (1980), 98–105.

10 Emphasis in original. 'The new nation', *The Nation* (1 September 1849).

11 Keith Thomas, *Man and the Natural World: Changing Attitudes in England 1500–1800* (London: Penguin, 1983), p. 37.

12 See, for example, Harriet Ritvo, *The Animal Estate: The English and Other Creatures in the Victorian Age* (Harvard, MA: Harvard University Press, 1987); Erica Fudge, 'A left-handed blow: writing the history of animals', in Nigel Rothfels (ed.), *Representing Animals* (Bloomington: Indiana University Press, 2002), p. 15; Kathleen Kete, 'Introduction: animals and human empire', in Kete (ed.), *A Cultural History of Animals in the Age of Empire* (London: Berg, 2008), pp. 1–24.

13 Mrs Maberly, *The Present State of Ireland and Its Remedy* (London: James Ridgway, 1847), p. 8.

14 Thomas Carlyle, *Reminiscences of My Irish Journey in 1849* (New York, 1882), p. 70.

15 'Condition of Ireland', *Illustrated London News* (15 December 1849).

16 Cormac Ó Grada, *Eating People is Wrong, and Other Essays on Famine, its Past, and its Future* (Princeton, NJ: Princeton University Press, 2015), pp. 30–6.

17 'Hunger and destitution of the people: the peasantry in the city', *Freeman's Journal* (9 January 1847). They claimed not to believe the report of peasants approaching the city but nonetheless circulated it in the newspaper several times.

18 'The new nation', *The Nation* (1 September 1849), emphasis in original.

19 *Report and proceedings of the General Relief Committee of the Royal Exchange from the 3rd of May to the 3rd of September, 1849* (Dublin: G. O'Shea, 1849), p. 42.

20 *Report … General Relief Committee … 1849*, p. 20.

21 Maberly, *The Present State of Ireland*, p. 5.

22 Sandham Elly, *Potatoes, Pigs, and Politics: The Curse of Ireland the Cause of England's Embarrassments* (London: Kent and Richards, 1848), p. 7.

23 Elly, *Potatoes, Pigs, and Politics*, p. 35.

24 See *Thom's Irish Almanac and Official Directory for the Year 1846* (Dublin: Alexander Thom, 1846), p. 678.

25 'Spalpeen' is an Irish word for migrant farmer. J. Stirling Coyne (draw-ings by WH Bartlett), *The Scenery and Antiquities of Ireland* (London: Mercury Books, 2003 [original publication 1842]), p. 407.

26 Peter Solar, 'Shipping and economic development in nineteenth-century Ireland', *Economic History Review*, 59:4 (2006), 717–42 (esp. 735).

27 'Irish Railways', *The Nation*, 27 October 1849.

28 Richard Perren, *The Meat Trade in Britain 1840–1914* (London: Routledge and Kegan Paul, 1978), p. 3.

29 Edward Dillon Mapother, *The Body and its Health: A Book for Primary Schools* (Dublin: Falconer, 1870), p. 20.

30 Nadja Durbach, 'Roast beef, the new Poor Law, and the British nation, 1834–63', *Journal of British Studies*, 52 (2013), 963–89.

31 *Twenty-eighth Report of the Inspectors-General on the General State of the Prisons of Ireland, 1849. With Appendices*, p. 3, HC 1850 [1229], xxix, 305.

32 Ian Miller, *Reforming Food in Post-Famine Ireland: Medicine, Science, and Improvement, 1845–1922* (Manchester: Manchester University Press, 2014), pp. 22–4.

33 'Potato disease', *Irish Farmer's Gazette* (7 March 1846), 732.

34 Rev. George H. Stoddart, *The True Cure for Ireland, the Development of Her Industry; Being a Letter Addressed to the Rt. Hon. Lord John Russell, MP &c&c&c* (London: Trelawney W. Saunders, 1847), p. 12.

35 'A panegyric of potatoes', *The Nation* (11 April 1846).

36 'A panegyric of potatoes'.

37 'A panegyric of potatoes'.

38 'Finale of a cook's triumph, from the *Packet* of Tuesday night', *Freeman's Journal* (17 April 1847).

39 See, for example, *Twenty-ninth Annual Report of the Managing Committee of the Association for the Suppression of Mendicity in Dublin: For the Year 1846* (Dublin: printed for the Mendicity Association, by Shea and Co., 1847).

40 *Transactions of the Central Relief Committee of the Society of Friends During the Famine in Ireland in 1846 and 1847* (Dublin: Hodges and Smith, 1852), appendix X, pp. 358–60.

41 Miller, *Reforming Food*, pp. 34–5.

42 'M. Soyer's soup for the poor', *Irish Farmer's Gazette* (6 March 1847), p. 716.

43 Letters to the editor, *Freeman's Journal* (25 February 1847).

44 'Scene from the soup kitchen', *Freeman's Journal* (5 April 1847).

45 Information taken from title page of John Aldridge, *The Present State of Vegetable Physiology* (Dublin: Hodges and Smith, 1848).

46 'Royal Dublin Society's proceedings', *Irish Farmer's Gazette* (13 April 1847), pp. 804–5.

47 'Articles of food—the potato', *Philanthropist* (2 November 1846), pp. 7–9.

48 Haughton later broke with Young Ireland. See Frances Clarke and James Quinn, 'Haughton, James', in James McGuire and James Quinn (eds), *Dictionary of Irish Biography* (Cambridge: Cambridge University Press, 2009), https://dib-cambridge-org.dcu.idm.oclc.org/viewRead-Page.do?articleId=a3858 (accessed 20 May 2020).

49 *Memoir of James Haughton With Extracts From His Private and Published Letters by his son Samuel Haughton* (Dublin, 1877), p. 86.

50 'The Vegetarian Society. Public meeting. How to stop Irish emigration by feeding men instead of bullocks', *The Nation* (27 September 1866).

51 Catherine De Courcy, *Dublin Zoo: An Illustrated History* (Cork: The Collins Press, 2009), p. 24.

52 *Classification of Black Cattle, Sheep, Swine, Horses, Poultry, Farm Implements, etc. etc. Entered for Competition at the Cattle Shew [sic] to be Held on the Premises of the Royal Dublin Society on Tuesday, the 6th, Wednesday, the 7th, and Thursday, the 8th April, 1847* (Dublin: M.H. Gill, 1847).

53 'Royal Dublin Society's Spring Exhibition of Farm Stock, Farm Implements, &c., &c.', *Freeman's Journal* (25 April 1848).

54 *Classification of Black Cattle, Sheep, Swine, Horses, Poultry, Farm Implements, etc. etc. Entered for Competition at the Cattle Shew [sic] to be Held on the Premises of the Royal Dublin Society on Tuesday, the 17th, Wednesday, the 18th, and Thursday, the 19th April, 1849* (Dublin: M.H. Gill, 1849).

55 'Royal Dublin Society's Spring Exhibition'.

56 Henry Inglis, *A Journey Throughout Ireland: During the Spring, Summer and Autumn of 1834* (London: Whittaker and Co., 1835), vol. 1, p. 12.

57 Inglis, *A Journey Throughout Ireland*, p. 13.

58 See, for example, 'Export of Irish provisions', *The Nation* (16 October 1847).

59 'Royal Dublin Society Cattle Show', *The Nation* (10 April 1847).

60 'Food for pigs', *Irish Farmer's Gazette* (22 August 1846), p. 267.

61 For an overview of early sanitary reform in England see Christopher Hamlin, *Public Health and Social Justice in the Age of Chadwick: Britain, 1800–1854* (Cambridge: Cambridge University Press, 1998).

62 Edwin Chadwick, *Report on the Sanitary Condition of the Labouring Population of Great Britain*, p. 369 (Contained within *Report to Her Majesty's Principal Secretary of State for the Home Department from the Poor Law Commissioners, on an Inquiry into the Sanitary Condition of the Labouring Population of Great Britain, with Appendices* (London: Her Majesty's Stationery Office, 1842).

63 Chadwick, *Report on the Sanitary Condition*, pp. 370, 371.

64 See also David Dickson, *Dublin: The Making of a Capital City* (London: Profile Books, 2014), pp. 372–8.

65 See, for example, Dublin City Council Minutes, vol. 14, Minutes for 7 April 1847, MS C2/A1/14, Dublin City Library and Archive [Hereafter DCC Mins].

66 DCC Mins, vol. 14, Minutes for 22 September 1848.

67 There were similar bodies concerned with hygiene and public health founded in Dublin during the nineteenth century. The Dublin Sanatory [sic] Association appears to have been founded in 1848 and continued until around 1850. One of its goals was civic reform, particularly legislation that would assist in sanitation. It seems to have lapsed around 1850. In the 1870s a new Dublin Sanitary Association was founded, principally to call the Corporation to account for perceived failings. This second body is discussed in Chapter 4 and Chapter 5.

68 *Report of the Transactions of the Dublin Sanatory Association, from the 4th of June 1848 to 30th April, 1849* (Dublin: James McGlashan, 1849).

69 See Mary E. Daly, *Dublin, the Deposed Capital: A Social and Economic History, 1860–1914* (Cork: Cork University Press, 1984), chapter 8; and Jacinta Prunty, *Dublin Slums 1800–1925: A Study in Urban Geography* (Dublin: Irish Academic Press, 1998), pp. 47–60.

70 John Aldridge, *Review of the Sanitary Condition of Dublin* (Dublin: Hodges and Smith, 1847), pp. 3, 7.

71 'Dublin Sanatory Association', *Freeman's Journal* (19 September 1848).

72 See DCC Mins, vol. 14, 1 December 1848.

73 'Dublin Sanatory Association', *Freeman's Journal* (6 September 1849).

74 'Borough sanatory court', *Freeman's Journal* (9 December 1848).

75 'Dublin Sanatory Association', *Freeman's Journal* (6 September 1849).

76 The close links between country and city, especially in terms of the supply of meat, are discussed in Gergely Baics and Mikkele Thelle, 'Introduction: meat and the nineteenth-century city', *Urban History*, 45:2 (2018), 184–92.

77 Christopher Hamlin, 'The rise and fall of the city as chemical system and of the chemist as urban environmental professional, 1780–1880', *Journal of Urban History*, 30 (2007), 702–28.

78 Aldridge, *Review of the Sanitary Condition*, pp. 4–5.

79 Aldridge, *Review of the Sanitary Condition*, p. 6.

80 Thomas Antisell, *Suggestions Towards the Improvement of the Sanatory [sic] Condition of the Metropolis* (Dublin: James McGlashan, 1847), p. 8.

81 'Practical agricultural association', *Irish Farmer's Gazette* (10 April 1847), p. 789.

82 'Practical agricultural association', p. 789.

83 William Hogan, *The Dependence of National Wealth on the Social and Sanitary Condition of the Labouring Classes: On the Necessity for Model Lodging Houses in Dublin and the Advantages They Would Confer on the Community* (Dublin: Hodges and Smith, 1849), p. 11.

84 Aldridge, *Review of the Sanitary Condition*, p. 17.

85 'Borough sanatory court', *Freeman's Journal* (9 December 1848).

86 Catherine McNeur, 'The "swinish multitude": controversies over hogs in antebellum New York City', *Journal of Urban History*, 37:5 (2011), 639–60.

87 Antonio Santoyo, 'De cerdos y de civilidad urbana. La descalificación de las actividades de la explotación porcina en la ciudad de Mexico durante el último tercio del siglo xix', *Historia Mexicana*, 47:1 (1997), 69–102.

88 Brett Mizelle, *Pig* (London: Reaktion, 2011); see also Thomas, *Man and the Natural World*, pp. 68–9.

89 'On the hog and horse', MS 256, folio 55–6, n.d., *c.* 1840s, National Library of Ireland.

90 'On the hog and horse', folio 56.

91 'On the hog and horse', folio 70.

92 A veterinarian, *The Cattle Keeper's Guide; Or, Complete Directory for the Choice Management of Cattle, Including Horses, Oxen, Cows, Calves, Sheep, Lambs, Hogs, &c. With a Description of the Symptoms and Most Approved Methods of Curing Every Disorder They are Subject to* (London: Joseph and W. H. Bailey, n.d., early 1800s), p. 52.

93 Samuel Sidney, *The Pig* (London: George Routledge & Sons, 1897), p. 143; H. D. Richardson, *The Pig* (Dublin: James McGlashan, 1852), p. 86.

94 Richardson, *The Pig*, p. 86.

95 Sidney, *The Pig*, p. 143.

96 Richardson, *The Pig*, pp. 95–103.

97 Richard Whately, *On Instinct: A Lecture* (Dublin: James McGlashan, 1847), p. 20.

98 Elly, *Potatoes, Pigs, and Politics*.

99 William Carleton, *Traits and Stories of the Irish Peasantry, Second Series* (Dublin: William F. Wakeman, 1833, vol. 1), pp. 209–64.

100 *Returns of Agricultural Produce in Ireland, in the Year 1850*. P. 256, [1404], HC 1851, l, 1.

101 Richardson, *The Pig*, p. 103.

102 Richardson, *The Pig*, p. 41.

103 'Peg Briggs and her pigs', *The Dublin Songster* (Glasgow: John S. Marr, n.d., *c.* 1846), pp. 19–20.

104 'Dublin Police: murder of a bonneen', *Freeman's Journal* (7 November 1846). Bonneen is the Irish word for a small pig.

105 *Report of the Transactions of the Dublin Sanatory Association, from the 4ᵗʰ June, 1848 to 30ᵗʰ April, 1849* (Dublin: James McGlashan, 1849), p. 7.

106 *Public Health Bill for Ireland: Report of the Dublin Sanatory [sic] Association on the Public Health Bill, and on the Nuisance Removal and Disease Prevention Act* (Dublin: James McGlashan, 1850), Appendix no. 1.

107 Eoin Bourke, '"Paddy and pig": German travel writers in the "Wild West", 1828–1858', *Journal of the Galway Archaeological and Historical Society*, 53 (2001), 145–55.

108 Fanny W. Hall, *Rambles in Europe; Or a Tour Through France, Italy, Switzerland, Great Britain and Ireland in 1836* (New York: E. French, 1839, 2 vols), vol. 2, p. 220.

109 'Dublin police—yesterday', *Freeman's Journal* (28 April 1847).

110 See, for example, Fudge, 'A left-handed blow', p. 15.

111 'Borough sanatory court', *Freeman's Journal* (9 December 1848).

3

The market metropolis:
cattle and urban development,
1850–65

This country will soon awake to find that it has ceased to be a nation, and is practically only an English grazing farm.[1]

During the Great Famine Dublin had experienced an enormous influx of migrants seeking relief and bringing fever. The city's work-houses filled beyond bursting during the hungry years with both the local poor and those arrived from the countryside.[2] The 1851 census recorded a surge in the non-Dublin-born population of the city to almost 40 per cent.[3] Much of this rural component probably trickled out again through the port and the city's population remained around a quarter of a million. In the post-Famine city, the migrations of cattle would prove at least as impactful as the movement of people. One of the Famine's most enduring legacies was an accelerating shift to live-stock farming, but the effects of this change on Dublin have been vir-tually ignored. As we shall see, the growing livestock economy had considerable impact on the capital city.

After the Famine, Dublin's middle classes sought recovery and renewal even more fervently. Chemist William K. Sullivan eloquently expressed the sentiment when he explained the city's first industrial exhibition in 1853 as an effort to see 'what we have done, what we might do, and what we ought to do'.[4] This chapter examines two different manifestations of post-Famine recovery: the regulation of slaughterhouses and the development of the Dublin Cattle Market. These changes demonstrate the importance of cattle in the story of

Dublin's post-Famine development. The growth of particular middle-class sensibilities demanded the reform of slaughter in Dublin as in many other Western cities at the same time.[5] Yet the specific politics of the Dublin Corporation (and Ireland) affected the direction of change. Reforms to the buying, selling and killing of cattle show a reformed Dublin Corporation trying to cope with changing attitudes towards the urban animal economy alongside changing expectations of civic authority.

The regulation of slaughterhouses and the creation of a new cattle market could be understood in a variety of ways. They are evidence of the emergence of what Michel Foucault has called 'governmentality'—a way of governing that sought to use expert knowledge of life to encourage the right way of living.[6] Both changes also reflect tensions caused by the human dilemma: how to reconcile a desire to consume meat with its undesirable side effects? What both perspectives help to emphasise is that a meat-eating and cattle-farming society has its ideas, practices and experiences shaped by this reality. From 1850 onwards a demand for meat, both at home and abroad, changed Dublin's geography and the daily lives of its citizens.

Before we consider these changes, brief mention should be made of the political and legal changes that intersected with them. The Dublin Improvement Act (1849) was a turning point for the Dublin Corporation. The Act brought the city closer into line with English municipal corporations in terms of its rights and responsibilities. Statutory bodies such as the Wide Streets Commissioners, the Paving and Lighting Board and the Pipe Water Board were gradually dissolved, and the Corporation took charge of their activities. By 1853, the Corporation controlled the city's markets and property, the provision of sewers and drains, the cleaning of streets, the supply of fresh water and the regulation of nuisance businesses. All of these activities had to be funded through rates (or taxes) levied on an impoverished city while wealthier citizens continued to migrate to the suburbs.

Underlying these challenges was the continued issue of sectarian and political divisions. Municipal reforms in 1841 combined with the Improvement Act had broken the Protestant, conservative hold over city governance. Efforts to pass an improvement bill had embroiled the city's political and business elites in years of unseemly and public disagreements. The old boards and commissions had been mostly in the hands of conservatives and Protestants and their dissolution left the city potentially in the control of the liberal and Catholic-dominated Corporation.[7] Yet a complete revolution was not realised. When the improvement bill had been passed and the dust had settled on the re-division of electoral wards, the newly elected council still contained significant conservative and Protestant representation. Between 1850 and 1865 an informal agreement ensured that the office of Lord Mayor alternated between conservative and liberal political allegiances.[8] A very restricted Dublin electorate, not much altered by the redrawing of voting districts, meant that the city's poor Catholic majority did not translate immediately into a fully nationalist Corporation.[9]

The type of person elected to city government changed slowly. The members of the committee tasked with public health in 1853, for example, included four solicitors and a barrister, two justices of the peace and a doctor alongside larger merchants and businessmen. In 1863, the same committee still had four solicitors, two justices of the peace and a surgeon but also a pawnbroker, a baker, a grocer and a cattle salesmaster.[10] The movement away from substantial businessmen, merchants and professionals towards small shopkeepers and publicans occurred more dramatically from the 1870s onward.[11]

Between 1850 and 1865, an evolving Corporation in a recovering city intervened in the cattle trades in ways that would change Dublin into the future. The public health department committed to a policy of containing slaughterhouses through surveillance and condemned many poor people to live among them. The Corporation built a new cattle market and thus embedded the city within the Irish livestock trade for the next century. Dublin embraced its status as an urban cowtown, Ireland's market metropolis.

The slaughterhouse problem

During the summer of 1861, the Dublin Metropolitan Police watched Denis Doyle. They watched as he drove animals into the rear of his house at 21 North Earl Street. When none of those animals came out again, they concluded 'beyond a doubt' that Doyle slaughtered animals inside his premises although he had no licence for a slaughterhouse.[12] Since the Dublin Improvement Act of 1849, any butcher who wished to slaughter on their site had to apply for a slaughterhouse licence from the Dublin Corporation.[13] Doyle had applied for a licence in 1857 and again in 1859 but the Corporation's public health committee had refused each application.[14] One of Doyle's neighbours, a Dr Harrison residing in 17 North Earl Street, complained that if a slaughterhouse be permitted,

> a dangerous and unwholesome atmosphere will be created pestilential in its influence as respects the health & lives of the inhabitants in its neighbourhood and as immediately degrading the respectability of the street and its property value.[15]

The police gave up watching Doyle that summer because 'the exertions of the Police seem to have no effect', but the Corporation's public health committee and its inspectors continued to watch Doyle in the years that followed.[16] The committee brought Doyle to court for violating the sanitary laws in 1865 and again in 1869.[17] Nonetheless Doyle continued to use the house for slaughtering as he claimed he had done for the previous eighteen years and intended to do for the next eighteen.[18]

What was going on behind Doyle's closed doors that required a police stake-out and pursuit by the Dublin Corporation? Between 1850 and 1865 Dublin contained over one hundred active slaughterhouses, and slaughtering cattle was a messy business. Doyle probably had at least two men working for him, depending on the volume of animals that he killed. In the killing shed, which may have been at the bottom of a garden or much closer to the house, the beast would have been restrained by a rope while one man tried to drive the pointed end of a poleaxe into her forehead with sufficient force to render her unconscious. If this failed, the man delivered further blows. Another man inserted a pole into the hole created by the poleaxe in order to destroy her brain. She was then tied up by the leg and her throat cut so that she bled to death.[19] A single animal might have produced sixty pounds of blood, all of it running into a drain, an open sewer or collected in a container recessed into the floor. Wherever it flowed, the blood might become 'a nuisance to the neighbourhood by the pestilential vapours evolved in decomposing'.[20] The butchers likely removed the hide and entrails in the slaughter shed while the carcass may have been cut up in the kitchens of the butcher shop. If the carcass had been prepared for another butcher without his own slaughterhouse, it might be carried through the streets on the back of a labourer or in an open cart for all to see.[21] Together the city's slaughterhouses killed an average of 300 cattle per week so each slaughterhouse might have killed just a few animals. Yet a single large heifer or ox, weighing around 800 pounds, could produce a plethora of potentially hazardous wastes from urine and manure to entrails and bones.

Slaughter had been conducted this way in the city for hundreds of years and both residents and city government had complained of its ill effects for at least as long.[22] Yet the post-Famine period saw a significant intensification of action on slaughterhouses that accompanied hardening middle-class attitudes to the dangers of meat production.

The first moves by the Dublin Corporation were new bye-laws introduced after the Dublin Improvement Act. A slaughterhouse had to have a flagged floor with no cracks in it to prevent blood from seeping into the soil. All manure, offal and general filth had to be collected and 'removed beyond the limits of the Borough of Dublin, at least once during every day'. The building had to be washed every day when in use and lime washed at least once per month. A butcher of cattle could not keep swine or other food animals on the premises and certainly could not feed them on the slaughterhouse slops. Any dog, the typical butcher's companion, had to be 'chained, fastened, and secured'.[23] Accumulations of animals or wastes would lead to contamination, and therefore should be rapidly swept beyond the city's boundary. A city contaminated by such wastes was a city whose population was vulnerable to disease, as writers on cholera pointed out.[24]

These bye-laws reflected middle-class concerns that the production of meat created both physical and moral hazards. The permeable human body was to be protected from environmental poisons generated by matter such as rotting blood, offal and manure.[25] Advocates of municipal abattoirs sought to remove animal slaughter from sight, particularly from the view of supposedly vulnerable women and children.[26] For example, anti-cruelty campaigners in London used scenes of slaughter to reinforce their message that humane treatment of animals ensured the humanity of people.[27] A combination of public health and economic needs during the nineteenth and twentieth centuries gradually transformed slaughter from a ritual act necessary to produce meat into an industrial process invisible to the urban consumers of meat.[28]

Yet there is no evidence that Doyle had violated the new bye-laws or that he ran a particularly filthy slaughterhouse likely to attract public attention and offend the senses. Doyle was not a rogue. An ordinary, respectable butcher, his premises had been valued at £47 and he advertised himself as 'Victualler to the Lord Lieutenant'. His neighbours were grocers, chemists, doctors and merchants.[29] It seems that

Doyle lived above his butcher shop and slaughtered animals in a shed enclosed in the yard, a situation that was not unusual in Dublin at the time. In 1862 a house on nearby Great Britain Street contained a butcher shop as well as two drawing rooms, three rooms on the upper floor, a parlour and separate kitchens 'with gas throughout' as well as a large yard, a pen for animals and a slaughterhouse. The sale advertisement for the business suggested that the previous owner had made 'a large independence' through the property and retired.[30] (For a view of a typical nineteenth-century butcher shop, see Figure 3.1.) Doyle had not yet made his independence but had enough money to hire a lawyer to represent him when he appeared in court to counter the claims of the Corporation's public health committee.[31] He made regular donations to charitable causes including the Catholic school for the deaf in Cabra (just outside of Dublin) and a memorial for the Archbishop of Dublin.[32] He had tried to comply with the sanitary legislation by applying for a licence. The Corporation's own sanitary inspector, Charles Branagan, had recommended that the public health committee grant the application because of the seclusion of the proposed site.[33]

So how could a respectable owner of a secluded butcher shop merit so much attention from the Dublin Corporation and the Dublin Metropolitan Police? Doyle reveals the contradiction at the heart of the Corporation's pursuit of the slaughterhouse nuisance. Put simply, the Corporation was more interested in implementing a system of surveillance than creating change. They used public health surveillance as a performance of municipal power (not always successfully, as the case of Doyle demonstrates). The consequence of the Corporation's surveillance system was that the city retained a very unequal geography of slaughter with some Dubliners constantly exposed to the moral and physical hazards of killing cattle.

Ordinary Dubliners objected to seeing, hearing or smelling the process of killing animals. One described the slaughterhouses in his neighbourhood as 'nurseries of vermin and receptacles of filth'.[34] Another complained that the smell emanating from the local slaughterhouse was 'quite sufficient to breed a plague in the locality'.[35] At Smithfield Market, one promoter of a new market complained, 'animals were slaughtered in the full gaze of the public' who saw 'blood and filth rolling into the street'. Even worse, live animals mingled with dead and carcasses hung 'in the midst of that pollution' created by the terrified beasts awaiting their fate.[36]

3.1. Market stalls and secluded butcher shop (left) in a Dublin lane, *c.* 1880. From the collection of Walter Osborne in the National Gallery of Ireland. CSIA/OSB1/13.

The consequences of being surrounded by such sights were moral as well as physical. Those who lived in the vicinity of the city's slaughterhouses were suspected of being morally compromised by witnessing the deaths of so many animals. For example, the *Freeman's Journal* joked that a man arrested for drunk and disorderly conduct 'had great educational advantages, being always, when at home, within two minutes' walk of the Cole's lane slaughterhouses ... [which] developed the refined tastes of the accomplished Joseph'.[37] Only a single group of residents wrote to the Dublin Corporation to support the presence of a slaughterhouse in their neighbourhood between 1850 and 1865.[38]

Despite widespread agreement on the need to regulate slaughter, real change proved difficult. As Doyle's case demonstrates, it was easier to watch the slaughterhouse than it was to either eliminate or alter it.

The Corporation did not pursue Doyle because his slaughterhouse was dirty, they pursued him because he did not have a licence. He could not get a licence because the location of his slaughterhouse did not meet new expectations for urban improvement, where middle-class businesses and shoppers would be able to avoid the consequences of their meat consumption. The tension between control and consumption of cattle was further complicated in Dublin by politics. Control of slaughterhouses asserted the new powers of a majority liberal Corporation but it targeted the same people who elected that liberal majority: lower middle-class businessmen. The Corporation settled on a system of licensing and surveillance. They would hide their cow and eat it too. Licensing prevented slaughterhouses from encroaching on new neighbourhoods deemed unsuitable for such businesses and surveillance attempted to keep existing shops undetectable to the consumers of beef.

A more radical option would have been to close private slaughterhouses and centralise slaughter in a public abattoir. An ideal abattoir, provided with piped water and appropriate sewerage, could produce cleaner slaughter and facilitate the distribution of edible and inedible offal. This possibility was raised in May of 1851. The 'Corporation Powers Committee' reported that the borough contained 117 slaughterhouses paying over £1500 in annual rent. The committee argued that because of

> the great benefit to general health and cleanliness which necessarily would arise from the establishment of abbattoirs and the removal of slaughter houses from closely inhabited districts ... we submit the early attention of the council should be directed to the important subject.[39]

However, there is no evidence that the Corporation actively pursued a public abattoir before 1866 when they tasked the recently appointed City Analyst with reporting on the slaughterhouse problem.[40] Butcher resistance appears to have scuppered the plan.

Bypassing the abattoir, the Corporation introduced a system of licensing, registration and inspection of private slaughterhouses. Slaughterhouses in existence before 1849 had to register and submit to inspection. All new slaughterhouses required a licence. The Corporation could refuse or revoke a licence if the slaughterhouse did not comply with its bye-laws. By rapid removal of wastes, frequent cleansing and lime-washing, the slaughterhouse should become almost undetectable to its neighbours. At the same time, the licensed or registered slaughterhouse became more visible to the Corporation. A slaughterhouse had to cooperate with inspection, display a sign with a registration or licence number, and submit returns of animals slaughtered including details of where they had been purchased.[41] Killing now produced not just meat and mess but data.

This need to control the killing of cattle also changed city governance. For example, the Corporation increased the city's full-time public health staff to meet the demands of sanitary inspection. Slaughterhouse inspection comprised a significant proportion of their duties. The Dublin Metropolitan Police had played a role in detecting public health nuisances (such as filth that generated bad smells) and pursuing their removal since their establishment in 1836. From 1849 onward the Corporation employed an 'inspector of nuisances' (on a salary of around £100 per annum) and two or three assistant inspectors (between £26 and £65 per annum).[42] These inspectors made rounds of the slaughterhouses to ensure compliance with city bye-laws around sanitation and animal cruelty. In 1853, the Corporation reconfigured its committees and 'Committee Number 2' assumed responsibility for slaughterhouses, nuisances and markets.[43] From 1857 the Corporation further tasked the chief nuisance inspector with searching out diseased meat.[44] In 1858, the nuisance inspector claimed to have made 138 slaughterhouse inspections per week, more than any other type of sanitary inspection.[45] In 1864 the Corporation co-opted four members of the Dublin Metropolitan Police to use as sanitary sergeants.[46] By 1865, when they brought Doyle to the magistrate for a second time, the Corporation had ten full-time employees who each had some responsibility for the regulation of meat production.

Originally understood as a problem of filth, slaughtering cattle came to be seen as a problem of disease. The Dublin Corporation expanded its medical staff throughout the 1860s. Dr Charles Cameron, a chemist with a medical qualification, was appointed as city analyst under the

Food and Drug Act in 1862. He was tasked with, among other things, detecting diseased meat and adulterated milk. The seizure of diseased meat, the vast majority of which was beef, increased and reached a peak in quantity and prosecutions in the early 1870s.[47] In 1864, Dr Edward Mapother became the city's first Medical Officer of Health.[48] Mapother specialised in surgery and was also appointed to the chair of hygiene at the Royal College of Surgeons in Ireland.[49]

Both Cameron and Mapother applied themselves to the problem of meat. Cameron began to round up diseased meat, a task he believed would be facilitated by a public abattoir.[50] Outbreaks of cattle plague (1865) and cholera (1866) encouraged Cameron to direct attention to the passage of germs between people and animals and in 1866 he produced an extended report on the hazards of diseased meat.[51] Mapother proposed a solution to sanitation and cruel slaughter techniques when he suggested that cattle be killed by an injection of air into the jugular vein and butchered without draining the blood. Cattle, he claimed, would be killed in 'the most rapid and painless' way. Blood would not be spilled into the sewers to create a 'dangerous nuisance' for local residents. Finally, the meat would be more nutritious with the blood retained. Mapother backed up his nutritional argument with chemical studies of different types of meats and blood.[52]

The sheer size of the task complicated the Corporation's effort to reduce the impact of slaughterhouses in the city. Many of the city's private slaughterhouses were located in areas of dense population and were associated with the tenements and back lane in-fills that were such a feature of Dublin.[53] By tradition, killing usually took place on a Thursday, which was also the day of the cattle market.[54] Butchers reported the killing of around 300 cattle per week throughout the year, although the Corporation thought that slaughters were under-reported (see Figure 3.2). Dublin on a Thursday would have been awash in the produce of hundreds of cattle as meat, blood, bones, hides and offal found their way to butcher shops, bone boilers, manure makers, tallow chandlers and tanners.

Surveillance rarely resulted in reform because the Corporation often neglected its own bye-laws. For example, a good water supply in order to keep the shop clean and remove wastes was considered a prerequisite to hygienic slaughter and was required in the bye-laws. The public health committee even dismissed their inspector (although he was later reinstated) for failing to report that a slaughterhouse lacked a good supply of water.[55] In other cases, however, they granted licences

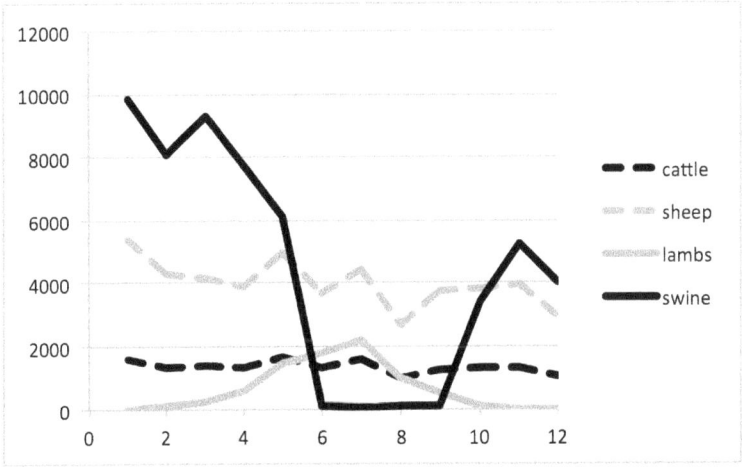

3.2. Graph of slaughters in Dublin slaughterhouses by month and type of animal, as per the records of the Dublin Corporation's Public Health Committee in 1865. Note that sheep and cattle remain relatively steady while swine drop off considerably during the summer. This is because pig meat was thought to 'taint' quickly in the heat. Although fewer cattle are slaughtered each month than other animals they are at least five times the weight of a sheep (on average) and almost four times the weight of a pig.

when street fountains provided the water supply and the shop had no access to a main sewer.[56] Applicants for slaughterhouse licences that failed to meet the standards were often given an opportunity to make alterations. As a result, surveillance never reduced the number of slaughterhouses. For example, the Corporation refused a licence in 1866 to John Hart for a slaughterhouse at 91 Camden Street on the grounds that 'no new premises will be licensed as slaughterhouses in the borough'. They then granted the licence several months later.[57]

Residents who sought to improve their neighbourhood (or at least prevent further decline) wished to see slaughterhouses removed. For example, in 1856 the residents of Trinity Ward in the south of the city appealed by way of a local doctor to the committee to refuse any new slaughterhouse licences and 'thereby relieve memorialists from the constant apprehension under which they labour'.[58] In 1858, the residents of St Mark's Parish, using the parish health inspector, asked for a reduction in slaughterhouse licences in their district.[59] The doctor on

Denis Doyle's street had complained of the potential for the slaughterhouse to create 'a dangerous and unwholesome atmosphere' but
was also concerned that the slaughterhouse would be 'immediately
degrading [of] the respectability of the street and its property value'.[60]
   But the process of licensing first revealed and then reinforced the
geography of slaughter. The Corporation's Public Health Committee
prevented change by continuing to allow slaughtering in places where
it already occurred. The committee might refuse a new licence in an
area without many slaughterhouses. However, residents attempting
to clean up their neighbourhood by reducing or eliminating slaughter faced an uphill battle. While the committee could do little about
the existing slaughterhouses as long as they remained in the same
hands, the transfer of a licence or the application for a new licence
provided an opportunity to intervene. The committee rarely did so
if the neighbourhood already contained slaughterhouses. In 1856, a
new slaughterhouse was approved for a premises in Clarendon Street
despite petitions from local residents and a physician who claimed that
it would be 'a public nuisance and most prejudicial to the health of all
in its immediate neighborhood'. The site itself was considered 'most
admirably adapted for a slaughterhouse' so that the presence on the
street of other slaughterhouses 'in a most disgraceful condition' did
not deter the committee from granting the licence.[61] A licence for a
new slaughterhouse was approved in 1860 because it was 'surrounded
by slaughterhouses of the same description'.[62] Even after resolving
to refuse a licence for slaughtering in Blackhall Place on account of
complaints about existing slaughterhouses, the committee granted a
licence for a new slaughterhouse because it had a drain and good ventilation.[63] The licensing of pig slaughtering followed a similar pattern.
When the intended slaughterhouse was near to similar premises or
in the region of the markets for bacon and the sites for bacon curing,
the applicant was certain to receive a licence.[64] Such decisions tacitly
defined a city of regions with varying degrees of nuisance businesses.
   Most of the city's slaughterhouses were in poor neighbourhoods
without a lot of low-value housing. A resident of Thomas Street felt
that callousness towards the poor resulted in unequal distribution of
slaughterhouses in the city. He complained to the *Freeman's Journal*
that 'if this nuisance existed near any of the aristocratic portions of
the city, it would be immediately removed, and, I ask, are not the lives
of the humbler classes just as precious and valuable as those of the
aristocracy?!'[65]

The pursuit of slaughterhouses between 1850 and 1865 offered a newly empowered Corporation the opportunity to express its power through licensing and inspection. However, the changing social, political and religious composition of the Corporation may have contributed to a failure to pursue slaughterhouse elimination. While many city councils balked at taking on the politically powerful traders, in Dublin the butchers also represented the expanding power of a Catholic 'shopocracy'.[66] The division over slaughterhouses in the council chamber showed clear support for butchers among liberal and nationalist councillors such as John Reynolds and John Gray. The latter, a licensed physician, claimed that no ill health effects attached to slaughterhouses.[67]

Through the policy of slaughterhouse surveillance the Dublin Corporation sought to implement new thinking in urban public health. Without the foundation of a public abattoir or the forced closure of existing slaughterhouses the net result was conservative: slaughterhouses tended to stay in the neighbourhoods where they had always been. The nineteenth-century ballad 'Dublin Jack of All Trades' recorded the employments of a roving 'Jack' who 'arriv'd to try for a situation'. As he moved from street to street his jobs changed:

In College-Green a banker was—in Smithfield a drover,
In Britain-st a waiter—in Georges-st a glover,
On Ormond-Quay I sold old books—in King-st a nailor,
In Townsend-st a carpenter & in Ringsend a sailor,
In Cole's Lane a job butcher—in Dame-st a tailor[68]

Of course butchers were not limited to Cole's Lane nor were drovers only in Smithfield. Nonetheless, the ballad indicates the way that people thought about the city, where each trade had its geographical niche. Many Dubliners agreed that slaughterhouses should be cleaner, but they were a part of the cityscape and few could imagine them completely absent. Similar attitudes about conserving Dublin's existing patterns of trade and its role in the booming cattle business affected how the Corporation handled demands to improve Smithfield cattle market.

The Dublin Cattle Market

The carcasses that so vexed the members of the Corporation had of course begun as living beasts. In the aftermath of the Great Famine,

cattle migration became as important for Dublin as human migration. A calf born on any farm in Ireland in 1850 was probably headed
for the city. She might spend the first two months of her life feeding
on her mother's milk but she was gradually weaned onto soft foods
and put out to grass. If she had been born in the poorer west of the
country she would be sold as a store animal at the Ballinasloe Market
and bought by a grazier who would arrange to have her driven on
foot to the richer pastures of Leinster for fattening.[69] The veterinarian's advice to 'buy cattle from a poorer ground than that you have to
feed them on' supported the movement of lean or immature animals
from the west and north to fattening fields in the east and south.[70]
Around the age of two (or perhaps as old as three or four) she would be
moved again: on a Wednesday night she would be driven 'on the hoof'
to Dublin where she would be sold early Thursday morning as a fat
heifer in the Dublin cattle market.[71] From the market she could be led
to a local butcher shop, such as Denis Doyle's, where she would await
her slaughter. Or, if she had been bought by an English dealer, her
migration would continue: driven around the city's North Circular
Road and down to the North Wall Quay, she would await a journey
by steamer across the Irish Sea, probably to Liverpool. From there she
might be forwarded by rail to almost any British city.[72]

   Along her journey, the heifer passed through many human hands.
Graziers owned or rented acres of grassland. In the counties near
Dublin, such as Meath, there might be as many as 250 cattle for every
thousand acres of land.[73] Once fattened, her sale was handled by a
salesmaster, who rented pens in the Dublin market and took a percentage of her price for himself. Market rules barred graziers from
acting as salesmasters.[74] Drovers, the lowest paid workers on the
cattle hierarchy, moved her from place to place. A drover might earn
less than 4s to drive fifteen beasts, each of which could fetch £15 for
the grazier.[75]

   The cattle trade connected Dublin to rural Ireland but also to
Britain. The industrialisation of England created the market for
beef. As industrial cities grew in population, the demand for meat
increased. In 1850, the average person in the United Kingdom consumed around eighty-seven pounds of meat annually. By 1914, he or
she consumed almost 127 pounds, or just less than two-and-a-half
pounds per week.[76] Not everyone ate the same amount: the English
consumed the most and the Irish the least per capita.[77] Both Scotland
and Ireland fed England, sending livestock by foot, railway and

steamship.[78] The cattle supply line created a tangible link between a Leinster pasture and a London dining table.

Thousands of cattle passed weekly through Dublin's market between 1850 and 1865. Calls to replace the old, crowded market in Smithfield eventually resulted in the foundation of a new Dublin Cattle Market under control of the Corporation. The new market on Prussia Street fixed Dublin's position in Irish patterns of cattle trading and cattle traffic for another century and influenced the area that grew around it. Even in the middle of the twentieth century Arran Quay Ward, where the market was situated, had 'a strong agricultural air about it'.[79] Figure 3.3 shows how the new market looked at the end of the century. The Dublin Corporation won the battle for civic control of the cattle trade but the brimming cattle pens, filled with beasts drawn from the Irish countryside on their way to Britain, suggested that Ireland had lost the war to establish economic independence.[80]

Dublin's busy cattle market provided a constant reminder of the consequences of the Great Famine. The failure of the potato crop

3.3. The new Dublin Cattle Market, opened in 1863 and photographed *c.* 1890. The photo gives a sense of its vast scale, once the largest live animal market in Europe. The housing seen at the edge of the market all developed in tandem with the market itself and to serve the needs of those working in it. Image courtesy of the National Library of Ireland.

accelerated a trend from tillage to pasture in rural Ireland as improving landlords replaced poor emigrants with herds of grazing cattle and sheep.[81] Contemporaries viewed this process with alarm, claiming that Irish landlords and the British government were complicit in deepening Ireland's economic subordination to England. One writer even blamed English newspapers, suggesting that 'the idea that cattle growing should be the natural and exclusive industry of Ireland has become a sort of fanaticism with the English press'.[82] In fact, the press repeated a widely held view that rainy Ireland should focus on livestock as a way out of poverty.[83] Livestock had always been an important element of Irish agriculture. The shift to exporting cattle from exporting grain was another swing of the pendulum between tillage and pasture that had occurred several times in Ireland's past.[84] If post-Famine Ireland was becoming an English grazing farm, then Dublin was becoming its barn. Here the future beef steaks of England were gathered together in the cattle market and the port before being packed onto steamships for export.

The numbers of cattle in Ireland roughly doubled between the Famine and the outbreak of the Great War.[85] Cattle herds increased throughout Ireland: the Irish provinces of Munster in the south and Connacht in the west saw overall increases. Only the northern province of Ulster recorded a decline, linked to post-Famine industrialisation. The west of Ireland grew store cattle while Leinster grew fat cattle and forward stores (those for further fattening at the site of slaughter). Fat cattle and forward stores filled the boats to England.[86] Figure 3.4 displays a map showing the relationship between Dublin and the Irish provinces.

The growing cattle trade altered the landscape around Dublin. Farmers devoted good soil to growing grass instead of crops. Large grazing farms dominated north Leinster: up to one fifth of all agricultural land was used as pasture.[87] This pattern had been evident from the eighteenth century but became increasingly prominent after the Famine. When landlords, bankrupt after the Famine, sold their holdings through the Encumbered Estates Courts, Dubliners bought up land for grazing.[88] Leinster's cattle herds increased by 19 per cent in the second half of the nineteenth century. County Dublin showed an even greater increase of 31 per cent (see Table 3.1).[89] Fattened cattle (over two years) increased in numbers while milch cows declined. Between 1855 and 1870 County Dublin lost about 1000 milch cows and gained more than 7000 cattle older than two years.[90] Outside of

3.4. Map showing the relationship between Dublin city, County Dublin and the province of Leinster. Image courtesy of Matthew Stout.

Leinster, at least 50 per cent of all cattle were milch cows. In County Dublin, despite the demand for milk from the city, milch cows made up only 30 per cent of all cattle.[91] The proximity of good grazing and the local demand for beef helped to ensure that Dublin remained the most important cattle market for fat cattle in Ireland.

Table 3.1 *Growth in Irish cattle numbers between 1855 and 1880. Numbers of cattle in the regions of Ireland, from the House of Commons Parliamentary Papers, reports of agricultural statistics for each year. Note that the late 1870s were a time of economic depression, particularly 1879 in which there was a return of potato blight and a subsequent famine.*

Region	1855	1860	1865	1870	1875	1880	Total % increase
Leinster	836,091	866,054	885,833	941,085	1,029,118	997,883	19%
(County Dublin)	(42,771)	(42,544)	(47,473)	(48,752)	(53,764)	(55,930)	(31%)
Munster	1,086,816	1,088,088	1,090,182	1,193,083	1,284,459	1,290,312	19%
Ulster	1,080,674	1,073,284	990,635	1,078,800	1,158,759	1,052,494	−2.6%
Connacht	571,235	571,809	526,764	583,412	642,645	580,337	1.6%
Total	3,556,616	3,599,235	3,493,414	3,796,380	4,111,990	3,921,026	10%

Infrastructure developed with the cattle trade in mind. For example, those who envisioned the most lucrative exploitation of the railway network had always viewed it as a way to funnel cattle towards Britain. When the Railway Commission made its second report on Ireland in 1838, they suggested that using the railways to transport cattle would facilitate economic improvement. Railways would place goods from the entire country within reach of the steam vessels that ran between the east coast of Ireland and the west coast of Britain. For these vessels, the commissioners believed, 'nine-tenths of the traffic thus carried on may be said to be new, such as the trade in fattened cattle—a most important item in the present exports of Ireland'.[92] The traffic could be expanded by 'a Railway [sic] intersecting the country from Dublin, [which] would place the cattle of those rich pastures within reach of Liverpool, Manchester, and Birmingham'.[93] During the second half of the nineteenth century, the growing Irish railway network radiated out of Dublin and helped to pull livestock from west to east.[94] Kingsbridge (now Heuston) Station was completed in 1848 as the terminus for the Great Southern & Western Railway line, which ran from Dublin to Cork. Broadstone Station was completed in 1850 as the terminus for the Midland & Great Western Railway line with its opposing terminus originally in Athlone, the heart of Leinster's grazing midlands. The line was later extended to Galway on the west coast. Amiens Street (now Connolly) Station was completed in 1846 and served first the Dublin & Drogheda Railway line and later the line to Belfast.[95] Initially these lines did not replace transportation of cattle by road and canal, but the hopes of converting them into a cheap means of moving cattle from west to east were a common refrain throughout the 1850s and 1860s.

Dublin's quays also facilitated the cattle trade. Beef cattle left from other Irish ports, but Dublin remained the most important throughout the nineteenth century.[96] The flow of beef on the hoof was almost entirely one way, with some return of breeding animals for the improvement of Irish stocks.[97] The development of the steam packet companies in Dublin depended upon the growth in cattle exports, especially fattened cattle.[98] By 1866, the Dublin Steam Packet Company alone had ten cargo ships devoted to the cattle traffic between Dublin and Liverpool.[99] Other companies specialised in passage to Holyhead. Between 2000 and 2800 cattle travelled each week to Liverpool, usually on a Friday or a Saturday. About 1000 of these beasts met the demand in Liverpool; the others were forwarded by rail to numerous

English cities. The shipping companies relied on cattle exports: the ships carried little or nothing with them on the return voyage.

As the demand for meat grew and the Irish cattle industry expanded in response, critics suggested that Dublin's Smithfield Market was no longer fit for purpose. A 'free' market with roots stretching back to the seventeenth century, Smithfield was small, poorly paved and surrounded by housing. Some aspiring cattle sellers accused established salesmasters of forming a cartel to control the market and prevent competition.[100] Other sellers bemoaned the market's poor facilities, unable to meet the needs of the stock that 'poured in by railway facilities from all quarters'. Smithfield was 'thronged' and the cattle suffered 'vile abuse' as a consequence.[101]

Popular culture reinforced the idea that Smithfield Market was far from modern. *The Omnibus*, a Dublin bi-weekly magazine published in 1862, condemned the market in a variety of different formats. A farcical song entitled 'Souvenir De Smithfield' lambasted the liberal politician John Reynolds for his supposed nostalgia for the old and dirty market. Reynolds sang of his love for all the backwardness of Smithfield including 'the riot and the row' as well as the smell of the sewers 'as nice as nice could be'. Finally Reynolds celebrated the butchers' cruelty: 'I was merry, I was merry/When some beasts were to be slain,/And I thought it funny, very,/When they made them howl with pain'.[102] Of course Reynolds never sang such a song, but the lyrics encapsulate many of the concerns over the old market, from raucous behaviour by drovers to bad smells and cruelty to animals. They also highlight the political importance of the cattle market and the cattle trade in Dublin.

A group of private businessmen and reformers with a conservative political orientation proposed a scheme to eliminate the problems of Smithfield. Their proposed new market on the North Wall of the River Liffey also would have centralised cattle export and broken the monopoly of certain traders in Smithfield. The new market would have reorganised Ireland's cattle trade and Dublin's role within it. As we shall see, there were a number of reasons for opposing the scheme. One difficulty was that the scheme favoured the store cattle trade while the fat cattle trade dominated the Dublin cattle market and the port.[103]

Those promoting a new market saw an opportunity to sever the cattle trade from the city. A new cattle market in the North Wall, its supporters believed, would create a barrier between the cattle and

Dubliners. The plans, produced by engineer George Willoughby Hemans in 1861, linked all railway lines approaching Dublin at a single terminus on the North Wall to facilitate cattle rather than human passengers. Hemans proposed a co-located abattoir to develop the trade in dead meat, which he argued would reduce the impact of cattle slaughtering in the city and benefit local trade in the use of offal.[104] The market and abattoir would be contained and separated from the city by a wall. Slaughter wastes would never enter city streets: paved with impervious materials and provided with drainage channels, wastes would be removed with ample water for 'complete purification' after market days. Rather than a market, it would 'present very much the appearance of an unusually large railway station'. The cattle within would become passengers either in this world (on steamships) or to the beyond (via the abattoir).[105] One salesmaster, although proposing a different location on the city's western outskirts, echoed this idea of a complete separation between a rural business and the city. His chosen site would 'keep the cattle, pigs, loads of straw and hay &c., outside [Dublin]' and avoid the need for driving cattle through the city as they moved between pasture and market and port.[106]

The idea of keeping the cattle trade out of the city may have appealed to the Corporation on the grounds of public health, but the needs of revenue and civic importance outweighed them. The Corporation had only recently fought hard to secure significant control over other aspects of city life through the Dublin Improvement Act and it was hardly going to relinquish control of its role in one of the largest trades in the country.

The Corporation's opposition to legislation that would enable the establishment of a new market reveals the central importance of the market to Dublin. The most forceful argument against the creation of a new cattle market in a different location was the probable disruption to trade. Over its two hundred years in existence, Smithfield Market had become an agricultural hub within the city. Surrounding the market were:

> farm-implement factories, seed shops; offices and places of business of brokers, salesmen and others; hotels and inns of different classes, livery stables, and those of dealers in horses; veterinary surgeons' establishments, and blacksmiths' forges; hay, straw, and corn stores, wool-cranes; offices of weigh-masters, and shops of other persons engaged in

the various trades connected with agriculture, stock feeding and the
breeding and rearing of cattle ...[107]

In addition, the market was located at the axis of a number of droving
roads and within reach of grazing pasture. Droving routes and pastures had been little disrupted by urbanisation and indeed the post-
Famine growth of grazing continued to favour the same areas for
cattle fattening. Members of the Corporation representing Arran
Quay Ward argued that its withdrawal would 'seriously injure that
portion of the city in which the present market is situate[ed]'. They
claimed that 15,000 houses in the district 'were dependent in some
degree or other for their support upon Smithfield'.[108] These outspoken
representatives depended upon Smithfield for their own support: one
was a cattle salesmaster and the other a manager of a livery stables.[109]

Another obstacle to moving the market was the new market's
reliance on the use of the railway network. In the 1860s, driving on
foot was the favoured means of moving cattle. A repeated refrain of
Irish witnesses to the Railway Commission of 1866 was the need for
railway companies to better facilitate the cattle trade. The railways
had succeeded in capturing the majority of the long-distance trade
in pigs, but store cattle continued to be driven by road, sometimes
walking next to railway tracks. James Cooper, who was involved in
the cattle trade, suggested to the Commission that one seventh of all
cattle reared in Ireland were moved by rail in 1863, compared with
three quarters of all pigs.[110] A variety of other witnesses pointed
to high rates for cattle, around 6d per head per mile, as a barrier.
However, directors and chairpersons of the various railway lines
expressed doubts about the possibility of expanding the traffic in store
cattle. John Ennis, MP for Athlone and chair of the Midland and Great
Western Railway, suggested that lowering prices would make no difference as 'there are some people, who if you offered them to carry
their cattle at a minimum price would prefer to drive them along the
road'. Such men resisted the very promise of the railroad, because for
them 'time is of no moment'.[111] Despite disparaging this behaviour,
Ennis admitted to having his own cattle driven sixty-six miles to
Dublin rather than sending them by the railway.

The resistance of the trade and the provision of an improved market
by the Corporation combined to defeat the North Wall scheme. Some
members of the trade accused the scheme's promoters of forgetting
that cattle were living beings that must be fed to maintain their value.

The North Wall site had no grass and stall-feeding was little used in the Irish cattle trade. The scheme's supporters imagined a Chicago-style stockyard before the Union Stockyard (1865) had been built. The Union Stockyard utterly transformed the collection of animals and their processing for meat while also transforming the landscape of the American West.[112] Promoters of a new market sought a similar transformation of the Irish cattle trade to a modern system oriented around railways and steam ships, cattle from the west barely touching a hoof to land as they were sped from field to butcher. Detractors believed this would be 'inconvenient in every possible respect to the general body of the landed gentry, Graziers, and Agriculturalists'.[113] The rejection of such a radical alteration of the railway networks and the cattle trade had a number of long-term impacts. Firstly, the Irish cattle trade continued to focus on live animals fed outside on grass. Although the export of meat gradually replaced the export of cattle in the twentieth century, much Irish beef is still grass-fed. Secondly, Dublin retained a cattle market within the city limits until 1973, complete with cattle driven across town to the port and a population of city-dwelling drovers.[114]

The triumph of the Corporation's improved market at the intersection of Prussia Street and Aughrim Street was total. The Lord Mayor opened the new Dublin Cattle Market in 1863, with 134 permanent pens and a number of temporary pens. The market could hold approximately 3000 cattle and another 10,000 sheep.[115] Soon after, the North Wall project folded. The Corporation had retained its control over Dublin's place in the lucrative fat cattle trade. This victory had a symbolic value beyond its associated revenue, ensuring that Ireland's most important industry could not simply bypass the capital city. The new market also introduced charges for the rental of pens and a toll of 3d for every ox, heifer or bull presented for sale in the market.[116] The tolls thus collected allowed the council to repay the substantial costs of developing the market without raising rates.[117] The new site was within easy walking distance of Smithfield and the other city markets north of the River Liffey. Perhaps most importantly, the new market remained convenient to the fertile pastures of north-west Leinster where some of the largest herds in Ireland grazed.[118] Dublin remained the largest market town for an area encompassing Meath, West Meath, Louth, Offaly and County Dublin (see Figure 3.4).

Accommodating cattle altered the city's socio-economic geography. Arran Quay became the ward that cattle made. The Arran

Quay electoral division, created in 1849, contained both the old Smithfield Market and the new Dublin Cattle Market. A commission had drawn new electoral boundaries with the aim to balance population numbers and rateable valuation so as to make 'equal' districts in voting terms. Arran Quay Ward combined a large wedge of under-populated and valuable land with a very small wedge of densely settled urban area. Parts of the district had been fashionable during the seventeenth and eighteenth centuries, but by the middle of the nineteenth century Arran Quay contained a large proportion of tenement housing.[119] The main arteries between the ward and the city's fringes were lined with houses. Beyond that, much of the ward was composed of grassy fields that were used to refuel cattle after droving and before market day.

The new cattle market slowly drove development. The population of the ward declined by a little more than 10 per cent between 1851 and 1871.[120] However, the city as a whole grew little in these decades and some wards lost a much greater proportion of their population than Arran Quay. The impact of the market and of the trade is reflected in the growth of cattle dealers recorded by the census. Between 1861 and 1871 the number of cattle dealers grew from 114 to 211.[121] While these numbers must be taken with some caution, the growth is echoed in the number of dealers listed in the city trades directory.[122] Most of these dealers were located near to the market in Arran Quay. House building also followed the fortunes of the market. The number of houses in the ward increased between 1851 and 1871. The Ordnance Survey Maps of the area surrounding the cattle market clearly show the appearance of new housing on Prussia Street, Aughrim Street and the North Circular Road. Most houses included large yards with cattle sheds, presumably for those involved in the area's principal trade (see Figure 3.5).

Arran Quay was an urban cowtown and the rhythms of the cattle market regulated the daily lives of its residents well into the twentieth century. The numbers of businesses catering to the market has already been noted, but it would be hard to overstate the impact of the movement of thousands of animals through the weekly market. On Wednesday nights cattle and sheep were driven in from the edge of town and from early morning the market was packed with animals and people engaged in the trade.[123] On Thursday, as the market closed, the animals were driven through the streets on their way to city butchers and to the port. By evening the drovers had their

3.5. Comparison of Sheet 6 of the Ordnance Survey maps of Dublin between 1847 and 1864 showing development around the new cattle market. Note the extension of housing on Aughrim Street, Prussia Street and the North Circular Road in tandem with the market. The top map is from 1847 before the new cattle market and the bottom map from 1864. The market is circled in black. Images courtesy of Joe Brady and the Ordnance Survey of Ireland. © Ordnance Survey Ireland/Government of Ireland Copyright Permit No. MP 000220.

payment for the week and filled the local pubs.[124] The lowest rung on the cattle industry ladder, drovers often worked only for the one or two days required to bring the cattle from surrounding pastures in to market and then on to the port.[125] Some continued their journey with the cattle on Friday and Saturday, taking ships to Liverpool, Holyhead and Glasgow.[126] Droving continued to be an urban occupation into the twentieth century. More than 14 per cent of all Irish drovers in the 1901 census lived in Dublin and most of these lived in Arran Quay.[127] Although butchers were scattered throughout the city, Arran Quay had a large number and these were also busy on Thursday and Friday converting their purchases into meat in backyard slaughterhouses.

The cattle trade shaped Arran Quay's politics. The councillors elected to represent the ward often included men engaged in the trade. Between 1850 and 1865, the ward was represented by three councillors and an alderman. Councillor Robert O'Brien was a salesmaster while Alderman Lawrence Reynolds owned a livery stables and hotel for several years. John Jameson came from a family of distillers whose land was purchased as a site for the new market. These representatives were all liberals. James Nugent, another liberal, remarked that as far as conservative candidates went, 'there is not the remotest chance of their success in our ward'.[128] In all parliamentary elections after the ward was created it voted heavily for liberal candidates (as did most of Dublin). In Arran Quay Ward this political alignment may have reflected a link with the cattle trade. The North Wall market scheme had been promoted by conservative politicians while the streets adjoining the new cattle market, Aughrim and Prussia Street, voted predominantly for the liberal candidate in the 1865 parliamentary election.[129]

The decision by the Corporation to fight to retain an urban cattle market under civic control was a choice about the future of the city. The cattle market ensured that Arran Quay remained a corner of the city where daily life was a negotiation between the needs of people and the needs of cattle. But the decision also had broader effects consequent on accepting the presence of thousands of cattle in the city. The Corporation surely had in mind the potential economic benefits of the market, rather than the public health problems of cattle manure and cattle slaughter.

An outbreak of cattle plague in 1865 revealed that not everyone was pleased by Dublin and Ireland's accommodation of the cattle export trade. The new cattle market had barely been opened for two years when cattle plague threatened both the safety of meat and the security of Irish livestock farming. The disease first appeared in a dairy outside of London and spread rapidly in England, resulting in a campaign of mass slaughter to 'stamp out' the contagion.[130] In Dublin and Ireland the disease never established itself. Yet responses to the disease reveal the contested nature of the compromise with cattle farming and meat production that the Corporation had made.

In October of 1865 Paul Cullen, Catholic Archbishop of Dublin, claimed that Ireland was 'menaced by scourges which, if not averted by the mercy of God, may sorely afflict us, and bring ruin on many'. Aside from cholera and potato blight, Cullen pointed to the threat from cattle plague. The disease was a punishment for the reappearance of 'a mitigated sort of cattle worship'. According to Cullen, Irish horse-fanciers and cattle owners cared more for their animals than their fellow humans: 'The excessive attachment of man to the beasts of the field appears to be punished by the diseases which now fall on them.'[131] Since the Great Famine, landlords had replaced people with cattle across Ireland, especially on the valuable grazing lands around Dublin. But the disease offered the possibility of redemption: God brought the cattle plague in order to demand that people restore 'the order of nature and religion' and stop placing cattle before humans.[132]

Cullen was not the only Irishman who saw cattle plague as an opportunity to set right something that had gone wrong in Ireland's relationship with livestock. A few months after his pastoral letter, a member of the North Dublin Poor Law Guardians claimed that farmers had become 'cattle worshippers, and exterminated the people to make way for the beasts'.[133] In August of 1865 the nationalist newspaper *The Nation* declared that 'the promise of the pest [cattle plague]' was to make the grazier 'tremble before such a visitation'. Landlords who had 'cleared away the people' would have their cattle cleared away by God.[134] In September of 1865 John Martin, a nationalist politician and the founder of the Irish National League, told a Dublin meeting that the plague punished England for 'making Ireland into her cattle farm'. The plague was also an opportunity for nationalists to exploit an English weakness. English dependence on imported food, especially Irish cattle, could assist the country's bid for independence. The way to an Irish parliament was through English stomachs.[135]

A combination of concern for the interests of the country and concern for the metropolitan role of Dublin ensured that the municipal council of the Corporation was among the first bodies in Ireland to press for an import ban to prevent the spread of cattle plague. They sent a deputation of the Lord Mayor and three members of the Corporation to wait on the Lord Lieutenant and encourage him to place a ban on imports of cattle.[136] A crisis committee was formed in Dublin, consisting of MPs, city councillors and a veterinarian. As a letter to the *Freeman's Journal* put it, 'there is but one opinion in Ireland'.[137] The way to protect Irish interests was to close the ports to all cattle, separating off the Irish herd from contact with British or foreign animals. Neither government nor the British public was easily convinced that banning cattle movement into Ireland was necessary and appropriate. The Prime Minister (Lord John Russell) initially took the view that enacting such a ban was outside his legal powers. English newspapers argued that cattle, like other property, resided within the United Kingdom rather than within a particular region.[138] By 25 August the Home Office had relented and cattle imports from Britain were banned.[139] This act did not end the Corporation's involvement, however. Instead city councillors now received, and acted upon, advice from the graziers in Leinster on how to deal with the cattle disease if and when it arrived.[140] A new committee was appointed consisting of the mayor, six aldermen and four councillors. The committee was empowered to call a meeting of the council in case of emergency and to consult with Dublin Castle on the measures to be taken, particularly in Dublin's port and markets, if cattle plague should appear.

The Corporation's actions cannot be explained solely by the body's duty in the oversight of Dublin port or a desire to protect urban meat supplies. The response is a further indication of the cattle market as Dublin's primary economic site and an integral part of its national role. Dealers and salesmasters were rate-payers and potential voters, but the Corporation also responded to pressure from rural groups.[141] Just as the Dublin Corporation appeased graziers and salesmasters by retaining the cattle market in the north-west of the city, they now preserved the city's role in the Irish economy. The rinderpest outbreak brought the identity of Dublin as the capital of cattle into sharp relief.

Decisions made about slaughterhouses and the cattle trade were ultimately conservative even if made by a liberal and nationalist Corporation. Instead of conserving elite privileges, they conserved the privileges of their rate-paying voters in the form of cattlemen and butchers. These decisions also conserved a geography of cattle growing and killing in and around Dublin. Slaughterhouses remained in the urban core as part of a landscape of poverty and nuisances while the cattle market remained in the north-west of the city and thus preserved the relationship between the city and the grazing fields of Leinster. As the story of cattle in Dublin shows, attempts to resolve the 'human dilemma' did not inevitably result in the concealment of animal exploitation. Sometimes, instead, exploitation became more permanently embedded in the urban landscape.

Attempts to police slaughterhouses also secured the role of the Dublin Metropolitan Police in sanitary policing. As the next chapter will show, the police became ever more important in regulating human–animal relationships in the city.

Notes

1 Anonymous [Francis M. Jennings], *The Present and Future of Ireland as the Cattle Farm of England and Her Probable Population* (Dublin: Hodges and Smith, 1865).

2 Cormac Ó Grada has demonstrated an excess of mortality in Dublin during the Famine, mostly due to epidemic disease rather than starvation. See Cormac Ó Grada, *Black '47 and Beyond: The Great Irish Famine in History, Economy and Memory* (Princeton, NJ: Princeton University Press, 2000), pp. 165–71. On the workhouses see Timothy W. Guinnane and Cormac Ó Grada, 'Mortality in the North Dublin Union during the Great Famine', *Economic History Review*, 55:3 (2002), 487–506.

3 David Dickson, *Dublin: The Making of a Capital City* (London: Profile Books, 2014), p. 308.

4 William Kirby Sullivan, 'Raw materials', *Exhibition Expositor*, 1 (1853), 5–6.

5 See, for example, Dorothee Brantz, 'Animal bodies, human health, and the reform of slaughterhouses in nineteenth-century Berlin', *Food & History*, 3:2 (2005), 193–215; Ted Geier, *Meat Markets: The Cultural History of Blood London* (Edinburgh: Edinburgh University Press, 2017); Paul Laxton, '"This nefarious traffic": livestock and public health in mid-Victorian Edinburgh', in Peter Atkins (ed.), *Animal Cities: Beastly Urban Histories* (London: Routledge, 2012), pp. 107–72; Paula Young Lee, 'Hide, seek, slaughter meat: the slaughterhouse as site', *Food & History*, 3:2 (2005), 241–90; Paula Young Lee (ed.), *Meat, Modernity, and the Rise of the Slaughterhouse* (Durham: University of New Hampshire Press, 2008); Ian MacLachlan, 'A bloody offal nuisance: the persistence of private slaughter-houses in nineteenth-century London', *Urban History*, 34:2 (2007), 227–54; Keith Thomas, *Man and the Natural*

World: *Changing Attitudes in England 1500–1800* (London: Penguin, 1984), pp. 287–300.

6 See Michel Foucault, 'Governmentality', in Paul Rabinow and James D. Faubion (eds), *Power: The Essential Works of Foucault 1954–1984*, vol. 3 (New York: The New Press, 2000), pp. 201–22. See also Simon Gunn, 'From hegemony to governmentality: changing conceptions of power in social history', *Journal of Social History*, 39:3 (2006), 705–20; Johanna Oksala, 'From biopower to governmentality', in Christopher Falzon, Timothy O'Leary and Jana Sawicki (eds), *A Companion to Foucault* (London: Blackwell, 2013), pp. 320–36.

7 Stefanie Jones, 'Dublin Reformed: The Transformation of the Municipal Governance of a Victorian City, 1840–1860' (PhD dissertation, Department of History, Trinity College Dublin, 2 vols, 2001), pp. 69–70.

8 Mary E. Daly, *Dublin, the Deposed Capital: A Social and Economic History, 1860–1914* (Cork: Cork University Press, 1986), pp. 208–10.

9 Daly, *Dublin*, p. 204; Jones, 'Dublin Reformed', pp. 273–5.

10 Committee member names culled from Dublin City Council Minute Books, vol. 16 C2A/16, vol. 17 C2A/17, vol. 23 C2A/23 and vol. 24 C2A/24, Dublin City Library and Archive [Hereafter DCC Mins]. Information on occupation from *Thom's Irish Almanac and Official Directory, with the Post Office Dublin City and County Directory, for the Year 1853* (Dublin: Alexander Thom, 1853) and *Thom's Irish Almanac and Official Directory, with the Post Office Dublin City and County Directory, for the Year 1863* (Dublin: Alexander Thom, 1863).

11 Daly, *Dublin*, p. 205.

12 Dublin City Council Public Health Committee Minutes, vol. 3, entry for 16 August 1861, Dublin City Library and Archive [Hereafter DCC PHC Mins].

13 Jacinta Prunty, *Dublin Slums 1800–1925: A Study in Urban Geography* (Dublin: Irish Academic Press, 1999).

14 This is according to Doyle's testimony. 'Police court', *Freeman's Journal* (4 May 1865). See also DCC PHC Mins, vol. 3, 14 January 1859.

15 DCC PHC Mins, vol. 3, 14 January 1859.

16 The committee was officially called 'Committee Number 2' until the name was changed after the Sanitary Act of 1866.

17 'Police Courts', *Freeman's Journal* (4 May 1865); Criminal Index, volume for 1867–1870, entry for Denis Doyle, 1869, National Archives of Ireland.

18 'Police Courts', *Freeman's Journal* (4 May 1865).

19 Ian MacLachlan, '*Coupe de grace*: humane cattle slaughter in nineteenth-century Britain', *Food & History* 3:2 (2005), 145–71.

20 'Royal Dublin Society', *Freeman's Journal* (17 March 1863).

21 See DCC PHC Mins, vol. 2, 14 January 1859.

22 Ian Cantwell, 'Anthropozoological relationships in late Medieval Dublin', *Dublin Historical Record*, 54:1 (2001), 73–80.

23 'Dublin Corporation', *Freeman's Journal* (18 June 1851).

24 See, for example, 'Review of the *Quarterly Journal of Public Health and Record of Medicine*', *Dublin Quarterly Journal of Medical Science*, 19 (1855), 429.

25 Linda Nash, 'Purity and danger: historical reflections on the regulation of environmental pollutants', *Environmental History*, 13:4 (2008), 651–8.

26 MacLachlan, '*Coup de grâce*'.

27 Diana Donald, '"Beastly sights": the treatment of animals as a moral theme in representations of London, *c.* 1820–1850', *Art History*, 22:4 (1999), 514–44.

28 Paula Young Lee, 'The slaughterhouse and the city', *Food & History*, 3:2 (2005), 7–25.

29 *Thom's Directory* (Dublin: Alexander Thom, 1862), entry for North Earl Street.

30 'To salesmasters ...', *Freeman's Journal* (20 August 1862).

31 'Unlicensed slaughterhouse', *Freeman's Journal* (4 May 1865); and 'Police Courts', *Freeman's Journal* (30 May 1860).

32 For example, 'Catholic Institution for deaf and dumb', *Freeman's Journal* (19 January 1861); 'Monument to the most Rev. Archbishop Murray', *Freeman's Journal* (20 March 1852).

33 DCC PHC Mins, vol. 2, 14 and 21 June 1859.

34 'Correspondence', *Freeman's Journal* (12 December 1853).

35 'Correspondence', *Freeman's Journal* (5 October 1857).

36 'The Dublin Cattle Market Bill', *Freeman's Journal* (26 June 1862).

37 'Police Courts, Head Office', *Freeman's Journal* (27 May 1862).

38 DCC PHC Mins, vol. 3, 17 June 1859.

39 DCC Mins, vol. 15, 26 May 1851.

40 See DCC PHC Mins, vol. 5, 19 October 1866.

41 Monthly returns were submitted at first and later weekly returns. See DCC Mins, vol. 16, 5 April 1852.

42 DCC PHC Mins, vol. 3, 1 and 4 November 1864.

43 DCC Mins, vol. 16, 5 January 1853.

44 DCC PHC Mins, vol. 2, 22 May 1857.

45 DCC PHC Mins, vol. 2, 7 January 1859.

46 DCC PHC Mins, vol. 3, 1 and 4 November 1864.

47 Ian Miller, *Reforming Food in Post-Famine Ireland: Medicine, Science, and Improvement, 1845–1922* (Manchester: Manchester University Press, 2014), p. 108.

48 Lydia Carroll, *In the Fever King's Preserves: Sir Charles Cameron and the Dublin Slums* (Dublin: A. & A. Farmar, 2011), p. 111.

49 Carroll, *In the Fever King's Preserves*, p. 111.
50 DCC PHC Mins, vol. 4, 20 October 1865.
51 DCC PHC Mins, vol. 4, 21 September 1866. See Juliana Adelman, 'Contagious bovine pleuropneumonia, germs and public health in Dublin, 1862–1882', *Social History of Medicine*, 30:1 (2017), 71–91.
52 'Royal Dublin Society', *Freeman's Journal* (15 December 1862).
53 DCC PHC Mins, vol. 4, weekly records of slaughter throughout 1865.
54 *Report of the Committee Appointed for the Local Government Board for Ireland to inquire into the Public Health of the City of Dublin and Minutes of Evidence*, minutes of evidence, p. 104 [Cd 243] HC 1900, xxxix, 681, 707.
55 DCC PHC Mins, vol. 3, 7 March 1862.
56 For example DCC PHC Mins, vol. 3, 31 December 1861 and 24 October 1862.
57 DCC PHC Mins, vol. 5, 11 September 1866 and 16 November 1866.
58 DCC PHC Mins, vol.2, 10 October 1856.
59 DCC PHC Mins, vol. 2, 8 October 1858.
60 DCC PHC Mins, vol. 2, 14 January 1859.
61 DCC PHC Mins, vol. 2, 29 August 1856.
62 DCC PHC Mins, vol. 3, 25 September 1860.
63 DCC PHC Mins, vol. 3, 20 September 1861.
64 See, for example, DCC PHC Mins, vol. 3, 24 January 1862, 1 February 1861, 25 September 1860, 3 March 1860, 26 August 1859.
65 W. J. R., letter to the editor, *Freeman's Journal* (5 October 1857).
66 Dickson, *Dublin*, p. 336.
67 'The Corporation. Election of Lord Mayor for 1859', *Freeman's Journal* (2 December 1858).
68 'Dublin Jack of All Trades', traditional ballad, nineteenth century, *Irish Traditional Music Archive*, 18123-BS, Lesley Shephard Collection.
69 David Seth Jones, *Graziers, Land Reform and Political Conflict in Ireland* (Washington, DC: Catholic University of America Press, 1995), pp. 3–5.
70 A veterinarian, *The Cattle Keeper's Guide; Or, Complete Directory for the Choice Management of Cattle, Including Horses, Oxen, Cows, Calves, Sheep, Lambs, Hogs &c. With a Description of the Symptoms and Most Approved Methods of Curing Every Disorder They Are Subject to* (London: Joseph and W. H. Bailey, n.d.), p. 28. See also Richard Perren, *The Meat Trade in Britain, 1840–1914* (London: Routledge and Kegan Paul, 1978), p. 9.
71 Matthew Milburn, *The Cow: Dairy Husbandry and Cattle Breeding* (London: W. S. Orr, 1851), pp. 104–6; *Select Committee on the Home and Foreign Trade in Animals by Sea and Railroad*. H.C. 1866 (427), xvi, 423, Evidence of Samuel Garnett, p. 280 [Hereafter *Select Committee on Trade in Animals*].

72 On the British market for Irish beef on the hoof see Perren, *The Meat Trade in Britain*, pp. 94–8. A third option was possible: she may have calved and been brought to Dublin as a milker, where she would have lived for about a year in a shed before contracting disease and being slaughtered for meat. Dairy cattle are dealt with in more detail in Chapter 5.

73 Jones, *Graziers*, pp. 3–5.

74 Liam Clare, 'The rise and demise of the Dublin cattle market', *Dublin Historical Record*, 55:2 (2002), 166–80.

75 Lodge Park Stock Book, MS 23,573, National Library of Ireland; see, for example, entries for 1856.

76 Perren, *The Meat Trade in Britain*, p. 3.

77 Perren, *The Meat Trade in Britain*, p. 80.

78 Perren, *The Meat Trade in Britain*, p. 22; Clare, 'The rise and demise of the Dublin cattle market'.

79 Paddy Crosbie, *'Your Dinner's Poured Out!'* (Dublin: O'Brien Press, 1981), p. 41.

80 Raymond Crotty has made a similar argument and sees the beginnings of Ireland's colonial dependence on Britain as entangled with the emergence of cattle capitalism. See Raymond Crotty, *When Histories Collide: The Development and Impact of Individualistic Capitalism* (Walnut Creek, CA: Alta Mira Press, 2001), pp. 161–200.

81 James S. Donnelly, Jr. 'Landlords and tenants', in W. E. Vaughan (ed.), *A New History of Ireland V: Ireland Under the Union 1801–70* (Oxford: Oxford University Press, paperback edn, 2010), pp. 332–49; and R. Vincent Comeford, 'Ireland 1850–1870: post-Famine and mid-Victorian', in the same volume, pp. 372–95. Note that 'cattle' often referred to any livestock during the nineteenth century. I will use it in the more specific modern sense to refer to bovines, although much of what is said in this chapter applies relatively well to sheep.

82 Papers of Thomas Larcom, extract from *The Post* (4 August 1865), MS 7748, National Library of Ireland.

83 Comeford, 'Ireland 1850–1870', p. 381.

84 John O'Donovan, *The Economic History of Livestock in Ireland* (Cork: Cork University Press, 1940), pp. 15–17, 34–9, 50–1.

85 Joseph Lee, *The Modernisation of Irish Society: 1848 to 1918* (Dublin: Gill and Macmillan, 1973), p. 10.

86 Jones, *Graziers*, pp. 5–6, 45–8.

87 Jones, *Graziers*, p. 115.

88 Jim Gilligan, *Graziers and Grasslands: Portrait of a Rural Meath Community, 1854–1914* (Dublin: Four Courts Press, 1998), pp. 23–4.

89 *Returns of Agricultural Produce in Ireland, in the Year 1850* [1404], HC 1851, l, 1; *Returns of Agricultural Produce in Ireland, in the Year 1855* [2174] HC 1857, xv, 81; *Returns of Agricultural Produce in Ireland, in*

the Year 1860 [2997] HC 1862, lx, 137; *Returns of Agricultural Produce in Ireland, in the Year 1865* [3929] HC 1867, lxxi, 435; *Returns of Agricultural Produce in Ireland, in the Year 1870* [C 463] HC 1872, lxiii, 299.

90 *Returns of Agricultural Produce in Ireland, in the Year 1870* [C 463] HC 1872, lxiii, 299.

91 *Returns of Agricultural Produce in Ireland, in the Year 1850* [1404], HC 1851, l, 1; *Returns of Agricultural Produce in Ireland, in the Year 1855* [2174] HC 1857, xv, 81; *Returns of Agricultural Produce in Ireland, in the Year 1860* [2997] HC 1862, lx, 137; *Returns of Agricultural Produce in Ireland, in the Year 1865* [3929] HC 1867, lxxi, 435; *Returns of Agricultural Produce in Ireland, in the Year 1870* [C 463] HC 1872, lxiii, 299.

92 *Second Report of the Commissioners Appointed to Consider and Recommend a General System of Railways for Ireland*, Part III, p. 90 [145], HC 1837–1838, xxxv, 449 [Hereafter *Railway Commission 1838*].

93 *Railway Commission 1838*, Part III, p. 91.

94 David Miller and Leonard J. Hochberg, 'Modernisation and inequality in Pre-Famine Ireland: an exploratory spatial analysis', *Social Science History*, 31:1 (2007), 35–60.

95 Christine Casey, *Dublin: the City Within the Grand and Royal Canals and the Circular Road with the Phoenix Park* (New Haven, CT: Yale University Press, 2005), p. 687.

96 Jones, *Graziers*, p. 6.

97 William Nielson Hancock, *Report on the Importation of Cattle into Ireland: In the Year Ended 16 August 1865* (Dublin: Alexander Thom, 1865).

98 Peter M. Solar, 'Shipping and economic development in nineteenth-century Ireland', *Economic History Review*, 59:4 (2006), 717–42.

99 *Select Committee on Trade in Animals*, Evidence of William Watson, p. 283.

100 Clare, 'The rise and demise of the Dublin cattle market'.

101 Ganly, Sons and Parker, 'Letter to the Irish press', *Dublin Builder* (1 February 1861), 423.

102 'Souvenir de Smithfield', *Omnibus*, No. 1 (14 June 1862), p. 10.

103 George W. Hemans, 'Proposed junction of the Dublin railways with a cattle depot', *Dublin Builder* (1 February 1861), 422–3.

104 Hemans, 'Proposed junction'.

105 Hemans, 'Proposed junction', 423.

106 Ganly, 'Letter to the Irish press', 423.

107 Michael Cahill, *Remarks on the Present State of the Cattle Market of Dublin, with Suggestions for the Improvement of Smithfield, and the Erection of a General Abattoir and Carcase Market. With a Map &c.* (Dublin: Hodges, Smith & Co., 1861), p. 11.

108 'North Wall vs. Smithfield as a cattle market', *Dublin Builder* (15 December 1861), 716.

109 *Thom's Irish Almanac and Official Directory, with the Post Office Dublin City and County Directory, for the Year 1855* (Dublin: Alexander Thom, 1855), pp. 857, 1008.

110 *Royal Commission on Railways in Ireland. Evidence and Papers Relating to Railways in Ireland,* Evidence of James Cooper, pp. 156–7 [3607] HC 1866, lxiii, 279 [Hereafter *Royal Commission on Railways 1866*].

111 *Royal Commission on Railways 1866,* Evidence of John Ennis, p. 171.

112 William Cronon, *Nature's Metropolis: Chicago and the American West* (New York: W. W. Norton, 1991), pp. 209–12.

113 Cahill, *Remarks on the Present State of the Cattle Market of Dublin,* p. 4.

114 Clare, 'The rise and demise of the Dublin cattle market', 177.

115 Clare, 'The rise and demise of the Dublin cattle market', 171.

116 DCC Mins, vol. 25, 20 June 1864.

117 Clare, 'The rise and demise of the Dublin cattle market'.

118 Jones, *Graziers,* p. 140.

119 Maurice Craig, *Dublin 1660–1860* (London: The Cressett Press, 1952).

120 Joseph V. O'Brien, *Dear, Dirty, Dublin: A City in Distress, 1899–1916* (Berkeley: University of California Press, 1982), Appendix B, p. 284.

121 *Census Ireland for the Year 1861. Part IV. Reports and Tables Relating to the Religious Professions, Occupations and Ages of the People. Vol. 1* [C 3204] HC 1863, lix, 1; *Census of Ireland 1871: Part I, Area, Population and Number of Houses; Occupations, Religion and Education. Volume I. Province of Leinster* [C 662] HC 1872, lxvii, 1.

122 *Thom's Irish Almanac and Official Directory for the Year 1865* (Dublin: Alexander Thom, 1865), p. 1791; and *Thom's Irish Almanac and Official Directory for the Year 1875* (Dublin: Alexander Thom, 1875), p. 1813.

123 Pigs arrived by rail or cart. Kevin C. Kearns, *Dublin Street Life and Lore* (Dun Laoghaire: Glendale, 1991), pp. 58–9.

124 Kearns, *Dublin Street Life and Lore,* p. 58.

125 Kearns, *Dublin Street Life and Lore,* p. 58.

126 These were the most common ports of export used throughout the century. See *Report on the Transit of Animals from Ireland to Ports in Great Britain with an Appendix* [C 2097] HC 1878.

127 National Archives of Ireland, Census of Ireland for 1901, www.census.nationalarchives.ie (accessed 15 May 2020).

128 James Nugent, 'To the editor of the Freeman', *Freeman's Journal* (12 March 1853).

129 Clare, 'The rise and demise of the Dublin cattle market'; S. Tudor Bradburne, *City of Dublin Election, July 15th, 1865. Candidates: John Vance Esq., D. L.; Benjamin Lee Guinness, Esq. D. L., L. L. D.; and Jonathan Pim, Esq. List of Electors for the Year 1865, Distinguishing the Names of Those*

Who Exercised their Franchise at the Above Election, and Showing for Whom they Voted (Dublin: J. Atkinson, 1865).

130 On cattle plague see Arvel B. Erickson, 'The cattle plague in England, 1865–1867', *Agricultural History*, 35 (1961), 94–103; Terrie M. Romano, 'The cattle plague of 1865 and the reception of "the germ theory" in mid-Victorian Britain', *Journal of the History of Medicine*, 52 (1997), 51–80; Michael Worboys, *Spreading Germs: Disease Theories and Medical Practice in Britain, 1865–1900* (Cambridge: Cambridge University Press, 2000).

131 'Pastoral of the Most Rev. Dr. Cullen', *The Nation* (14 October 1865).

132 'Pastoral of the Most Rev. Dr. Cullen', *The Nation* (14 October 1865).

133 'North Union', *Freeman's Journal* (15 February 1866).

134 'The promise of the pest', *The Nation* (12 August 1865).

135 'The National League', *The Nation* (9 September 1865).

136 DCC Mins, vol. 26, 7 August 1865.

137 Ornamore and Browne, 'To the editor of the *Freeman*', *Freeman's Journal* (25 August 1865).

138 MS 7748, National Library of Ireland, Thomas Larcom papers, newspaper clipping from *The Telegraph*.

139 National Archives of Ireland, Registry of State Papers for 1865, paper 8633.

140 DCC Mins, vol. 26, 10 January 1866.

141 DCC Mins, vol. 26, 10 January 1866.

4

Enforcing values and controlling animals: dogs, pigs and police, 1865–80

> There has been a raid made against the pigs; there are some, but nothing like the number there used to be.[1]

> The dog nuisance has long been a subject of complaint in Dublin, but the public will be surprised to learn how much the police have done to abate it.[2]

On a designated date in July, constables of the DMP fanned out across the city to gather the annual agricultural statistics. The men were unmistakable in their helmets bearing the crest of the DMP, a wooden baton at their side. The Registrar-General and the Under Secretary at Dublin Castle asked the DMP to conduct themselves with 'utmost civility' to ensure the public's cooperation as they combed the police district counting pigs, horses, cattle, sheep, chickens, mules, asses and goats. In the municipal borough they would go street by street, listing the livestock numbers by owner.[3] Control and enumeration of animals demanded a surprisingly large proportion of police power, not just during the weeks when they collected agricultural statistics. Between 1865 and 1880 the police were called upon to enforce sanitary laws regulating the keeping of livestock and a new dog licence regulating the ownership and control of dogs.

By the later decades of the nineteenth century, certain animals were no longer welcome in the modern city. In New York, a campaign eliminated free-range pigs in the 1840s.[4] In London and Paris, fear of rabies led to increased controls on how one could keep a pet dog in the city streets.[5] In Dublin, policemen captured roaming or unlicensed dogs and removed pigs from homes and yards. The regulation of pigs and dogs demonstrates the growing importance of the Dublin Metropolitan Police as the enforcer of middle-class values. The story of dogs and pigs also shows how middle-class Dubliners sought to resolve the human dilemma created by conflicting desires. On the one hand, they wanted to keep dogs and eat pork. On the other hand, they wanted to reduce the urban nuisances created by dogs and pigs. The solution was to regulate animal-keeping, changing who could own a pig or a dog in Dublin.

Such regulations represent a form of governmentality: they sought to cement ideas of acceptable urban street life.[6] They also demonstrate the ways in which regulation of animals and animal businesses could disproportionately impact the lives of the poor. Middle-class reformers, aided by the police and the Corporation, sought to eliminate the street dog and the house-bound pig.

The need to control dogs and pigs in Dublin involved reconceptualising the role of the police. When a bill to regulate dogs in Ireland was introduced, Sir Robert Peel, former chief secretary for Ireland and sitting MP for Tamworth, favoured legislation to solve the 'great evil' of roaming curs. However, he objected to 'throw[ing] on the constabulary of Ireland [the job] of registering three millions of dogs'.[7] Such a duty was too onerous for a police force already tasked with nuisance inspection, census taking and collection of agricultural statistics, not to mention detecting and preventing crime.[8] *The Mail*, by contrast, asked why the constabulary should object to registering dogs when they had agreed to count pigs. They were, the paper observed critically,

> unwilling to stoop from their military eminence to take part in anything so vulgar as abating the dog nuisance. There is a vast difference between a pig and a dog. They have consented to 'enumerate' the one but to take the smallest notice of the other is utterly beneath them.[9]

In terms of improving the city, reformers saw no 'vast difference' between a pig and a dog. Both animals created nuisances in the city, both animals provoked new control measures between 1865 and 1880 and the DMP, however reluctantly, implemented those controls.

New controls on urban pigs and dogs affected who could own them. The restriction of pig-keeping practices occurred across Europe and America, spurred on by public health activists and local health administration.[10] Changes affected the poor in particular as middle-class reformers sought to remove pigs from crowded districts, small yards and the inside of homes. These changes concentrated pig-keeping in the hands of middle-class business owners such as butchers and bacon factors. Pet-keeping, and particularly dog-keeping, also became a middle-class activity. From London to Paris to New York City, the idea of the dog as a pet and a human companion came to dominate human–dog relationships.[11] City authorities no longer tolerated stray animals and human owners usually had to pay a tax for the privilege of keeping a pet. Humane legislation restricted the working roles of dogs while at the same time dog-keeping expanded significantly. Middle-class urban residents often initiated these changes, new laws formalised them and the police enforced them.

New ways of controlling dogs and pigs appeared alongside a variety of bourgeois-led reforming initiatives in Dublin. Voluntary associations proliferated to address perceived needs from education for artisans to temperance promotion to the scientific study of social reform. The middle classes flocked together in professional societies, scientific societies, humane societies, musical societies, sanitary societies, literary societies. They organised and attended industrial exhibitions, agricultural shows and dog shows.[12] Through these activities they sought to create a city that was more modern, more sanitary, more cosmopolitan. The middle of the century has been identified by historians of Dublin as particularly significant for middle-class life in the city.[13] Social, economic and even geographic changes echoed their increased importance. Suburban housing multiplied, particularly on the south-eastern side of the city. Successful speculation and development drew the professional classes out of the crumbling city centre and into the prosperous suburban townships. Transportation networks followed them in the form of omnibus and tram routes. Shopping adapted to the needs of these wealthy suburban residents, most evident in the success of the 'monster' department stores.[14]

At the same time as middle-class influence increased, the Irish police force expanded. Police numbers per head of population in Ireland outstripped the rest of the United Kingdom. The Irish constabulary became a centrally administered and educated force in the 1830s and by 1870 Ireland had twice as many police per head of population as England or Wales.[15] The DMP was among the largest urban police forces in the nineteenth century. In 1850, there was one policeman per 250 persons in Dublin. In London there was one policeman per 418 persons. The DMP made similar numbers of arrests in Dublin as their counterparts in London despite a much smaller population.[16] Through their actions the DMP helped to bring middle-class values into the streets. This chapter examines dogs and pigs in turn. In each section, I show how cultural ideas about animals were translated into the realm of law enforcement and consider the impact on human and animal lives.

Dogs

At the first Dublin dog show in 1864 the 'canine deputies' assembled in two large, temporary wooden buildings that filled the pleasure gardens behind the Rotunda maternity hospital. The buildings sat at the northern end of the city's main commercial thoroughfare, Sackville Street (now O'Connell Street). Dogs and owners who arrived on foot from the busy omnibus stops on Sackville Street would have passed hotels, clothing shops, grocers, solicitor's offices, printers and associations such as the Royal Agricultural Improvement Society of Ireland and the Irish Farmers' Club. Approaching the building they may have noted the noise coming from more than 450 dogs 'keeping up a perpetual growl'. Once inside, it was 'scarcely necessary to mention that the noise is fearful' as the assembled animals protested the circumstances of their confinement. Chained dogs, contained in stalls lining the walls of the oblong buildings, kept the sixteen caretakers busy providing food and water and removing wastes. Among them were tiny lap dogs, including the Lord Lieutenant's own miniature terrier, and a gigantic Maltese lion dog. The *Freeman's Journal* noted with approval that 'types of the whole human family are represented, or rather indicated, in the dogs now prepared to be exhibited'.[17] A military band bravely attempted to play over the sounds of barking. On the day of judging, the Lord Lieutenant (the Earl of Carlisle), accompanied by military officers, perambulated the show among the hundreds of 'fashionable' visitors who had paid the half-crown entrance fee. And so arrived in Dublin a new form of entertainment that, predicted the *Irish Times*, 'will unquestionably amuse and interest the public, who are ever ready to grasp at a novelty' (see Figure 4.1).

The Dublin show extended the English dog show circuit, which had begun in Newcastle (1859) before spreading to Birmingham (1860), Leeds (1861), Manchester (1861) and London (1862).[18] The chief

4.1. Prize winners at the first Dublin dog show in 1864 (16 April 1864, *Illustrated London News*). Image courtesy of the Board of Trinity College Dublin.

organiser of the first Dublin show (John Sillitoe) was based in London, but the baton soon passed to Irish enthusiasts. In the gap between the first Irish show in 1864 and the next in 1872, Irish exhibitors participated in English dog shows, including a combined fat cattle, poultry and dog show in Liverpool in 1868.[19] The Ornithological Society of Ireland hosted the Grand National Poultry and Dog Show of 1872 in the newly built Exhibition Palace. Further shows were held throughout the 1870s, including the first show hosted by the Great National Dog Show Society of Ireland in 1874.[20]

The arrival of the dog show in Dublin signalled a new way of valuing dogs. Dog shows turned dogs into consumer goods. Dogs became a kind of living currency whose value was judged at shows, recorded in books of lineage and linked to the pedigrees of owners. By shaping the dog show and the dog fancy, the English middle classes verified their own social status and further differentiated themselves from the working classes.[21] Pet-keeping became an integral part of bourgeois life in nineteenth-century European and North American cities. Veterinarians and entrepreneurs took advantage of new opportunities to make money out of caring for pets by producing tonics, remedies, collars and cages.[22]

The dog show exhibited animals in a way that was both novel and familiar to Dubliners. The cattle shows of the Royal Dublin Society exhibited and valued livestock twice per year. Fat pigs, for example, often commanded prices higher than pedigree dogs and encouraged similar attention to their breeding. Yet the *Freeman's Journal* thought the dog show departed from such 'mere exhibitions of animals' because dogs held a different status to livestock, being 'amalgamated with society'.[23] Despite the feeling that a pedigree dog was different to a fattened pig, the dog show introduced a similar method of valuing dogs as exemplars of careful breeding. The dog show became a giant, noisy dog market. Prizes only added symbolic flourish to animals already valued at hundreds of pounds. Prices told visitors which dogs were of greatest interest. In the 1864 show, the owner of the 'Maltese lion dog' sought more than £500 to part her from her pet.[24] Perhaps in an effort to deter buyers at the 1874 dog show, one owner priced their prize mastiff at £1000.[25] By contrast, first prize in most classes did not exceed £5.

Dog shows also pushed Irish dogs towards conformity with standards set by the English Kennel Club. The Irish naturalist Robert Scharff saw the rise of the dog fancy as a turning point for dog breeds in Ireland. For example, Scharff recognised the Irish terrier as a distinct breed after its first exhibition at a dog show in the 1870s, although he traced the breed to an ancient race of dogs. In the case of Irish water spaniels and Kerry Beagles, Scharff compared characteristics of the modern show variety to those of possible ancestors found in medieval records. While tracing ancient pedigrees of Irish dogs, Scharff accepted the dog-show definition of each breed.[26]

Dog shows permanently altered the appearance of Irish dogs. For example, Irish dog breeders rapidly eliminated colour variety among setters. By 1866, patches of white or black were out of fashion. Harry Blake Knox, a breeder resident in one of Dublin's south-eastern suburbs, argued that the proper colour for an Irish setter was 'blood-red'; white should be excluded or at least limited to 'the centre of the forehead and the centre of the breast'. Black streaks were unacceptable and eye, nose and whisker colour was limited. Red colour assured purchasers of 'pure' breeding. When Knox's male red setter impregnated a black-and-tan setter bitch, the resulting puppies showed black streaks and Knox 'of course, drowned them'.[27] This new standard departed from that of the past, a historian of the breed noted: 'The sportsmen of one hundred years since were evidently not very particular about the dogs as long as they did their work well, but since the days of dog shows, breeders have been breeding their dogs free from white.'[28] By the twentieth century almost all Irish setters were dark red. Prizes at the dog shows were awarded for red setters so breeders abandoned the red and white variety. This variety was 'indeed not quite extinct, but being less popular than the other, is eliminated'.[29] The setter's colour became the index of pure breeding and a proxy for a wide range of other characteristics. Knox didn't wait to find out if his mixed-breed puppies were good hunting dogs: they were the wrong colour and impure in their pedigree, and therefore of no value.

The pet dog began to appear more frequently in the newspaper classifieds. Dublin's dog owners valued their pets enough to pay for their safe return if they strayed. Between 1864 and 1874, lost dog advertisements appeared regularly in the *Freeman's Journal* where owners offered rewards ranging from 5s to £2.[30] By 1874 most owners offered £1. Lost dogs included pedigree breeds such as Skye terriers, Pomeranians and King Charles spaniels.[31] But the distraught owner of the terrier described as 'old; fat; his fore-teeth gone' surely sought the return of a companion rather than a prize.[32] By 1876 dogs had anchored themselves in the 'lost and found' column alongside dropped valuables such as jewellery. By the mid-1880s, lost dog notices were numerous and a further dedicated column contained notices of dogs for sale. For example, on 7 September 1886 the 'lost' column contained seven lost dog notices, all for pedigree animals. One reader offered the substantial sum of £5 for a dog's return.[33] On 3 May 1887, the column contained eleven notices relating to lost or stolen dogs. Six of the owners listed an address in the suburbs.[34]

The same trend appeared in other periodicals. The *Irish Sportsman*, first published in Dublin in 1870, included advertisements for pedigree dogs in its first issue. 'Highly-bred setters' cost £1 for a puppy while other dogs 'whose pedigree can be given from Champion prize blood on all sides' cost two guineas for a puppy.[35] By 1880, the *Irish Sportsman*'s advertisers included more sophisticated accounts of pedigree and even higher prices. The owner of the Irish setter 'Palmerstown' offered his stud services at a fee of £5 5s, a comparable price to stallions. Palmerstown had 'taken cups and first prizes at all the leading shows'.[36] Breeders used the dog show as a shop window to market their kennels. J. J. Gilltrap (owner of the famous prize-winning red setter Garryowen) offered his winning water spaniel for sale just after the 1880 show had finished.[37]

Over the first two decades of dog showing in Dublin, Dubliners embraced a changed way of valuing dogs. By 1876, the *Irish Times* claimed that 'dog shows have taken deep root in Ireland'.[38] The foundation of the Irish Kennel Club in 1877 supports this. Prospective Kennel Club members believed that a voluntary association of the large and growing number of 'dog breeders and dog fanciers of Ireland' would allow for more frequent and more satisfactory dog showing leading to the 'steady improvement' of existing breeds and the introduction of new ones.[39] The club hosted annual shows in Dublin from at least 1878.[40]

Valuable dogs also created a market for dog portraits. Photographers M. Allen and Co. on Westland Row had a special 'Studio for Children and Animals'.[41] The demand for painted pet portraits supported at least one specialist. William Osborne, father of more famous painter Walter Osborne, made a career in Dublin as a painter of animals. Originally a warehouse clerk, Osborne trained in painting at the Royal Hibernian Academy and began exhibiting in 1851. He began by painting the prized sporting animals of the landed gentry. As the gentry's money dried up, his focus shifted to the pet-owning urban middle classes and he began painting more scenes of dogs.[42] He painted so many dogs and horses that his biographer described his work as leaving 'an overall impression of dark brown'.[43] Osborne's catalogue of paintings shows the impact of the dog fancy. His first exhibition in 1851 included portraits of dogs. However, his first portrait of dogs with an identified master appeared in 1863. The Italian greyhounds were said to be 'the property of the Hon. Mrs. Plunkett'. Throughout the 1870s and the 1880s, dogs became as common as horses in his work.[44] Perhaps the most famous example is his painting of the champion Irish red setter Garryowen (*c.* 1880), which now resides in the National Gallery of Ireland.[45]

Satirical literature made fun of the rising cultural and financial value of the pedigree dog. The comic magazine *Zoz*, for example, lampooned the pampered, middle-class dog. In the story 'Mountain View', Mr Crump's dog Charlie and Mr Crump's daughter (called only 'little Crump') wrestle. Worried about his pet, Crump inquires after Charlie to be told that the dog is uninjured but 'little Crump' has broken her neck. Crump announces, without sympathy for the child, 'I am very glad to hear it, she deserves it richly'.[46] A fake advertisement for

'Dog Lost' suggested a £1 reward 'if the finder will keep this valuable animal tied up lest he find his way home'.[47] Writers who did not love dogs crafted violent ends for the spoiled pets of their friends and relatives, such as when one character converted a friend's dog into sausages.[48] A poet wrote of 'Timotheus' who 'belonged to our opulent aunt'. The aunt's heirs 'feared Aunt Jemima might alter her will,/If she found that we used her pet animal ill'. In order to get their inheritance they resolved to kill both dog and aunt.[49] A poet writing in the *Dublin University Magazine* lamented of a lady's lap dog that 'the moral now, 'tis well to know-/should you not love this creature—go!/Her doting mistress is your foe!/Ah! Odious Spitz!'[50]

The dog show craze alone might have changed how dogs were owned and controlled in Dublin. Dog shows and specialist breeders created a self-reinforcing circle with the middle-class market. English ideas about dogs found a ready audience among better-off Dubliners of all political and religious persuasions much like English periodicals and fashions found ready consumers.[51] The addition of legislation and policing enforced new practices of dog ownership.[52] The only acceptable urban dog would soon be the middle-class pet. A hierarchy of swine, dependent upon the social status of their owners, would also emerge.

The dog show arrived in a city where dog ownership was widely distributed among the social classes. Some dogs lived a cosseted life among the wealthy where they were fed and groomed and housed indoors. Surgeon General Philip Crampton could afford to keep a kennel of sporting dogs in his mansion on Merrion Square, where a groom cared for them and he took them hunting at weekends.[53] Some wealthy ladies were partial to the lap dog, 'lazy, furry, warm and bright,/Peeping from a fringe of white;/Blinking, sleeping, day and night'.[54] Arthur Tracy could make a living as a dog thief, stealing pedigree animals and reselling them.[55] Yet the working classes also kept pets that may have been less confined and perhaps scavenged for their food. A police magistrate recalled hearing numerous cases of owners brought before court during the 1840s and 1850s on the charge of letting their dogs wander off a lead. The working-class man was often represented by his wife, who reassured the judge that the dog had been disposed of. One woman declared: 'He's hung, sir; he was very owld and stupid and hadn't a tooth in his head, so we hung him, not to be bother'd with him any more.' Another woman brought the skin of the sacrificed dog as proof.[56] A different magistrate lectured his court on delinquent owners who 'had scarcely half enough of food for their children' but insisted on keeping a dog or two which were therefore 'always afflicted with a tremendous appetite'.[57] Advocates of artisan dwelling schemes discouraged shared yards as a 'never-ending source of annoyance' because of noise, quarrelling children and 'contention as to dogs'.[58] Other Dubliners kept dogs to protect their businesses or to help with work. One witness to the public health inquiry claimed that knackers had 'very powerful and dangerous dogs that feed on the refuse'.[59] Butchers also kept such dogs and both butchers and knackers were associated with dog fighting. Under the humane legislation discussed in Chapter 1, the police rounded up several butchers 'for the barbarous act of dogfighting'. Fighting dogs often died or were 'dreadfully mutilated', a far cry from the pampered life of the lap dog.[60]

The dog tax, introduced in Ireland in 1865, reinforced the idea of the dog as a middle-class commodity. The dog shows suggested the superiority of dogs bred according to new pedigree standards, while the dog tax attempted to exclude the lower classes from legal dog ownership. Although presented to parliament as a solution to the plague of curs that roamed the countryside and killed sheep, the tax always had a class element. Poor Irish farmers, supporters of the bill claimed, wasted resources they could ill afford by keeping useless pets.[61] The expectation was that these owners would avoid the tax by killing their dogs. The *Freeman's Journal* joked that the dogs of the city would know 'they had been legislated for by the number of kicks and other kinds of hard usage' they received from frustrated owners. The paper suggested that 'worthless' dogs would find themselves turned out on the street or 'sacrificed' to avoid the tax.[62]

After the dog tax, dog numbers indeed declined in Dublin and Ireland. Owners had to register each dog for a fee of 2s 6d. Some types of working dogs were exempt or incurred a reduced tax. Owners purchased fewer than 500,000 dog licences in Ireland in the first year of the tax, a fraction of the estimated three million Irish dogs. The figures continued to decline thereafter.[63] The Dublin Metropolitan Police annually made hundreds of convictions for 'not complying with the dog act'.[64] Yet registered dogs also continued to decline in Dublin. In 1866, over 10,000 dogs were registered in the city.[65] By 1871, the number had dropped to 4178. The trend slowly began to reverse at the close of the century, but by 1896 there were still just 4851 registered dogs in the city.[66]

Licensed dogs were middle-class dogs and their decline mirrors the declining middle-class population of inner-city Dublin. All locations suffered a dip in the aftermath of the tax, but dog numbers in Belfast and the Dublin suburbs quickly recovered and surpassed those prior to the tax. For example, in Belfast dog numbers fell between 1867 (5065 registered dogs) and 1871 (3230 dogs). However, the number had trebled by 1896 when there were 9115 registered dogs despite the introduction of a higher level of tax.[67] Belfast at this time had a substantial middle-class industrial elite.[68] While dog numbers in the city of Dublin itself declined or remained static, numbers in the suburban townships increased. Booming Rathmines showed the most dramatic increase, from 904 in 1871 up to 1559 in 1896. Kingstown and Pembroke, the other important south-eastern townships, showed increases from around 600 dogs in 1871 to more than 900 dogs in 1896. Dogs are thus another register of the embourgeoisement of the suburbs and the economic decline of the municipality.[69]

The cost of owning a licensed dog discouraged working-class ownership. The initial fee of 2s 6d per dog was high for the average working wage. The increased fee of 7s 6d (from 1876) was prohibitive. This higher fee was out of reach for most urban residents, whose wages probably averaged around fifteen to twenty shillings per week. Weekly rent cost on average more than two shillings and food took the majority of the remaining wage, leaving little extra to pay the licence fee and feed the dog.[70] Small butchers, victuallers and shopkeepers made up the majority of lower-middle-class dog owners as they had ready access to supplies of food. Even these shopkeeping classes found the increased tax in 1876 prohibitive as it was accompanied by further taxes on tobacco and on income. A cartoon entitled 'Put that in your pipe and smoke it' (see Figure 4.2) made the predicament of the average 'Pat' clear. A man, pipe in hand and dog at his feet, dolefully observes his added expenses posted on a wall. The taxes are linked to an impending conflict with Russia over the Middle East, and Pat declares: 'Begorra! if a body can't smoke nor keep a dog, nor have an income before they begin fightin', what will it come to when they are in grips with Rooshia?' Pat appears to be considering whether to dispose of the pipe or the dog first. The dog cowers, tail between its legs, as though aware his future demise is contemplated.

Just as the Zoological Gardens provided a respectable space for consuming animal spectacle in the right way, the dog tax sought to

4.2. 'Put that in your pipe and smoke it': Cartoon showing a man contemplating the new taxes on tobacco, income and dogs. From *Zoz* (13 April 1878). Image courtesy of the Board of Trinity College Dublin.

encourage the 'right' way of keeping a dog. Opposition to the dog tax linked this 'right' way with social class and political identity.

Opponents of the dog tax perceived it as an attempt to restrict freedom and prevent the working classes from owning dogs. 'A new song on the saucy dogs of Ireland' suggested that 'each poor man that has a dog and cant the tsxes [sic] pay, sir,/Must wear a muzzel and a log, and hunt his dog away, sir'. The dog tax treated owners like dogs: unjustly muzzled and controlled by government. The dogs in the ballad opposed the bill on the grounds that it would restrict their freedom to roam and claimed they would protest by withdrawing their service to humankind. A terrier claimed that 'a rat he'd never kill, sir,/Unless he'd see his comrades free from this obnoxious bill, sir'. As revenge, dogs planned to pillage their food. The pointer and the greyhound would 'murder every rabbit, hare & phessant [sic]' while the bull dog would 'eat the legs from under every bobby'. The only dog undisturbed by the bill was 'the lap dog that was fed on every deinty [sic]'. This dog had 'house and home, along with full and plenty' and was certain that 'my master will pay them [dog tax] for me that I may please the ladies'. After the dog tax, the ballad implied, only lap dogs would remain in Dublin where they would live idle lives as homebound pets of the middle classes (see Figure 4.3).[71]

Similar themes of class and freedom appear in the poem *An Evening in the Green Hills* but with a political message. The poet took the point of view of a traveller returning to Dublin via the Green Hills, a location where Dublin Fenians had assembled prior to the rebellion in 1867. The Fenians were nationalists who pursued separation from England through violence during the 1860s.[72] Now the dogs, meeting 'free from muzzles, collars, logs', echoed Fenian cries for freedom from British rule. A wolfhound, found in Ireland 'Ere Saxon footprints stain'd the shore', led the meeting. He decried 'Britain's vaunted liberty' as false and cited the dog tax as evidence: 'the most damning stain of all/Is the tyrannic new taxation,/Whereby each dog of hut or hall/Must have a license in this nation'. One after the other, the dogs echoed the twin complaints of Irish and canine oppression under British rule. No dog wanted 'A sordid, slavish, licens'd life'. Instead they were full of 'thoughts of glorious liberty'. They agreed that they would bear the tax if the proceeds went to erect a monument to Henry Grattan, an eighteenth-century opponent of the Act of Union dissolving the Irish parliament. The only exception was

A New Song on the

SAUCY DOGS OF IRELAND

Air the Old Dogs Story

You dog-fanciers of Ireland wheaever that you be,
I hope you'll pay attention and listen unto me,
'I's about the dogs I'm going to sing, do not think I'm larking,
You must shell out 2s 6d, now if you keep a dog a barking,

Now each poor man that has a dog and cant the tsxes pay, sir,
Must wear a muzzel and a log, and hunt his dog away, sir,
And if he dares to grumble, into Harolds Cross they'll bang him
Unless he goes and buys a rope the wretched dog to hang him

4.3. 'A new song on the saucy dogs of Ireland', written in response to the new dog tax. The printer seems to have lacked any images of dogs with which to top the ballad and has used an array of mostly mythical animals instead. Image courtesy of the National Library of Ireland.

'a dog of some distinction' whose 'coat was finer than the rest'. This dog lived with a wealthy man who, the dog argued, was a stalwart member of society and 'gives relief in many ways/Asylums, hospitals, and schools/And houses built for crazy fools'. According to this dog, the tax prevented the unnecessary violence of dog fights and any deserving owner could afford it.[73]

Neither the poem nor the ballad can be read as simply a critique of the dog tax. Each engaged with social and political critique that might be interpreted many ways. Yet both suggest that the impact of the tax was to favour a particular way of keeping a pet dog, one that was most common among wealthier Dubliners. The dog tax reinforced the cultural changes brought about through the rising popularity of the dog fancy in Dublin. The dog shows implied a greater value for middle-class pedigree dogs and the dog tax made this value concrete. The poem and the ballad strike at a crucial aspect of changing human–dog relationships: only certain dogs could live in the city while others would be rounded up and euthanised.

The dog tax had not eliminated the problem of the stray dog and in 1879 a tragic case of rabies encouraged further action. On 30 July 1879, Miss Anna Maria Collins of Zion Terrace in Rathgar died from hydrophobia at the age of twenty-five. Rathgar, part of the wealthy suburban township of Rathmines, was home to around 1000 dogs.[74] Over a month before, Miss Collins had welcomed home her wounded fox terrier after a disappearance of two days. The dog had been in a fight and as Miss Collins attended to his wounds, 'he suddenly flew at her, and fastened upon her lip'. Miss Collins sent for a doctor who cauterised the wound. She may have thought nothing more of the incident but given the dog had strayed and that it was the 'dog days' of summer when rabies often became more prevalent, perhaps Miss Collins waited in dread for symptoms of the disease to develop. She complained of a twitch in her lip on 26 July and the next day her cousin accompanied her to the Meath Hospital where she was attended constantly by medical staff and family but eventually died. The hospital matron described Miss Collins, who asked that relatives not come too close lest they become infected, as 'a girl of great courage and kindly feeling'. The city coroner was less sympathetic. He worried that Miss Collins had failed to notice the symptoms of rabies in her pet and had allowed him to be 'wandering about the neighbourhood of Rathmines' possibly infecting other dogs. He concluded that 'All our lives ... were really in jeopardy, owing to the folly with which people persisted in these useless pet dogs'.[75]

Newspaper columns soon filled with comments stirred by the 'melancholy case' of Miss Collins. One letter to the editor of the *Freeman's Journal* complained that observing women and their dogs 'often filled me with sickening disgust to witness the caresses bestowed on those dirty brutes' and suggested that even pedigree pets should not be allowed in carriages, trams or railways.[76] Such a reaction against the middle-class suburban dog was, however, unusual. The finger of blame pointed squarely at the roving, unregistered dog. The *Irish Times* claimed that hydrophobia 'very seldom declares itself spontaneously in the well-fed dog, though many such were infected by being bitten by strange curs'.[77] The death of Miss Collins from the bite of her own pet suggested that Dublin required greater vigilance around rabid dogs, but particularly around stray dogs. Within a week of her death the city had established a home for lost dogs and the Dublin Metropolitan Police had begun to round up strays and kill them.

The creation of the middle-class pet required the elimination of its opposite—the roaming, unregistered dog. The initial impact of the dog tax had been, observers claimed, to increase this very class of unwanted dog. Owners turned unlicensed dogs out into the streets where they were 'roaming about in a half starved and disgusting state'.[78] The DMP enforced the laws about logging and muzzling dogs and, from 1866, the dog tax. By 1879, however, these laws had not eliminated '*canis vagrans*'.[79]

Although Sir Robert Peel had expressed doubts about asking police to control and license dogs, the DMP had engaged with their duties under the Dog Act (at least in the early years). To the question: 'What are you responsible for when on your beat?' the catechism from the force's manual suggested the response: 'The security of life and property, the preservation of peace, and general good order.'[80] Control of dogs, if they appeared to threaten life, peace or good order, could be justified. In 1865 police summoned 884 individuals for 'suffering dogs to be at large without a log or muzzle'. In 1866, the first year the dog tax was in operation, they summoned 193 persons for non-compliance. By 1867 this number had climbed to a peak of 2523 while summonses for dogs wandering without a log or muzzle had fallen to 146.[81]

Enthusiastic enforcement was short-lived and soon all types of summonses for dog-related offences began to fall. In 1870, the police summoned only 829 persons for improper keeping of dogs and of these the vast majority (732) were for failing to pay the dog licence fee rather than possessing an uncontrolled animal. Summonses reached a low of 313 in 1877. Despite concerns over rabies, only nine of these summonses were for stray dogs.[82] Either Dubliners had learned to comply with the laws or the police had decided not to enforce them. Letters to newspapers complained of the dog nuisance. In 1874, 'no less than twenty-four curs', at least nine of them lacking any licence, menaced 'Pro Bono Publico' in his own street.[83]

Fear of rabies eventually changed the policing of dogs in Dublin. This fear had been slow to develop and was directed mostly at *canis vagrans*. In Paris, where Louis Pasteur later produced a vaccine, the fear of mad dogs far exceeded the frequency of their appearance. Hysteria over the horrible effects of rabies on humans could make those bitten by dogs behave strangely even if they never developed the disease. Because dog control laws, including a dog tax, shifted dog-owning onto the bourgeoisie, the cultural context of rabies also changed. From a disease associated with the working classes and their improperly cared-for dogs, rabies became a disease associated with the middle classes and their improperly pampered dogs.[84] In London, the resurgence of a rabies panic in the 1860s was strongly associated with stray dogs and the working classes, although by the late 1880s the blame had begun to shift to pampered pets.[85] Disgust for the feminised, pampered pet is evident in Dublin but the focus of dog policy was firmly on the roaming cur between 1865 and 1880. Rabies neither captured the imagination nor influenced dog policy to a substantial degree in Dublin until 1879. The local papers considered Ireland to have a low rate of rabies. In 1877, for example, the *Freeman's Journal* spoke of the 'great alarm' felt in England and Scotland because of 'the increasing frequency of hydrophobia cases' there. The writer believed that 'something very like a panic' about rabies in Britain was not matched in Ireland.[86] In 1878, the presence of rabies in Dublin encouraged some councillors to propose a ban on all dogs wandering without 'being under the control of any person'. Yet the debate on the proposed order lacked both consensus and urgency. While one councillor raised the spectre of 'children being torn by rabid dogs', others suggested that recognising madness in dogs (or people) was nearly impossible and a distraction for police officers with more important duties.[87]

The death of Miss Collins prompted the successful campaign to establish a dogs' home. Within a week, the Corporation and the DMP opened the home in a 'spacious but dilapidated' building in the city centre (formerly a bacon-curing establishment). The police soon filled the home with stray dogs using a new Corporation order that allowed them to seize any animal not under human control.[88]

The DSPCA had proposed such a home in 1878 to combat the perceived dog nuisance in a humane way. The Society sought annual subscriptions to set up a home for 'lost and starving dogs', which it believed would solve a number of ills. Firstly, the dogs would be saved from 'misery and starvation' on the streets while the public would be spared the predations of these dogs. Secondly, the dogs would be killed by a 'merciful, instantaneous, and painless scientific method' if they could not be rehomed. Finally, no owner would have to offer a reward for the return of a lost dog.[89] Dubliners did not flock to support the DSPCA's home. Instead, the Corporation and the Dublin Metropolitan Police established a home between them. The Dublin police commissioner complained, however, that the collection and disposal of stray dogs 'certainly cannot be construed into legitimate police duty'.[90]

The new dogs' home shows how the police and the Corporation put into practice changed cultural ideas about dogs. The dogs were collected together and restrained 'in the usual manner that we see them tied at dog shows'. One of the city's dog dealers inspected the dogs and sorted them according to their monetary value. Dogs he deemed 'above the ordinary mongrel class' received five days' board to allow their owners to claim them before police sent them to a city horse repository for auction. 'The annoying guerrilla or nomadic species', however, received only three days' grace before being poisoned by way of their food dish.[91] The Corporation's street scavengers carted away the dead dogs as they did manure or night soil.[92] Thus the fate of a dog was determined by its perceived value according to the aesthetic standards of the dog fancy. If the dog tax threatened the mongrel cur of the working-class urbanite, the combined efforts of the Corporation and the police now sought to eliminate him. Despite the complaints of the police commissioner, twelve police constables were employed full time to capture and destroy large numbers of dogs.[93] Between August of 1879 and December of 1880, the DMP brought over 2000 dogs to the home and killed over 1800 of them.[94]

If Dublin had co-opted the dog show and its standards of pedigree pets from England, the city responded differently than London to the problem of stray dogs. By 1860 Londoners (mostly women) had established the Battersea Dogs' Home, where stray dogs could be rescued and homed until resold. Although dogs were killed in the home, its advocates resisted the idea that policemen should be involved in the containment of stray dogs. The Battersea Dogs' Home was imagined as a rescue agency for reviving poor starving dogs, rather than a solution to eliminate the roving cur.[95] Yet the dog rescuers in Battersea also classified their dogs by something akin to social status. By the 1870s, cooperation with the police and a change in attitude meant that the home killed the vast majority of dogs that entered rather than rehoming them.[96] In Dublin no voluntary project of dog rescue masked the intentions of the city's home for lost and starving dogs. Government, specifically the Corporation and the police, directed the city's approach to stray dogs and, from 1879, they were treated as a public health problem and a nuisance.

The celebration of special dogs at the dog show masked the brutal truth of dog breeding: people such as Harry Knox killed animals they deemed worthless in the pursuit of a perfect specimen of the breed. For every prize-winning hound, there were probably many others that had not been allowed to live to adulthood. The practice of collecting and killing stray dogs in the Corporation's dogs' home replicated the same process of selection with the added justification of securing public health. This culling put into action a set of middle-class ideas about dog appearance and dog behaviour, which taxation and policing imposed on the city as a whole. Strongly influenced by English trends in dog fancying and dog showing, Dublin's reforming middle classes defined the acceptable urban dog as a taxed, pedigree animal under the control of its (middle-class) owner. Eventually the threat of rabies encouraged the Corporation and the DMP to begin killing stray dogs. Nonetheless, the DMP's commissioner maintained that control of dogs was not an important duty of the police but a distraction from more serious work such as the policing of sanitary faults and nuisances.

Pigs

Like the urban dog, the urban pig attracted scrutiny by the middle classes, inspired new legislation to control its presence and was policed by the DMP. While dogs declined, pigs increased in Dublin. As discussed in Chapter 2, Dublin pigs lived wherever a small space could contain them. Summoned for insanitary pig-keeping on one day in 1873 were Rose Smyth, Patrick Foley, James Balfe and John Gibbins, each of whom kept pigs 'in a filthy state' in a disused stable. Also summoned were John Parker and Laurence, who kept pigs 'underneath the dwelling', and William Davis and Mary Doyle, whose pigs resided

4.4. People and their animals fleeing the whiskey fire that erupted in June of 1875 on Chamber Street in the south inner city. These images from *The Graphic* (26 June 1875) depict pigs (and a donkey) being driven to safety and a woman fleeing with her child and a pig bundled in her arms. Image courtesy of the National Library of Ireland.

in a small yard.[97] Pigs crowded into rooms with the poor, collected in the yards of tenement buildings and populated the lanes filled with small cottages. But they also lived in the large piggeries of businessmen who supplied the city's slaughterhouses and bacon-curing establishments.[98] A wide variety of Dubliners from very poor tenement dwellers to wealthy businessmen kept pigs. The prevalence of pig-keeping can be seen in the image of Dubliners fleeing the 'whiskey fire' of 1875 (Figure 4.4).

The pig was 'a profitable creature, where there is convenience to keep him'.[99] In Ireland, the price of pigs rose throughout the century, as did the price of pig meat and of bacon.[100] Just feeding a piglet from suckling to 'store' (an animal requiring further fattening) could provide more than a 100 per cent return on the price of the piglet. In 1850 the *Irish Farmer's Gazette* reported that suckling pigs cost ten to sixteen shillings each in the Smithfield pig market while stores fetched thirty to sixty shillings each. In 1870 their prices were eighteen to twenty-five shillings for piglets and thirty-five to sixty-five shillings for stores.[101]

When parliament extended the Sanitary Acts to Ireland and Dublin in 1866, more than 9000 pigs lived within the municipal borough. In the immediate aftermath of the Act, the Corporation asked the city analyst and the chief medical officer to report on the manner in which pigs should be kept 'so as not to prove objectionable to health and the senses of the inhabitants near them'.[102] At the same time, some areas of the city had also begun to fill in with denser housing. Attitudes towards the keeping of pigs changed over the following decade and complaining of pig-related nuisances became routine. From a concern of a small number of sanitarians, the pig became a widely disparaged nuisance subject to increased regulation by the Corporation and enforcement by members of the DMP acting as sanitary sergeants. By 1880, the year that the first parliamentary commission to investigate Dublin's public health reported, only 4600 pigs remained in the city.[103]

Pigs, like dogs, could be arranged in a hierarchy. Gentlemen breeders of fancy livestock exhibited pigs at shows where prize specimens sold for high prices. At the Royal Agricultural Society's National Horse and Cattle Show in 1867 the prizes offered for swine came to £197. Lords and ladies, doctors and politicians all visited the prize pigs.[104] Swine at a similar Royal Dublin Society show in 1865 sold for prices considered 'exceedingly large'.[105] Pigs described as 'thoroughbred prize taking boars' were included in advertisements for country house auctions.[106] These were special pigs, reared in rural areas as a part of profitable and respectable farming operations. In the city, as we saw in Chapter 2, sanitary reformers defined pigs as filthy risks to urban health. Deprived of value while degrading their surroundings, such pigs could be eliminated in the name of improvement. In Dublin, existing prejudice against pigs combined with the popularisation of sanitary reform during the 1860s to further devalue the urban pig. From a figure of fun and an acknowledged aid to the poor man's survival, pigs became markers of filth, poverty and backwardness.

By the 1860s, the Irish pig was widely associated with laziness, filth and vice in popular culture despite (or perhaps because of) the high rate of pig-keeping. The filthy pig signified low value and reduced the worth of its surroundings. Consider for example the ballad 'The House Pat Built'. Circulated in Ireland and Britain in multiple forms from around 1865, the ballad told the life of lazy 'Pat'. Pat's 'illigant mansion' in 'Dublin town' was a thatched cottage 'on lease from the lord of the manor'. In his cottage Pat lived a slovenly life of poverty, which he made no effort to improve. He chose as his companion 'the pig that eat the spud, that lay in the House that Pat built'.[107] The pig signified that 'Pat' was to blame for his own poverty, clinging to 'potatoes, pigs and politics' against the warnings of post-Famine improvers.

Pigs also signified the poverty of Irish migrants. Irish émigrés brought their pigs (or the habit of keeping one) when they migrated to British and American cities. The Irish enclave of Shepherd's Bush in London became 'the pigsty of the metropolis'.[108] Friedrich Engels claimed that in English cities the Irish introduced 'new, abnormal methods of rearing livestock', allowing the pig to live in the house with the family.[109] The *British Medical Journal* saw the methods of Irish pig-keeping as an indication of a total lack of sanitary knowledge amongst the poor Irish.[110] In New York City, pig owners tended to be Irish immigrants or African Americans. Both groups were poor and used pig-rearing as an extra source of income. As a result, campaigns to target the pig were associated with racist and anti-immigrant feeling.[111] In nineteenth-century Montreal, the rearing of pigs represented an important supplement to household income and was dominated by low-income groups including Irish immigrants. As in New York and London, particular neighbourhoods with high numbers of Irish became associated with pig-keeping and were targeted by city ordinances seeking to remove the pigs.[112] Urban pig-keeping by Irish migrants represented, in the words of one historian, the maintenance of 'the habits of another society and another economy'.[113] Urban reformers considered keeping pigs a dirty activity, so the Irish pig-keeper became dirty by association.

Urban sanitary reformers in the 1860s and 1870s expanded upon the efforts of the Famine era to try to reduce Dublin's pigs. Popular criticism increased pressure on the Dublin Corporation to make changes in sanitary policy. In 1865 the *Dublin Builder* complained that

> some of the best houses in the city will be found to abut on the most filthy localities, and the pursuits more particularly of pig-keeping and cattle-keeping, and of overcrowding tenements are carried on in the most dangerous manner, literally under the most aristocratic noses.[114]

The *Dublin Builder* had a wide middle-class readership despite the implied specialism of its title.[115] Here cattle-keeping was complained of alongside pig-keeping as part of a complex of sanitary problems including general filth and overcrowded human housing. These 'dangerous' practices threatened to contaminate the adjacent buildings housing the city's wealthier residents. In a different article the same journal complained that Dublin compared badly with London where 'pigstyes[sic] are banished altogether'. The writer misunderstood sanitary legislation in the metropolis but the article underscores the importance of the pig nuisance.[116]

The revival of the Dublin Sanitary Association (DSA) in 1872 reflected the growing public interest in sanitary reform. The DSA sought to hold the Corporation to account for urban public health by performing its own sanitary inspections. A sanitary association had been founded in 1848 (noted in Chapter 2) but had gone into abeyance after the Great Famine. The new DSA was an alliance of philanthropic medical men (such as William Stokes and Thomas Wrigley Grimshaw) and philanthropic businessmen (such as Arthur E. Guinness).[117] Grimshaw held the post of General Registrar for Dublin and used the DSA as an outlet for his frustration with the Dublin Corporation's public health activity. The DSA performed sanitary inspections and gained publicity through periodicals. The DSA's inspections used 'pig' to signal 'filth'. In 1872, for example, the DSA's subcommittee of inspection described a house in Mary's Lane thus: 'Extremely dirty and dilapidated—smell in house, pool of filthy water at end of back hall—pigs in yard, valuation £6'.[118] Filth, bad smells and dirty animals corroborated the low value of the house. In 1873, Macleans's Lane was a nuisance because it contained 'several score of pigs, over 150 loads of offensive manure'. The 'very dirty yard' at 37 James's Street contained pigs and a 'foul smelling ashpit and privy'. The residents of 7 Hoey's Court kept pigs alongside a dirty privy and ashpit. In 1874, DSA inspectors visited the 'fever nest' at 18 Ardee Street over and over until the residents removed their pigs. Although the reports highlighted other potential nuisances, the presence of pigs needed no qualification. A privy or an ashpit had to be deemed filthy or smelly to be a nuisance. A pig, according to sanitary reformers, was always filthy and smelly.[119]

The DSA brought public health matters into the press and campaigned for a parliamentary commission of inquiry into the state of Dublin's sanitation. Journalists declared the pig to be among the worst urban nuisances. In 1873, for example, the *Freeman's Journal* enumerated 'violations of the first principles of sanitation' including 'filthy yards, collections of stagnant water, dung heaps, pigsties and other centres of foulness and infection'.[120] Yards must be 'filthy' and water 'stagnant' but a pigsty was always a 'centre of foulness'. Journalists used the presence of pigs to emphasise the poor sanitary condition of a location. A yard behind a tumbledown house was described as 'in a shocking state' containing a 'reeking pool of filthy fluid' but also pigs and pigsties. The pigs underscored the urgency of abating the nuisance.[121] Changes to public attitudes and the increased vigilance of sanitary reformers outside of city government both reflected and influenced the changed status of the pig vis-à-vis public health regulations. The *Irish Builder* echoed the DSA's sentiments about the filth of the pig and added its own. From the 1870s onward the journal voiced increasing frustration at the sanitary failings of the Corporation. The public health impacts of urban animals, especially cattle and pigs, were among the journal's particular concerns. Expressing this outrage in poetic form, 'The Reign of the Gutter' satirised the supposed view of the Corporation that 'Dirt is only another name/for a very useful matter'. The poet singled out the pig for special mention:

> The pig has often paid the rent,
> Though housed in the human dwelling;
> The landlord does not mind the scent,
> Except when it is a selling.
> Snug in the chimney corner still,
> It grunts if it cannot mutter.
> Leave it alone till fit to kill—
> Hurrah for the reign of the gutter![122]

Silly verses made serious accusations against the Corporation. The journal lambasted the Corporation for taking little interest in eliminating disease among the poor and instead protecting the interests of slum landlords and ratepayers. Prose repeated the themes of poetry. In 1874, the *Irish Builder* argued for more rigorous sanitary inspection and claimed that 'piggeries should at once be got rid of, not only within human habitations, but wherever situated near to them'.[123] The journal challenged the Corporation and its sanitary sergeants to perform more inspections and to remove more animals from the city.

Members of the public who gave evidence to the sewerage and drainage inquiry in 1879 continued to use the presence of pigs to indicate overcrowding and dirt. One witness complained of the lanes surrounding Fitzwilliam Square, among the city's finest Georgian developments, where poor housing mingled with urban farming of pigs, goats and poultry.[124] Landlords converted disused stables into either unsuitable human habitation or piggeries.[125]

Judicial opinion, necessary for the enforcement of sanitary laws, also changed during the 1860s. In 1859, for example, a complaint about a free-ranging pig was treated by the Dublin police court as an occasion for humour rather than a grave sanitary concern. Instead of fining those brought before him, the police magistrate declared that 'it was lawful for any person finding a pig or pigs straying about the streets of Dublin to seize it, take it home, kill it and eat it', a suggestion that he believed would encourage more caution by pig keepers. He evinced greater concern for the menace of roving dogs: he ordered them destroyed and further suggested that they ought to be subject to a licence.[126] However, by 1871 at least one Dublin magistrate had decided that all pigs were nuisances that required removal and had 'repeatedly declared that he will not allow one pig within the city'.[127] Key to these changes was the redefinition of the pig in public health law and the enforcement of new laws by the Dublin Metropolitan Police.

Despite criticism by the Dublin Sanitary Association and the popular press, the Corporation's expanding public health system reflected the same negative attitudes towards the keeping of pigs in Dublin. New legislation expanded the sanitary powers of the Corporation and provided new means of financing their activities, including pig removal.

There had been a lengthy gap in parliamentary legislation after the passing of the Dublin Improvement Act of 1849. In 1866, the Sanitary Act was extended to Ireland, followed by the Public Health Acts of 1874 and 1878. The Sanitary Act required the foundation of a public health committee by the sanitary authority of each district and increased the range of actions that body was permitted to carry out. The Act also allowed for greater borrowing to finance these actions. In the wake of the Act, Dublin Corporation renamed 'Committee Number 2' as the Public Health Committee and streamlined its activities. The 1874 and 1878 acts brought further borrowing powers, increased taxation powers for sanitary matters, gave a greater weight of authority to the Corporation and made the dispensary medical officers as public health employees.[128] Instead of the Poor Law commissioners, the Local Government Board became the highest sanitary authority in Ireland.[129]

Rising pig numbers may have drawn the attention of the Corporation's enlarged sanitary workforce. Pig-keeping had suffered a blow across the country as a result of the Famine. The agricultural statistics, in which the DMP counted pigs street by street, suggest that during 'Black 47' (the worst year of the Famine) the police could find only eighty-seven pigs in the city. By 1850, the number had increased to almost 7000 and rarely dropped below this number throughout the 1860s and 1870s. The pig population occasionally reached much higher peaks—approximately 11,000 in 1858, 9000 in 1866 and 12,000 in 1872. While the agricultural statistics are flawed, they are a good indication of trends. These peaks occurred against the backdrop of a nearly stagnant human population and thus represented a noticeable increase from lows of around two pigs per 100 persons to almost five pigs per 100 persons (see Figure 4.5). In a city of Dublin's size, one could hardly avoid noticing a doubling in pig numbers. Yet there was a gap between the increased pig population and increased vigilance against pig-keeping. Between 1856 and 1860, for example, the sanitary department received few complaints about nuisances

4.5. Graph charting numbers of pigs per one hundred persons in Dublin and Ireland between 1865 and 1880. Although the numbers in Dublin are considerably smaller than those in the country as a whole, it is possible to see a small city peak coinciding with the country peaks in 1865–66 and 1870–71. The third country peak in 1876–77 is not mirrored in the city. Statistics all taken from the parliamentary reports of the annual agricultural statistics.

arising from piggeries and granted numerous licences for pig slaughterhouses.[130]

Local legislation enabled the Corporation to create a local definition of how a pig or a pigsty might become a nuisance. In 1877, the Public Health Committee had asked the chief medical officer, the medical officers of health and the city analyst to inspect all places where animals were kept and to provide a recommendation 'on the keeping of animals so as not to be injurious to health'.[131] Their findings are lost, but after the 1878 Act the Corporation defined a pigsty or manure heap as a nuisance when kept within fifty feet of any house. Pigs were banned from the yards of public lodging houses.[132] Although legislation allowed for the keeping of pigs in large yards, sanitary sergeants were instructed to always notify their superior officer if they noticed a pig being kept in *any* yard.[133]

As time went on, the Corporation tightened the restrictions on pigs even further. Regulations made it more acceptable for a business to keep numerous pigs than for a poor family to keep a single pig. Clause 107 of the Public Health (Ireland) Act of 1878 prohibited 'any animal so kept as to be a nuisance or injurious to health'. This allowed the Corporation to fine owners of a wide range of urban animals. The pig, however, was singled out for special notice. Clause 57 named pigs as a specific nuisance and allowed the sanitary authority to levy a large fine for them. Any person who 'keeps any swine or pig stye in any dwelling house, or so as to be a nuisance to any person' was subject to a penalty of up to forty shillings when discovered and five shillings for each day 'during which the offence is continued'.[134] The urban sanitary authority could define in what way a pig might be considered a nuisance. However, the Public Health Act prioritised the punishment of those keeping individual pigs or animals at home, as opposed to business premises. Clause 57 was grouped under 'Regulations as to Streets and Houses' and thus implied the detection of health hazards in residential areas. The definition of a nuisance allowed any 'accumulation or deposit' (even malodorous pig manure) kept for purposes of business as long as it was regularly removed.[135]

After the Public Health (Ireland) Act of 1878, some were convinced that there had been an effective 'raid made against pigs'. Witnesses reported to the sewerage and drainage commission in 1879 that the Corporation had reduced pig numbers. One inspector from Britain had seen pigs during his walk around the city but fewer than during his last visit to Dublin. He had 'only seen two houses with pigs this morning' when in Clanbrassil Street. Others disagreed, claiming that although keeping pigs in the city was 'most objectionable' it was 'commonly done' and that 'large quantities of manure are allowed to remain undisturbed in many parts of the district for months'. Another witness complained of pig-keeping in the proximity of the city's wealthiest squares, while yet another noted that 'the houses occupied by poor people overlook yards, and no matter what precautions are taken, pigs will be kept'.[136]

Creating public health law to control pigs entailed trying to convert complex attitudes into simpler regulations. Not all pigs were considered filth and the public health threat from pigs was ill-defined. Even the Corporation's public health staff did not agree on the working definition of a filthy pig. On the one hand, the nuisance inspector James Boyle bragged of the successful abolition of 231 piggeries in three months.[137] On the other hand, he argued that

> so long as pigs are kept clean, and that there is sufficient air space and that they are not too near a dwelling, pigs may be kept not only without prejudice to the health or comfort of the public, but also with benefit to the industrious poor.[138]

Nonetheless the Corporation's policies tended to limit the ability of the industrious poor to keep pigs. Only the poor kept pigs in their homes and this was considered the most offensive nuisance. Within three months of the introduction of the 1866 Sanitary Act, inspectors had removed 1100 pigs from the city, 417 of these from inside homes.[139] The fact that pigs would thrive in small spaces made it possible for the poor to keep them. But the Corporation wished to eliminate pig-keeping in small spaces, arguing that certain lanes were 'too crowded to permit of pigs being kept'.[140] By contrast, they often allowed bigger businesses to keep pigs in large numbers. The Corporation's public health committee viewed swine-only slaughterhouses that kept and killed many pigs in a week as the best kind of slaughterhouse because 'they must keep all their premises scrupulously clean—otherwise the pork will become tainted'. Even better, they were only open during the cold months of the year.[141] In one case a woman was summonsed for keeping one pig in a small yard when her neighbour had been allowed to keep twenty-six pigs. He was running a breeding business with frequent turnover of piglets and high-value fattened animals. Calls for further inspection reports of his premises were never followed up.[142]

Pigs, whose wastes were perceived as particularly malodorous, were associated with sanitarian notions of 'all smell is disease'. The Dublin Corporation, like other public health authorities from the 1860s onwards, retained sanitarian ideas while also accommodating new ones about germs as the source of disease. They still advocated for increasing space, light and air with the corresponding reduction of crowding, darkness and bad smells. However, public health experts such as Charles Cameron (the city analyst) had begun to point to ways of transmitting disease that had little to do with the bad air produced by urban pollution and more to do with means of transferring organisms between bodies.[143] He focused considerable energy on eliminating diseased meat, which he saw as a medium for the passage of disease.[144] By contrast, Cameron did not link the removal of pigs directly to specific diseases. Seizures of diseased meat were weighted towards beef consumed by the middle classes rather than pork consumed by the poor.[145]

The DMP started their engagement with pigs, as *The Mail* had satirised, by enumerating them. We know approximately how many pigs lived in Dublin because of the work of police officers who counted them for the annual agricultural statistics. More important for changes to pig-keeping was the role that police officers played in the Corporation's expanded sanitary administration.

Just as dogs were added to policing duties from the 1860s, so too was sanitary enforcement. Rather than hire Poor Law doctors or independent inspectors, as many other towns had, the Corporation turned to the Dublin Metropolitan Police. Four policemen were added as inspectors in 1864 as part of an initial expansion of the city's sanitary staff.[146] The Corporation paid these officers, although the police commissioners retained some control as orders were passed from the city's Medical Officer of Health to the police department before being given as orders to the inspectors.[147] By 1879, the Corporation employed twenty-one policemen as inspectors with duties that ranged from general sanitary inspection to specialised inspection with a view to detecting diseased or contaminated foods.[148] They resisted calls to rely on medical men, even when forced to take Poor Law doctors onto the payroll as medical officers of health.[149] The Corporation relied on the DMP for effective implementation of sanitary law. The DMP had an important role in reducing a specific type of pig-keeping associated with the poor.

As discussed in Chapter 3, sanitary inspection by co-opted members of the DMP had a range of limitations. For example, one butcher evaded punishment for slaughtering without a licence by simply closing the door to his premises and refusing police admission. Frustrated police felt they could do nothing further without the support of prosecuting magistrates. Members of the police force were also of a similar social class to the small businessmen running the slaughterhouses that they inspected. The *Irish Builder* accused the DMP of failing as sanitary inspectors because of their involvement in businesses that caused sanitary offences. The journal's claim that 'several of these police sergeants who have acted as sanitary inspectors are owners of tenement houses in different parts of this city' could have been applied to members of the Corporation in some years. Since 'we all know the general state of most tenement dwellings', one could not expect their owners to be scrupulous about sanitation.[150]

A familiarity with tenements may have aided sanitary sergeants in their inspections. They appeared to enter private homes and rooms unimpeded and to conduct intimate sanitary inspections with little resistance. In December of 1868, for example, the sanitary sergeants reported visiting 2830 dwelling houses and 5180 rooms as they hunted for sanitary defects.[151] In October of 1870 they visited 3757 houses and 8046 rooms.[152] Only such detailed examination of the lodgings of the poor would have rooted out the home-reared pig. Without these police inspections the identification of nuisances relied on the complaints of neighbours. Such complaints rarely came from poor tenement dwellers; instead the police complained on their behalf by issuing summonses to the sanitary court or demanding that nuisances be abated.

Intimate inspection resulted in pig removals. In 1866, the sanitary department removed over 1100 pigs while in 1867 this rose to over 1500.[153] Enforcement responded to fluctuations in the pig population. In 1869 and 1880, both years of relatively low numbers of urban pigs, they removed just over 500 pigs. In 1870, as pig numbers increased, removals rose to almost 900 pigs.[154] In 1875, the chief sanitary officer, James Boyle, reported that his staff had removed 6270 pigs in just under a decade, including 728 from houses. Nevertheless, he felt the remaining 4600 pigs was a number 'twofold that which should, I would suggest, be permitted in it; many being kept where the air space is utterly insufficient, and others where their proximity to dwellings is opposed to every sanitary condition'. He also acknowledged that the same pigs may have been removed 'a second, and perhaps a third time', although he was certain that 4500 had been truly removed and that 'to their places no others have been brought'.[155] Despite the emphasis on housebound pigs, police inspectors actually found few such animals to remove. Monthly reports from sanitary sergeants suggest that they usually found and removed between five and fifteen pigs per month from inside of dwelling houses and a further ten to twenty from yards.[156]

By about 1875 the Dublin pig population no longer appeared to follow the pattern of the Irish pig population; pig removal seemed to be suppressing numbers (see Figure 4.5). Up until then, when fluctuations of the human population are taken into account, Dublin followed the rise and fall of pig numbers nationally. In the city this meant approximately three pigs per 100 persons compared with a national average of approximately twenty-two per 100 persons. The number of Dublin pigs per 100 persons went into a decline after 1874 and hovered around two pigs per 100 persons. It is not clear whether this can be attributed to policing, attitudinal change or economic decline, but the link in time with new public health legislation and an increased police inspectorate is suggestive.

Yet opinions about the keeping of urban pigs continued to be divided, as the debate over the location of the city's pig market in 1883 demonstrates. In that year the Corporation moved the pig market to the new cattle market at the edge of the city as a temporary measure to help arrest the spread of foot and mouth disease. They intended to reopen Smithfield Market for pigs once they had laid improved paving for efficient cleansing. Residents of Smithfield and the residents in the area of the new cattle market both objected to moving the pigs. Householders and business owners near the new market at the northern edge of the city appealed to the Corporation to the keep the pigs out. Unperturbed by their proximity to a huge live cattle market and the public abattoir, residents argued that the addition of pigs would be unbearable. The residents petitioned the Corporation, claiming that the pig market 'would create a nuisance from which we would seriously suffer, not alone in the enjoyment of our houses, but also it would depreciate the value of property in the district'.[157] The residents and business owners of Smithfield, by contrast, were concerned about the loss of the pig market. They claimed that its removal would cause the area to decline through loss of trade.[158] The Corporation moved the pigs to the new cattle market despite the objections. The temporary measure became permanent, suggesting that while the Corporation was not always rigorous in its public health campaigns, most councillors accepted the idea that the pig was dirty and unfit for inner city life. When some councillors raised the issue of reopening the pig market at Smithfield, one opponent claimed that 'they would gain nothing for tact or intelligence if they proposed to bring swine into the city or near congested districts'. Others claimed the potential return of the pig market was 'fraught with danger to the public health'.[159] One councillor objected on the grounds that the presence of pigs would be an insult to St Paul's Church.[160]

By 1880, Dublin contained noticeably fewer pigs than it had in 1865. Stray dogs still pestered citizens, but their days were numbered: hundreds of them were collected and killed each year. These changes reflected the prevailing influence of the bourgeois on the reform of urban life and the introduction of a bourgeois form of urban civility. It was the poor man's (or woman's) pig in the cellar, the yard or the house that the policeman removed, and the unlicensed dog of no fixed abode that he captured and killed. The policemen who enforced these changes were themselves barely elevated above the class of those whose animals they seized. The lower ranks of the police force earned 26s per week, less than twice the weekly wage of a poor city labourer.[161] Policemen, who were mostly Catholic and from rural areas, became an important arm of urban reform. We have already seen their significant role in enforcing humane legislation. By examining their impact on human–animal relationships in the city we can see the Dublin Metropolitan Police force as key players in the attempt to create an improved, modern city along the ideals of a globalised middle class. The streets of Dublin should resemble those of Paris and London and New York, free from the smell of pig manure and the menace of vagrant curs.

The city's poor, like their counterparts in London and Paris and New York, could resist by ignoring regulations and risking fines or imprisonment. Many did just that; the police court's weekly litany of sanitary violations and the dogs' home full of stray dogs each testify to incomplete acceptance of the new urban order. The regulations, of course, affected animal lives as profoundly as those of their human keepers. The stray dog risked execution or at least imprisonment; the pedigree pet soon outnumbered his unwelcome opposite. The solitary family pig would be replaced by the commercial pigsty and a few commercial breeds of pigs would replace variety. Both pigs and dogs would become ever more standardised items of consumption.

While these changes made Dublin more like other Western cities, they also reveal ways in which it was unique. The Dublin bourgeoisie, regardless of religion or politics, appeared to embrace the same vision of urban modernity. This sense of shared bourgeois identity is well described by Ciaran O'Neill's suggestion that the middling sort pursued 'bourgeois badges', or signifiers of social status achieved.[162] But hints of the entanglement between class, religion and politics can be seen in the response to both the dog tax and sanitary reform.

The dog tax could be portrayed as a triumph of British rule and the pedigree pet mocked as a symbol of the Protestant Ascendancy like in the 'Saucy dogs of Dublin' and the tale of nationalist dogs meeting in the Greenhills. The same Dublin Metropolitan Police who rounded up strays had also rounded up Fenians. The DMP was an arm of the state and thus control of dogs was on a continuum of efforts to control Irish behaviour in urban space through policing.

Even the policing of pig-keeping, widely accepted across political and religious lines, could hold greater symbolic significance in the relationship between Ireland and Britain. What was at stake for Dublin was more than public health and hygiene. The association of pigs with a condemned system of rural subsistence farming made the animals symbolic of a supposed lack of progress. In the final decades of the nineteenth century the improving city appeared in stark contrast to the backward crumbling city. These cities shared one set of boundaries but contained different populations of humans and animals.

Notes

1 *Report of the Royal Commissioners Appointed to Inquire into the Sewerage and Drainage of the City of Dublin and Other Matters Connected Therewith, Together with Minutes of Evidence, Appendix, Index &c.*, Evidence of Thomas W. Grimshaw, p. 41 [C 2605] HC 1880, xxx, 1 [Hereafter *Sewerage and Drainage Inquiry 1880*].

2 Untitled, *Irish Times* (16 July 1880).

3 *Report of the Select Committee of the House of Lords, Appointed to Inquire into the Best Mode of Obtaining Accurate Agricultural Statistics from all Parts of the United Kingdom*, 1855, Appendix C, pp. 170–3.

4 Catherine McNeur, 'The "swinish multitude": controversies over hogs in antebellum New York City', *Journal of Urban History*, 37:5 (2011), 639–60.

5 Philip Howell, *At Home and Astray: The Domestic Dog in Victorian Britain* (Charlottesville: University of Virginia Press, 2015), chapter 6; Kathleen Kete, '*La rage* and the bourgeoisie: the cultural context of rabies in the

French nineteenth century', *Representations*, 22 (1988), 89–107; Chris Pearson, 'Stray dogs and the making of modern Paris', *Past and Present*, 234 (2017), 137–72.

6 See, for example, Patrick Joyce, *The Rule of Freedom: Liberalism and the Modern City* (London: Verso, 2003), pp. 9–12.

7 This was the son of Prime Minister Sir Robert Peel who also held a parliamentary seat for Tamworth and served as chief secretary for Ireland, and had died in 1850. 'Sheep Protecting (Ireland) Bill', *Freeman's Journal* (31 March 1865).

8 W. E. Vaughan, 'Ireland *c.* 1870', in W. E. Vaughan (ed.), *A New History of Ireland V. Ireland Under the Union 1801–1870* (Oxford: Oxford University Press, 2010), pp. 726–800: 766.

9 'Sheep Protectors', *The Mail* (31 March 1865).

10 See, for example, Peter Atkins (ed.), *Animal Cities: Beastly Urban Histories* (London: Routledge, 2012); Bettina Bradbury, 'Pigs, cows, and borders: non-wage forms of survival among Montreal families', *Labour/Le Travail*, 14 (1984), 9–48; Brett Mizelle, *Pig* (London: Reaktion, 2011).

11 See, for example, Katherine C. Grier, *Pets in America: A History* (Orland: Harcourt, Inc., 2006); Harriet Ritvo, 'Pride and pedigree: the evolution of the Victorian dog fancy', *Victorian Studies*, 29:2 (1986), 227–53; Howell, *At Home and Astray*.

12 R. J. Morris, 'Voluntary societies and British urban elites, 1780–1850: an analysis', *Historical Journal*, 26 (1983), 95–118.

13 For example, evidenced in the building of grand homes in the suburbs. Susan Galavan, *Dublin's Bourgeois Homes: Building the Victorian Suburbs, 1850–1901* (London: Routledge, 2017). On the development of the Irish middle classes more broadly see Ciaran O'Neill, 'Bourgeois Ireland, or, on the benefits of keeping one's hands clean', in James Kelly (ed.), *The Cambridge History of Ireland. Volume III 1730–1880* (Cambridge: Cambridge University Press, 2018), pp. 517–41.

14 Mary Daly, Mona Hearn and Peter Pearson, *Dublin's Victorian Houses* (Dublin, 1998); Galavan, *Dublin's Bourgeois Homes*; Stephanie Rains, *Commodity Culture and Social Class in Dublin, 1850–1916* (Dublin: Irish Academic Press, 2010).

15 R. V. Comeford, 'Ireland 1850–1870: post-Famine and mid-Victorian', in W. E. Vaughan (ed.), *A New History of Ireland V. Ireland Under the Union 1801–1870* (Oxford: Oxford University Press, 2010 paperback edn), pp. 372–95: 390.

16 Anastasia Dukova, *A History of the Dublin Metropolitan Police and its Colonial Legacy* (London: Palgrave Macmillan, 2016), p. 61.

17 'The Dublin Dog Show', *Freeman's Journal* (26 March 1864).

18 Charles Henry Lane, *Dog Shows and Doggy-People* (London: Hutchinson, 1902), pp. 263–75.

19 'The Liverpool fat cattle, dog, poultry show', *Irish Times* (18 December 1868).
20 'Great National Dog Show', *Freeman's Journal* (26 September 1874).
21 Ritvo, 'Pride and pedigree'.
22 See Grier, *Pets in America*: on products see chapter 6, on veterinarians see pp. 118–19.
23 'The Dublin dog show', *Freeman's Journal* (26 March 1864).
24 'The Dublin dog show', *Freeman's Journal* (26 March 1864).
25 'Great National Dog Show', *Irish Times* (14 October 1874).
26 Robert Scharff, 'On the breeds of dog peculiar to Ireland and their origin (Conclusion)', *Irish Naturalist*, 33:9 (1924), 89–95: 91.
27 Colonel J. K. Millner, *The Irish Setter, its History and Training* (London: H. F. & G. Witherby, 1924), p. 46.
28 Millner, *The Irish Setter*, p. 45.
29 Scharff, 'On the breeds'.
30 I used the Irish Newspaper Archive to search for 'dog' and 'lost' in the named years and then eliminated spurious results. Such a search is likely to under-represent the number of such notices. Five shilling rewards, for example, 'Dog lost', *Freeman's Journal* (4 April 1864); '5s reward—Skye terrier dog lost', *Freeman's Journal* (31 July 1874). Ten shilling rewards, for example, 'Red setter dog lost', *Freeman's Journal* (19 March 1864); 'Ten shillings reward', *Freeman's Journal* (14 July 1869); 'Dog lost-ten shillings reward', *Freeman's Journal* (13 January 1874). Higher rewards, such as '£1 reward', *Freeman's Journal* (30 June 1874); '£2 reward-lost', *Freeman's Journal* (3 December 1874); '£1 reward lost', *Freeman's Journal* (29 January 1869); '£1 reward', *Freeman's Journal* (29 July 1864).
31 Pomeranian: 'Dog lost', *Freeman's Journal* (21 June 1864); King Charles: 'Lost', *Freeman's Journal* (27 July 1869); Skye terrier: 'Lost', *Freeman's Journal* (21 December 1874).
32 'Lost', *Freeman's Journal* (3 October 1873).
33 'Lost', *Freeman's Journal* (7 September 1886).
34 'Lost', *Freeman's Journal* (3 March 1887).
35 Classifieds, *Irish Sportsman* (7 May 1870), 4.
36 Classifieds, *Irish Sportsman* (3 January 1880), 13.
37 Classifieds, *Irish Sportsman* (29 May 1880), 1.
38 'Resuscitation of the Irish wolf-hound', *Irish Times* (26 April 1876).
39 'The projected Irish Kennel Club', *Irish Times* (2 March 1877).
40 'Irish Kennel Club dog show', *Irish Times* (7 August 1878).
41 Advertisements, *Irish Sportsman* (19 February 1870).
42 Walter G. Strickland, *A Dictionary of Irish Artists* (Dublin: Maunsel and Company, 1913), pp. 207–8; Stephen Gwynn, 'Walter Osborne and Ireland', *Studies*, 32 (1943), 463–6.

43 Jeanne Sheehy, *Walter Osborne* (Ballycotton: Gifford and Craven, 1974), p. 12.
44 Exhibition catalogues, Royal Hibernian Academy of Arts, pp. 50–2.
45 Gwynn, 'Walter Osborne and Ireland'.
46 'Mountain View', *Zoz*, 5th quarter, 2nd year (*c.* 1878, unpaginated and undated copy held in Trinity College Dublin Library, date approximate based on other extant volumes).
47 'Dog lost', *Zoz* (13 April 1878).
48 'Why I don't eat sausages', *Zoz* (28 October 1876).
49 'Ye death of Timotheus', *Zoz* (2 December 1876).
50 'To a white pomeranian dog', *Dublin University Magazine*, 68:404 (August 1866), 218.
51 Rains, *Commodity Culture*; on periodicals see Tom Clyde, *Irish Literary Magazines: An Outline History and Descriptive Bibliography* (Dublin: Irish Academic Press, 2003), pp. 26–9.
52 See Howell, *At Home and Astray*, pp. 19–21.
53 William Gibson, *Rambles in Europe in 1839: With Sketches of Prominent Surgeons, Physicians, Medical Schools, Hospitals, Literary Personages, Scenery &c.* (Philadelphia, PA: Lea and Blanchard, 1841), pp. 226–8.
54 'To a white pomeranian dog'.
55 'Dublin Police', *Freeman's Journal* (16 July 1842).
56 Frank Thorpe Porter, *Twenty-Years Recollections of an Irish Police Magistrate* (Dublin: Hodges, Foster, and Figgis, 1880), pp. 95–6.
57 'Police courts', *Freeman's Journal* (12 November 1859).
58 Sloane, 'Some thoughts on artisans' dwellings. Part II', *Irish Builder* (15 July 1879), 220.
59 *Sewerage and Drainage Inquiry*, Evidence of Charles F. Moore, MD, p. 199.
60 'Cruelty to animals—dog fighting', *Freeman's Journal* (7 May 1856).
61 MS 7588, Thomas Larcom papers, newspaper clipping from *Freeman's Journal* (4 April 1865), National Library of Ireland.
62 'Great dog demonstration', *Freeman's Journal* (25 October 1865).
63 MS 11,241/1, Mayo Papers on the cattle plague, Richard Wingfield to Lord Naas (Richard Bourke, later Earl of Mayo), 22 March 1867, National Library of Ireland.
64 Dublin Metropolitan Police, *Statistical Tables*, table for 1885, p. xl.
65 'Dogs Regulation (Ireland) Act', *Irish Times* (10 July 1867).
66 *Dogs registration (Ireland). Copy of the regulations made by the Lord Lieutenant or the Treasury as to the appropriation in aid of the local county or borough cess of the sums received under the act 28 Vict. c. 50, for the registration of dogs in Ireland; and, return of the gross amount so received, and number of dogs registered in each petty sessional division during the year 1866.* HC 1867–1868 (499) lv, 757; *Dogs Regulation (Ireland) Act 1865. Accounts of Receipts and Expenditure Under the Dogs Regulation*

(Ireland) Act 1865, For the Year Ending 31ˢᵗ December 1896. HC 1897 (249), lxxvi, 781.

67 *Dogs Regulation (Ireland) Act 1865. Accounts of Receipts and Expenditure Under the Dogs Regulation (Ireland) Act 1865, For the Year Ending 31ˢᵗ December 1871.* HC 1872 (347), xlvii, 769; *Dogs Regulation (Ireland) ... 1896.*

68 See, for example, R. Bayles, 'Understanding local science: the Belfast Natural History Society in the mid-nineteenth century', *Science and Irish Culture,* 1 (2004), 139–69.

69 *Dogs Regulation (Ireland) ... 1871; Dogs Regulation (Ireland) Act 1865. Accounts of Receipts and Expenditure Under the Dogs Regulation (Ireland) Act 1865, For the Year Ending 31ˢᵗ December 1896.* HC 1897 (249), lxxvi, 781.

70 Charles Cameron, *How the Poor Live* (Dublin: J. Falconer, 1904), pp. 168–9.

71 MS 5159 (88), 'A new song on the saucy dogs of Ireland', National Library of Ireland.

72 Shin-Ichi Takagami, 'The Fenian Rising in Dublin, March 1867', *Irish Historical Studies,* 29:115 (1995), 340–62.

73 Patrick Byrne, *An Evening in the Green Hills; Or the Complaint of the Dogs on Taxation* (Dublin, 1869).

74 In 1879 there were 960 registered dogs while in 1880 there were 1018. *Dogs Regulation (Ireland) Act 1865. Accounts of Receipts and Expenditure Under the Dogs Regulation (Ireland) Act 1865, For the Year Ending 31ˢᵗ December 1879.* HC 1880 (199), lxii, 203; *Dogs Regulation (Ireland) Act 1865. Accounts of Receipts and Expenditure Under the Dogs Regulation (Ireland) Act 1865, For the Year Ending 31ˢᵗ December 1880.* HC 1881 (231), lxxix, 103.

75 'Sad death of a young lady from hydrophobia', *Weekly Irish Times* (2 August 1879).

76 Pax, 'The dog mania', *Freeman's Journal* (2 August 1879).

77 Untitled editorial, *Irish Times* (1 August 1879).

78 Amicus Canis, 'The dog nuisance', *Freeman's Journal* (6 June 1866).

79 Untitled editorial, *Weekly Irish Times* (9 August 1879).

80 *Instruction Book for Supernumeraries, Kevin-Street Depot* (Dublin: Alexander Thom, 1870), p. 36.

81 See *Statistical Tables of the Dublin Metropolitan Police, for the Year 1865* (Dublin: Alexander Thom, 1866), table LII; *Statistical Tables of the Dublin Metropolitan Police, for the Year 1866* (Dublin: Alexander Thom, 1867), table LII; *Statistical Tables of the Dublin Metropolitan Police, for the Year 1867* (Dublin: Alexander Thom, 1868), table LII.

82 *Statistical Tables of the Dublin Metropolitan Police, for the Year 1870* (Dublin: Alexander Thom, 1871), table LVII; *Statistical Tables of the*

Dublin Metropolitan Police for the Year 1877 (Dublin: Alexander Thom, 1878), table XLIX.

83 Pro Bono Publico, 'The dog tax', *Irish Times* (17 August 1874).

84 Kete, '*La rage* and the bourgeoisie'.

85 See Howell, *At Home and Astray*, pp. 153–7; see also Neil Pemberton and Michael Worboys, *Mad Dogs and Englishmen: Rabies in Britain, 1850–2000* (London: Palgrave, 2007).

86 *Freeman's Journal* (3 November 1877), 5.

87 'Wandering dogs', *Irish Times* (21 September 1878).

88 'Temporary home for stray dogs', *Irish Times* (11 August 1879); 'Temporary dogs' home', *Irish Times* (6 August 1879).

89 'Lost and starving dogs', *Irish Times* (24 June 1878); 'Lost and starving dogs', *Freeman's Journal* (18 June 1878); 'Lost and starving dogs', *Irish Times* (11 June 1878).

90 *Statistical Tables of the Dublin Metropolitan Police, for the Year 1879* (Dublin: Alexander Thom, 1880), p. viii.

91 'Temporary home for stray dogs', *Irish Times* (11 August 1879).

92 Dublin City Council Public Health Committee Minute Book, vol. 16, minutes for 15 August 1879, Dublin City Library and Archive [Minutes books referred to hereafter as DCC PHC Mins].

93 'The dog nuisance ...' *Irish Times* (16 July 1880).

94 *Statistical Tables of the Dublin Metropolitan Police, for the Year 1879*, p. viii.

95 Hilda Kean, *Animal Rights: Political and Social Change in Britain Since 1800* (London: Reaktion, 1998), pp. 88–91, 97.

96 Howell, *At Home and Astray*, pp. 73–101.

97 Saturday's police intelligence, *Freeman's Journal* (27 October 1873).

98 Samuel Sidney, *The Pig* (London: George Routledge & Sons, 1897), p. 143; H. D. Richardson, *The Pig* (Dublin: James McGlashan, 1852), p. 86.

99 A veterinarian, *The Cattle Keeper's Guide; Or, Complete Directory for the Choice Management of Cattle, Including Horses, Oxen, Cows, Calves, Sheep, Lambs, Hogs &c. With a Description of the Symptoms and Most Approved Methods of Curing Every Disorder They are Subject to* (London: Joseph and W. H. Bailey, n.d.), p. 52.

100 Liam Kennedy and Peter Solar, *Irish Agriculture: A Price History from the Mid-Eighteenth Century to the Eve of the First World War* (Dublin: Royal Irish Academy, 2007), pp. 51–60.

101 'Smithfield cattle market', *Irish Farmer's Gazette* (12 January 1850), 23; 'Smithfield market', *Irish Farmer's Gazette* (15 January 1850), 26.

102 DCC PHC Mins, vol. 5, 28 September 1866, 149.

103 'Corporation of Dublin Public Health Committee', *Reports and Printed Documents of the Corporation of Dublin ... 1875* (Dublin: Joseph Pollard, 1876), p. 11.

104 'Royal Agricultural Society's Grand National Horse and Cattle Show', *Irish Times* (29 August 1867).
105 'The Easter Cattle Show', *Irish Times* (20 April 1865).
106 'County of Waterford. Unreserved auction ...' *Irish Times* (10 December 1866).
107 *The Irish Comic Song Book* (Dublin: J. Harding, n.d.), pp. 33–4.
108 Richard Perren, *The Meat Trade in Britain 1840–1914* (London: Routledge and Kegan Paul, 1978), p. 43.
109 Quoted in Mizelle, *Pig*, p. 119.
110 'Poor relief and sanitary service in Ireland', *British Medical Journal* (7 June 1873), 649.
111 McNeur, 'The "swinish multitude"'.
112 Bradbury, 'Pigs, cows, and boarders'.
113 Mizelle, *Pig*, pp. 49–57; Perren, *The Meat Trade in Britain*, p. 43
114 'The sanitary state of the city', *Dublin Builder* (15 August 1865), 195.
115 Elizabeth Tilley, 'Trading in knowledge: the *Irish Builder* and nineteenth-century journalism', *Revue LISA/LISA e-journal*, 3:1 (2005), 110–20. Note that there was a magazine in England entitled *The Builder* with a similar scope. The *Dublin Builder* became the *Irish Builder* in 1866.
116 'The health of our metropolis and country towns', *Dublin Builder* (15 September 1865), 217.
117 *Report of the Working Committee of the Dublin Sanitary Association to the General Meeting, Held June 11th, 1873 ...* (Dublin: J. Atkinson & Co., 1873), p. 1.
118 DCC PHC Mins, vol. 11, 11 October 1872, 306.
119 Joseph Nugent, 'The human snout: pigs, priests and peasants in the parlor', *Senses & Society*, 4:3 (2009), 283–302.
120 Untitled editorial, *Freeman's Journal* (29 August 1873).
121 'Our sanitary commission', *Freeman's Journal* (19 September 1873).
122 'Civic Lyrics no. L. The Reign of the Gutter', *Irish Builder* (15 September 1873).
123 'Public rights and public nuisances. Inspection of trades', *Irish Builder* (1 June 1874), 152.
124 *Sewerage and Drainage Inquiry*, p. 174 [Evidence had been collected in 1879, the report was published in 1880.]
125 *Sewerage and Drainage Inquiry*, minutes of evidence, p. 136.
126 'Police courts', *Freeman's Journal* (12 November 1859).
127 DCC PHC Mins, vol. 10, 28 April 1871, 76.
128 For an overview of changing public health law in Dublin see Jacinta Prunty, *Dublin Slums 1800–1925: A Study in Urban Geography* (Dublin: Irish Academic Press, 1998), pp. 67–78. See also Juliana Adelman,

'Contagious bovine pleuropneumonia, germs and public health in Dublin 1862–1882', *Social History of Medicine*, 30:1 (2016), 71–91.

129 Mary E. Daly, *Dublin, the Deposed Capital: A Social and Economic History, 1860–1914* (Cork: Cork University Press, 1984), p. 259.

130 DCC PHC Mins, vol. 2, for example 29 August 1856 and 29 April 1859 (slaughterhouses), 7 January 1859 and 22 July 1859 (licence for pig slaughterhouse).

131 DCC PCH Mins, vol. 14, 26 January 1877, 133.

132 *Reports and printed documents of the corporation of Dublin ... 1880*, pp. 9–20, 88–90.

133 'Instructions for the use of sanitary sub-officers, 1880', *Reports and Printed Documents of the Corporation of Dublin ... 1880*, p. 10.

134 George T. B. Vanston, *The Law of Public Health in Ireland: Being the Public Health (Ireland) Act, 1878, and Amending Acts, and Other Statutes Affecting Sanitary Authorities* (Dublin: E. Ponsonby, 1892), p. 101.

135 Vanston, *The Law of Public Health in Ireland*, pp. 134–5.

136 *Dublin Sewerage and Drainage Inquiry*, minutes of evidence, pp. 41, 86, 174, 184.

137 DCC PHC Mins, vol. 5, 21 December 1866.

138 DCC PHC Mins, vol. 10, 28 April 1871.

139 DCC PHC Mins, vol. 5, 21 December 1866.

140 DCC PHC Mins, vol. 8, 19 March 1869.

141 DCC PHC Mins, vol. 6, 25 May 1867.

142 DCC PHC Mins, vol. 8, 7 May 1869.

143 Adelman, 'Contagious bovine pleuropneumonia'.

144 Adelman, 'Contagious bovine pleuropneumonia'.

145 Charles Cameron, *Annual Report of the Medical Officer of Health for the Dublin Corporation ... 1871*, p. 6.

146 DCC PHC Mins, vol. 4, 1 November 1864.

147 DCC PHC Mins, vol. 4, 4 November 1864.

148 DCC PHC Mins, vol. 16, 18 July and 25 July 1879.

149 See Adelman, 'Contagious bovine pleuropneumonia'.

150 'The Irish Public Health Bill', *Irish Builder* (15 June 1874), 163.

151 DCC PHC Mins, vol. 8, 22 January 1869.

152 DCC PHC Mins, vol. 9, 12 November 1869.

153 DCC PHC Mins, vols 5 and 6.

154 DCC PHC Mins, vols 8 and 9.

155 *Reports and Printed Documents of the Corporation of Dublin ... 1875*, p. 11.

156 See, for example, 'Corporation of Dublin. Public Health Committee. Annual Return of Sanitary Operations for the year ending March 31st, 1874', *Reports and Printed Documents of the corporation of Dublin ... 1874* (Dublin: Joseph Pollard, 1875).

157 *Minutes of the Municipal Council of the City of Dublin ... 1883*, p. 160.

158 *Minutes of the Municipal Council of the City of Dublin ... 1883*, p. 161.
159 'Meeting of the Corporation', *Freeman's Journal* (4 July 1899).
160 'The Corporation', *Freeman's Journal* (18 November 1898).
161 Fergus D'Arcy, 'The Dublin police strike of 1882', *Soathar*, 23 (1998), 33–44.
162 O'Neill, 'Bourgeois Ireland', pp. 534–6.

5

Progress or decline? Associating animals with urban success and failure, 1880–1900

In 1884 the writer Edwin Hamilton imagined Ireland 'eighty years hence'. The British parliament had granted Home Rule and Ireland was divided by a canal running through the middle of Dublin and westward to Galway. North of the canal lay the prosperous nation of Ireland while to the south lay 'Mud Island', at war with Britain. One city became two: Dublin on the north side of the canal and Ballymuckbeg on the south. When an inquisitive English visitor (John MacBull) snuck into the forbidden city, a local explained the origin of the town's name: 'Sir Joe Beggar, who was Prime Minister, suggested "muckbeg"; the pig ("muck") being the national animal, and "beg" meaning "small".' Beggar had rejected the alternative 'Ballymuckmore', or 'town of the fat pig', because 'a little pig was a much more sentimental object than a fat one'.[1] As MacBull wandered the capital of Mud Island he discovered the consequences of legislative independence pursued along radical lines. The abolition of property rights decimated agriculture and economy. Railway lines stood unused, covered in 'moss, weeds and ivy'. Empty streets were 'overgrown with weeds and moss' and heaps of rubbish abounded. While Dublin rang with the 'busy sounds of hammer, anvil, and wheel', in Ballymuckbeg he heard just 'the loud braying of an ass'.[2]

Ballymuckbeg might be the city depicted in Thomas Fitzpatrick's cartoon of 1908 for *The Lepracaun* (see Figure 5.1). A man representing the Dublin Corporation's public health department naps in the muck

5.1. 'Dear, dirty, Dublin' as drawn by Thomas Fitzpatrick for *The Lepracaun* in December of 1908. Image courtesy of the Royal College of Physicians of Ireland.

like a pig, oblivious to all around him. He dozes as 'private slaughter houses' send forth filth and attract rats, vegetable scraps rot and dead animals fill the slob lands. The men of the Corporation have grown fat while ignoring the filth threatening the poor. Dublin, resembling the goddess Athena, frowns down at him and presents him with the damning statistics of the city's death rate while holding a cat-o'-nine-tails in her other hand.

Fitzpatrick and Hamilton looked around late nineteenth-century Dublin and saw 'a city in distress'. For Hamilton, radical nationalism could reduce a metropolis to a mud pit. For Fitzpatrick, greedy and lazy civic politicians had mired the city in poverty and filth. At the close of the nineteenth century, some reformers imagined Dublin in a fight for her life. Chaos threatened urban civilisation in the Irish metropolis. Or as one witness to the public health inquiry put it, 'Dublin is ailing, and wants a sanitary physician'.[3]

Others disagreed. A witness to the municipal boundaries commission saw a thriving metropolis, 'a great city' and 'the centre of Ireland'.[4] Guidebooks touted the attractions of 'the city of broad streets, fine statues and noble edifices, the ancient stronghold of the Hibernian Danes, and the Irish metropolis for centuries'.[5]

These different ways of describing or imagining Dublin reflected a struggle to agree on the form a modern city should take. Animal histories have demonstrated that when the middle classes pursued urban improvement they tried to remove certain animals from cities.[6] By the close of the nineteenth century these animals still lived in Dublin. This chapter focuses on horses and cattle and argues that ideas about these animals and their role in the city reflected different interpretations of whether Dublin had improved or not.

Instead of asking whether Dublin failed or succeeded, modernised or declined, this chapter asks how different animals became entangled with different narratives of what a city should be. A middle-class ideal of the city included horses, which were associated with progress if not with modernity per se.[7] By contrast, many reformers agreed that food animals were obstacles to creating a modern city and that the removal of dairy yards, private slaughterhouses and the live cattle market would bring improvement. The proliferation of bye-laws to control animals, even when the Corporation failed to enforce them, created the potential for a powerful municipal administration in the future.[8] Yet the resistance to these changes reflected not only cleaving to tradition but also an idea of the modern city as a place of economic opportunity and freedom.

Fin-de-siècle Dublin was certainly an 'anthrozootic city', a 'city made by the close interaction and interdependence of humans and animals'.[9] People also used animals to define many ways of understanding the city: they could be signifiers of poverty or wealth, they could bring modernity or reflect tradition, they could assist with improvement or herald decline, they might advance civilisation or drag the city into chaos. We do not have to accept Hamilton's view that people who valued pigs could not be civilised nor do we have to accept that the elimination of certain animals from the urban core was inevitable. Instead, this chapter analyses how and why certain animals came to be identified with what was 'good' in a city while others suggested what was 'bad'. The first section argues that Dublin depended on horses to create a particular ideal of a modern city. The second section uses cattle to argue that food animals, upon which the city depended for sustenance and income, became strongly associated with the problems of public health and poverty.

Horses

In February of 1880 Mrs Nannie Lambert Power O'Donoghue attended a reception for the Empress of Austria just outside Dublin.[10] The Empress was a famous rider and so the great and the good of Dublin, including Mrs O'Donoghue, had gathered to meet her on horseback. As O'Donoghue took in the sight of the assembled ladies she pronounced herself appalled and depressed by the scene: 'Such horses, such saddles, such rusty bridles, such riding-habits, hats, whips, and gloves; and, above all such *coiffures!* My very soul was sorry.'[11] This formative experience drove O'Donoghue to write her first book instructing ladies on how to choose a horse, learn to ride and dress for riding. O'Donoghue, with practical briskness, advised her readers seeking a proper mount to look for 'soundness and suit-ability; everything else, including beauty, can be dispensed with'.[12] O'Donoghue saw horse and rider as a partnership. She described her relationship with her favourite horse, Pleader, as that of siblings: 'certainly no two ever loved one another better'.[13] Ladies, she advised, ought to choose a horse whose temperament matched their own personality. Yet a rider also had to contain and control her horse to ensure that the animal never discovered that 'he can be master if he pleases'.[14]

O'Donoghue's advice targeted prospective bourgeois horsewomen but she suggests much more about the understanding of the rela-tionship between humans, horses and civility. Through centuries of domestication the horse had become an acknowledged partner in the creation of human civilisation. The relationship required mastery by humans but cooperation from horses. When properly controlled, horses did more than provide power. Horses allowed humans to display power, self-control, civility and even beauty. They could be ignored as machines but also celebrated as siblings.

Special horses helped to perform human identities in the nineteenth century, from the bourgeois Dublin lady to the British colonist in South Africa.[15] Farm horses signified the social status of Irish farmers; their labour was of secondary value.[16] Dr Henry Marsh, an eminent physician, was remembered for 'his handsome open Victoria, drawn by a fiery pair of horses, always driven at full speed' as well as for his medical achievements.[17] The speed of his horses reflected the urgency and importance of his business: everyone noticed him passing. Peter O'Brien, Lord Chief Justice of Ireland from 1889 to 1913, demonstrated his identification with the British elite by keeping 'a scratch pack of harriers' and 'a horse called Chance, the most trustworthy of hunters' at his brother's estate in County Clare.[18] He later purchased his own estate, about fifteen miles from his court duties in Dublin, where he could indulge his interest in horses and hunting.[19] One Dublin memoirist claimed that a lady acquaintance kept two horses 'solely for the purpose of attending funerals'.[20] Funerals required an appropriate display of social status and therefore horses. The Guinness brewery maintained a stable of 127 horses with a value of around £5400.[21] The horses provided labour but they also became part of a recognisable display of the Guinness brand. Visitors admired the expensive Clydesdale horses (£50 to £100 each) as 'quite equal to the London dray-horse so greatly celebrated'.[22]

Horses could even help to physically separate Dublin's middle class from the city around them. In George Moore's novel of Dublin in the 1880s (*A Drama in Muslin*), the female characters spend their time in the city attending a series of dinners and dances at Dublin Castle where the mother hopes to capture the best possible husband for her preferred daughter. The horse and carriage in which they travel provides a barrier between comfort and poverty. On the way to the ball they pass 'squalor multiform and terrible', a part of the city 'black, plague-spotted, pestilential'. While waiting to approach the castle, 'never were poverty and wealth brought into plainer proximity'. Those in the carriages 'strove to hide themselves' from the appraising gaze of those on the streets.[23]

For the city, as opposed to the individual, reliance on horse power brought into being trades, professions and economic systems that facilitated the creation of the horse–human partnership. Just as Mrs O'Donoghue's ladies displayed their civility by riding correctly and using the right equipment, so Dublin demonstrated its progress by its ability to harness many horses to make the city a faster and cleaner place. To say that a nineteenth-century city could not have functioned without horses would be no exaggeration. A witness to the commission on municipal boundaries in 1880 claimed that a city was essentially a place of trade and trade required roads, therefore 'if you were to shut up and close the roads of a city, that city could not exist'.[24] And to use those roads you needed horses. The interdependence between horse and human helped to create the nineteenth-century city.[25] A single horse could become a 'willing servant' to its master, but a veritable army of horses served Dublin.[26]

Among the most important tasks of the willing servant in Dublin were those of powering transportation and assisting sanitation. Through these tasks the horse not only performed useful work but also symbolised the advance of civilisation. Dubliners depended upon horses to keep the city of free circulation and commerce in operation and to push back the tides of filth that threatened it. The horse was not easily replaced by steam or other engines. A journalist covering the Royal Dublin Society annual horse show in 1902 asked rhetorically: 'Can we picture that day in the future when, the horse being extinct in Ireland ... the extensive premises at Ballsbridge will be given over to a show of motors to which every county will send its crowds of enthusiastic admirers?'[27] No one could picture that day; a motor could not be admired as a horse could: it was not yet charged with the same symbolic values.

Reliance on horse power created local economies. Horses had to be reared and trained for harness in large numbers, they had to be fed and cared for, bought and sold and eventually slaughtered and turned into other products. As Mrs O'Donoghue recognised, people had to be trained to use horses effectively and other people had to produce the saddles, whips, bridles and harness required.[28]

These local horse economies were especially important in Dublin because there were more horses there than in any other Irish city. Horses projected a city of busy commercial and administrative importance. According to the *Pictorial and Descriptive Guide* Dublin in 1900 was still 'the most car drivingest city of Europe', as it was, in the days of 'Harry Lorrequer'.[29] Even the rise of electric trams had not removed Dubliners' reliance on horses. While Dublin's human population barely changed in the second half of the nineteenth century, the city's horse population rose significantly. Horse numbers in Dublin kept pace with growing cities such as Boston, increasing throughout the century and peaking in the early 1900s.[30] Between the census years of 1851 and 1871, for example, Dublin's horse population rose from around 7000 to 8000. In the same period, the change in the human population was almost zero. By 1891 the number of horses may have been as high as 11,500 while Dublin's human population remained stable.[31] The introduction of trams and the growth of railway lines since 1871 probably increased reliance on horse power as it did in most other cities.[32] At the height of the tram system in Dublin, the city housed 1577 tram horses alone.[33]

The supply of these horses drew on the Irish countryside as well as international trade networks. Reporting to a parliamentary commission on horse breeding, a member of the Irish Harness Horse Society presented evidence that horse breeding around Dublin was divided into districts, with cart horses mostly bred on the north side of the city and harness horses on the south side.[34] He also revealed that the importation of 'very poor' 'flat-sided animals' from America, already broken in, partly supplied demand for cheap harness horses in Dublin.[35] Another witness from the same society demonstrated that Dublin dominated the demand for horses to aid 'traffic and manufacture': 14 per cent of all horses raised in the province of Leinster were put to such purposes, the highest percentage of the four Irish provinces.[36] The shortfall in demand was made up by imports from the province of Ulster and abroad.

To train and use the horse, humans with various skills were also required. Craftsmen linked together the horse–human transportation machines through harnesses, coaches, saddles and whips. Craftsmen employed in these trades were over-represented among Dublin's population compared with London and Liverpool. Coachmaking, in particular, was a thriving trade and one in which multigenerational businesses persisted. The firm of John Hutton and Sons was particularly long-lived, lasting from 1779 to 1925, by which time it was building bodies for motor cars. During the nineteenth century, Hutton's built a state coach for Queen Victoria which is still in use by the royal family today.[37]

Cab drivers, coachmen and carters all relied on horse power to perform their jobs and each of these trades was also over-represented in Dublin. In Dublin, almost all males employed in domestic service were grooms and coachmen. The proportion of coachmen and grooms to overall male employment in Dublin was almost twice that of London in 1871 and more than three times that of Liverpool in the same year.[38] Although there was significant employment of men and horses for the movement of goods, movement of people seems to have been most important and distinguished Dublin from industrial cities of a similar size. Liverpool, London and Dublin, for example, had very different levels of employment in the categories of 'coachmen, cabmen, flymen' and 'carman, carrier, carter, drayman' which cannot be fully explained by different interpretations of job categories by the census takers. Carters and draymen, much more numerous in Liverpool, would have been employed to bring goods to and from the port. The importance of horses for the transportation of people seems to have been greatest in Dublin and London, reflected in the figures for drivers (coachmen and cabmen) and for the owners of different types of transportation businesses (omnibus owners and livery stable keepers).[39]

To keep those horses well, Dubliners employed almost ten times as many specialists in horse health than Belfast. In 1891, the census found 114 'veterinary surgeons and farriers' in Dublin (an increase from 1871). These individuals served around 8000 horses. Belfast, by contrast, required only sixteen veterinary surgeons and farriers for its nearly 6000 horses. London had even higher numbers in proportion to its horse population than Dublin, probably explained by the presence of a veterinary college where many Irish veterinarians had also trained.[40] The opening of a veterinary college in Dublin in 1900 marked the achievement of higher professional status for veterinary surgeons and a claim to the title required specific training.[41] By 1901, veterinary surgeon and farrier were separated on the census but the significant difference between Dublin and Belfast remained. The city and suburbs of Dublin were home to forty-eight qualified veterinary surgeons, more than the number of veterinary surgeons resident in the city of Belfast and its two neighbouring counties combined.[42]

Although cabs, carriages and the famous Irish jaunting car continued to serve passengers in late nineteenth-century Dublin, the most significant development in urban horse transportation was the introduction of horse-drawn trams. Approved by legislation in 1867, trams did not actually appear on Dublin streets until 1872.[43] They quickly overtook omnibuses as the principal means of circulation between the wealthy suburbs and the inner city, facilitating the

5.2. Sackville Street *c.* 1890, showing the operation of horse trams. They would soon be replaced with electric trams. Image courtesy of the National Library of Ireland.

middle classes to live in the healthier atmosphere of the urban fringes. By 1880, tramlines ran between the city and almost every suburban township, in most cases following the routes that had previously been plied by horse-drawn omnibuses. Figure 5.2 shows trams working in Sackville Street. The first lines were introduced along the roads to the most populous suburbs, Pembroke and Rathmines, and to the Phoenix Park because of its recreational and governmental importance. A few years later, further lines brought passengers north to the suburbs of Drumcondra, Glasnevin and Clontarf. The lines all converged on Sackville Street (now O'Connell Street) in the north-east of the city. This remained the heart of the commercial city even as the adjacent streets declined in value. The continuous flow of trams presented a busy and prosperous city. *Dignam's Dublin Guide* suggested that due to the 'enormous number of tram cars coming and going from all points ... One would think our city was far larger than Manchester and more densely populated'.[44] A French memoirist commented that the tram service was 'very well organised', with faster trams than London (if slower than Paris).[45]

The horse tram or horse railway consisted of a wooden car, sometimes containing two levels with seats, powered by a team of horses

5.3. Trams in front of Trinity College Dublin, *c.* 1890. There are three different types of tram car shown here, including a single level car. Image courtesy of the National Library of Ireland.

who pulled the carriage along a metal track. Figure 5.3 shows the variety of styles of car that plied the roads in Dublin. The track reduced the work for the horses, making it possible for them to carry more passengers at a faster pace and thus reduce the cost of the fare.[46] Reaching speeds of around six miles per hour with a somewhat smoother journey, they were viewed as a significant improvement on the omnibus.

Tramlines, their supporters argued, brought prosperity and health. William Barrington, a tram promoter and later board member of several tram companies, claimed that the new trams would rationalise the city's circulation, removing the

> disgraceful confusion as results from the crowding pell-mell together of full and empty cabs, chiefly the latter; lumbering omnibuses; Fishbourne's vans; private carriages; and every description of vehicle our city contains; with no more idea of extrication on the part of the drivers, than if they were a drove of pigs.[47]

The new tramlines would increase property values in the suburbs by 'bringing those localities into rapid, frequent, cheap, and comfortable communication with the business centres'. Finally, Barrington argued that the trams would become 'the arteries of a great city's ventilation' by allowing the poor to visit the countryside cheaply and thus refreshing those 'who have to live in dark, noisome, and often pestilential lanes and alleys'.[48]

The horse tramways connected the healthful and prosperous suburbs with the decaying yet necessary city centre. They facilitated the city's significant social segregation by making it easy to live outside the city and work and shop inside it. In 1880, when the tramways were well established, the Corporation attempted to extend the municipal boundaries to include the suburban townships. The councils of these relatively young townships objected to being pulled into the city, which they considered poorly run with higher taxes. The Dublin Corporation wished to include the suburbs as they felt suburban residents benefitted from the city without making a contribution to its upkeep. Among the arguments in favour of the inclusion of the suburbs was that the tramlines had already made this incorporation a practical reality. According to the Corporation, 'these townships were in fact part of the city, separated from it by an artificial boundary only'. Witnesses repeatedly cited the tramways as a reason that the 'townships are in reality portions of Dublin, and not separate places'.[49] Another claimed that 'the townships ... have become knit by tramways and railways to the centre of the city'.[50]

Horses allowed suburban residents all the benefits of the city without the need to pay city taxes. The extent of these connections was clear from the tram timetables, offering service to and from most suburbs every ten or fifteen minutes during the working day.[51] Further, horses hauled the 'daily supplies, including coal' from the city into the suburbs. Delivery was often by horse and cart, but Eaton's also delivered parcels to 'inhabitants resident along the tramlines'.[52] A parcel service was also offered by the Dublin United Tramways Company.[53] The building of those spacious homes that attracted the middle classes to the suburbs also relied on the labour of horses. The large supply yards and sawmills of Dublin's builders were located in the city itself.[54] Horses carried bricks, stones, wood and other building materials from the city to the suburbs.[55]

Until the late 1890s only horses were seen as suitable forms of transportation in crowded urban districts. The Dublin Corporation only supported horse traction within the municipal boundaries. In 1883, for example, they received a proposal for a new steam tramway

that would run between the city and the northern suburbs of Coolock
and Swords. By 1884 the tramway company had modified the proposal
to suggest that the use of steam power terminate at the city's edge to be
replaced by horses within it. Park Neville (the city engineer) reminded
the council that they had rejected the use of steam within the city on
the part of the South Dublin Street Tramways Company and it had
been struck out of the ensuing bill.[56] Horses were considered safer and
cleaner than steam trams within crowded districts.

The Corporation could not hold back the tide of mechanisation
forever. Perhaps the most significant contribution of the horse tram
was to make way for its replacement. The familiar and trustworthy horse helped to ease the transition to mechanised rail transport
within the city. By the end of the nineteenth century, electrification
rather than steam had emerged as the new direction for trams. The
Dublin Corporation initially resisted electrification within the city,
and tramway companies proceeded from the 'outside in' by electrify-
ing suburban routes first. Yet once the principal of electrification was
accepted, power stations and wires rapidly replaced horses. Dublin's
tram system went from all horse traction within the city boundaries
to almost all electrical traction in less than five years.[57]

Despite the apparent ease of the transformation, electric traction
raised new concerns and posed new problems. Dublin's nationalist
Lord Mayor in 1896 (Richard McCoy) initially opposed the introduction of electrification because he believed that it would disfigure the city
while rendering Irish agricultural land 'useless' by removing horses as
a major source of income. No longer would farmers be able to 'fall back
on … the raising of hay and oats and breeding of horses'. Other councillors defended 'horse haulage', citing the city's thousands of cab and
carmen.[58] There was also a big difference between a driver controlling
two sentient creatures and one controlling a machine. Horses could
be expected to avoid a certain amount of danger instinctively and did
not find the presence of other horse-drawn vehicles alarming. Electric
trams forced adaptation by both horses and humans. Trams initially
frightened the horses, although within a few years horses were being
advertised as 'used to electric trams'.[59] Drivers of carriages often drove
along the tramway, even ahead of electric trams, leading to furious
debate between car drivers, cyclists and tram passengers about
whether electric trams ought to be faster or slower than horse traffic.[60]
When the tramlines had been introduced, drivers of other horse-
drawn vehicles had complained of the dangers of the tracks. Indeed,

serious accidents resulted when traditional vehicles had to share the roads with trams.[61] Nonetheless, the horse trams had been a gentler introduction to mechanisation. Many mourned the loss of the horses, and the thousands of Dubliners engaged in related trades of caring for those horses must have certainly felt it in their pockets. However, the predicted agricultural collapse did not occur and horse-drawn carts and drays and vans and carriages continued to ply their trade on the Dublin streets in large numbers.

Even when they were no longer delivering suburban commuters, horses continued to power important city services. They hauled away wastes, watered roads and pulled the Corporation's disinfecting van.

Although the emergence of ideas about germs in the 1860s and 1870s had affected some aspects of public health, it had not diminished the desire of the Corporation to tackle 'filth of the most dangerous nature', especially 'the exhalations and the oozings from these abominable foecal accumulations'.[62] While privies were beginning to be replaced by water closets, the need to collect a variety of wastes only expanded throughout the latter part of the century. Both street cleaning and waste collection relied upon an expanding stable of horses.

In 1880, the Corporation kept seventy-seven horses in constant employment for the purposes of road maintenance. The Paving and Lighting Committee valued the horses at over £3000 and spent a similar amount annually on food and veterinary care. In return the horses worked most days (on average sixty-three were on duty each day) hauling thousands of pounds of waste from the streets and maintaining the surface by repaving and watering to keep down dust. The removal of household waste was a close alliance of human and horse labour. 'Wheelers' collected waste from inside and around the properties served by the Corporation's scavenging service. Offensive material was collected at night ('night soil') and left on the curb to be gathered up by carters. A team of eight men and one horse worked each scavenging district. Collected materials were delivered to scavenging depots where the waste was sorted and either resold for fertiliser or carried out to sea by barge.[63]

The number of horses employed in street scavenging increased steadily over the final two decades of the century despite the equally steady introduction of water closets. By 1884 the number of horses had increased to 105; by 1900 the number was 150. The number of men required also increased from around 400 in the 1880s to almost 600 in 1900. In 1884, Charles Cameron estimated that almost

60 per cent of the city's population used water closets and thus did not require their privies to be scavenged. Yet scavenging efforts only intensified in a desire to remove as much waste as possible. Rubbish had become an unacceptable component of the urban streetscape and an indication of Dublin's backwardness. As the superintendent of scavenging put it, 'there is no city in the United Kingdom, similar in extent, population or importance to Dublin, which the public thoroughfares are so abused as they are in this city, where in many instances they serve as receptacles for house, fish, vegetable and other shop refuse, and every kind of filth'.[64] Display was important even for horses hauling waste. Observers complained that the city's 'beautiful horses' were 'parading through the streets' but 'doing hardly anything'.[65]

Horses' role in improving urban sanitation presents an interesting contradiction. The average horse produces between three and four tons of manure per year, leading to a potential accumulation of over 30,000 tons on Dublin roads each year during the late nineteenth century.[66] Horses were also long known to directly pass the disease of glanders on to humans.[67] The 1880 'sewerage and drainage inquiry' considered manure accumulations to be a significant health hazard. Yet no one suggested the removal of horses from Dublin nor were they often spoken of as detrimental to public health.

Cattle

Few doubted the importance of the horse to urban development. Yet from a sanitary point of view, urban horses did have their detractors. One witness to the public health inquiry of 1880 accused Dubliners of 'allowing the effete matter from that large animal, the horse, to surround us on all sides'. He believed this laxness derived from the 'popular notion that a horse can do no harm'.[68] He was, as he knew, a lone voice: no other witness in hundreds of pages of testimony considered the urban horse to be a health hazard. When the pig market in Smithfield was closed for good on sanitary grounds, the Corporation suggested replacing it with a horse market to which no one might make a sanitary objection.[69] The public health hazards of horse manure and highly flammable stables attracted less attention than in American cities.[70] Instead, reformers focused on how to deal with dairy yards and private slaughterhouses. Dublin in 1880 was as much of a cowtown as it had been in 1860.

Although members of the DSA admitted that sanitary progress had been made by the final decade of the nineteenth century, they felt progress had been lamentably slow. Frederic Pim, a local business-man and president of the DSA in 1891, compared the sanitary task to the fifth labour of Hercules: 'So foul was the Augean stable which had to be cleansed, so enormous is the mass which still remains to be moved, that all that has been done seems as yet but a drop in the bucket.'[71] Just like the Augean stables, Dublin was loaded down with cattle manure. Clearing out the stables would not be enough: the DSA and many other reformers argued for the removal of the manure-producing animals. By 1880 the campaign against the urban pig, discussed in Chapters 2 and 4, had made a significant impact. From a height of nearly 12,000 pigs in 1872, numbers had fallen to fewer than 4000 by 1880. Starting in 1874, pig numbers as recorded in the agricultural statistics did not fluctuate in Dublin in line with Irish pig numbers as a whole, suggesting the beginning of a decoupling between town and country.[72] By 1900, witnesses to the city's second major public health inquiry reported that the Corporation had 'cleared away all the pigs with great energy and complete success'.[73] Ballymuckbeg did not materialise.

Reducing numbers of cattle proved more difficult. The Dublin Cattle Market had no rivals in the British Isles for the volume of beasts being bought and sold within it.[74] While these beasts moved through the city on their way to English or Irish plates, dairy cows were more per-manent residents. In 1878 James Boyle, the city's Executive Sanitary Officer, suggested that there were approximately 7500 dairy cows within the city.[75] By the time of the public health inquiry of 1900 the number was reduced to 5000.[76] Public health reformers continued to pursue their elimination from the city.

The idea that cattle and pigs were inappropriate in the city was not new in the 1880s, as previous chapters have demonstrated. The evi-dence of the 1880 sewerage and drainage commission sounded like weary repetition. Yet the discourse around removing cattle and pigs was growing louder and more widespread than in previous decades. Legislative changes, including the Public Health (Ireland) Act of 1878 and subsequent bye-laws, introduced greater stringency around animal-keeping and the increase in sanitary staff enabled better enforcement. Thus by the close of the nineteenth century public health advocates within the Corporation and without had reimagined Dublin as an urban environment free from certain types of animals.

They pursued this version of modernity through enhanced sanitary inspection and regulation.

Numerous witnesses to the 1880 sewerage and drainage inquiry cited cattle as sources of pollution. More importantly, cattle were explicitly linked to the problem of the city's sewerage and the pollution of the River Liffey that had instigated the commission in the first place. The commission's own report ranked the presence of slaughterhouses and manure depots in the inner city as among the city's chief public health problems after the prevalence of poor quality tenements and poor drainage.[77] These problems were interrelated according to chemist and witness Henry Hennessy: animal wastes rather than human wastes blocked up drains as they contained higher proportions of solid matter.[78] Dr Frederick Moore blamed the smell emanating from the River Liffey almost exclusively on the depositing of slaughterhouse waste and manure in it.[79] Albert Speedy reported to the inquiry that he objected to keeping pigs in the city not just because of the pigs themselves but because 'large quantities of manure are allowed to remain undisturbed in many parts of the district for months'.[80]

Other reforming interest groups echoed the concerns about animal-keeping voiced at the commission of inquiry. When the Royal College of Physicians of Ireland (RCPI) joined the Royal College of Surgeons of Ireland (RCSI) in condemning the city's high death rate and proposing solutions, among their principal concerns were the close associations between human populations, animals and their wastes. 'The presence and the unsatisfactory condition of numerous slaughter-houses, cow-yards, and manure depots within the most crowded parts of the city' ranked after housing and poor scavenging as the third most significant contributor to urban disease and death. The spread of infectious disease and the inadequate means of transporting people with disease, however, only ranked tenth and eleventh.[81] Among the suggested remedies was to 'abolish all slaughter-houses, dairy-yards, manure depots, swine-yards, &c., within the precincts of the city; and, until this be effected, to enforce the regular daily cleansing of such places'.[82] The medical men linked these concerns with the control of infectious diseases such as typhoid (understood to pass through milk) but they extended further than an interest in stopping the spread of germs. The presence of certain food animals within the city was, they claimed, a hazard that should be eliminated rather than controlled.

A growing pamphlet literature on public health also condemned urban cattle. For example, Frederick Moore's 1886 pamphlet on the Dublin dairy yards enumerated the many perceived hazards of urban animals. Moore advised that cattle should be removed from the most crowded districts: they should not be slaughtered there nor kept as milch cows. The greatest offence arising from urban cattle-keeping was the accumulation of manure. According to Moore, few could 'doubt the connection between manure collections and sickness'. The heaps produced an 'obnoxious and infectious kind of residue' that would 'accumulate if not speedily removed to the right place— namely, the land'. These accumulations could be found 'permeating masonry and pavement ... whilst rendering the localities odorous and pre-eminently unhealthy'.[83] The demand for meat and milk in the cities had brought the cattle there but both human and animal health now demanded their removal. Moore declared that 'the great importance of maintaining in a state of health and cleanliness the cattle on whom we and our children depend so largely for meat and butter and milk must be self-evident'. Yet these same cattle, 'especially in cities, towns and their suburbs', were 'so badly kept as to be productive of injurious effects on the health of those who depend so much on them for food'.[84]

Legislation also demonstrated an increasing concern with controlling cattle and pigs within the city. After the sewerage and drainage commission and the Public Health (Ireland) Act of 1878, for example, the Corporation enacted further bye-laws to circumscribe animal-keeping. These bye-laws were intended to enforce distance between humans and animals or animal wastes. For example, neither swine nor swine dung could be kept within fifty feet of a dwelling house. The same restriction applied to cattle and cattle manure. All animal manure (including horse manure) had to be contained, covered and removed every week. For comparison, human wastes in fixed privies had to be removed once per month.[85] The Corporation even sought further powers to regulate and license dairy yards in the same way as it regulated slaughterhouses (see Chapter 3). Some of these powers were granted to them in 1886, when the regulation of dairies and of cattle disease within the city boundaries was transferred from the Poor Law Unions to municipal authorities. The new duties were considered 'numerous and heavy' and included the detection and seizure of diseased cattle as well as the registration of dairy yards.[86]

Action against dairy yards had been slow to come. Poor Law Unions supervised dairy cattle until 1886 because of their role in detecting outbreaks of animal disease. Without the ability to license dairy yards the Corporation could not implement the same system of surveillance used on slaughterhouses. Milk and meat consumption also fell along class lines: the poor drank milk while the middle classes ate the most beef. Milk lacked the moral taint of death and killing associated with meat. It is therefore not hard to imagine that the Corporation's middle-class councillors had first focused their attention on meat (as we saw in Chapter 3) because they perceived it to be the bigger public health concern. Nonetheless the problem of slaughterhouses had not gone away by 1880.

Charles Cameron, city analyst and chief medical officer, had sought centralisation of slaughter in a municipal abattoir since the 1860s. In 1882, the Corporation opened a public abattoir across the road from the Dublin Cattle Market. The ten-acre site included an acre of buildings with the remaining nine given over to cattle pens. The abattoir, like many similar buildings throughout Europe, made slaughter aesthetically acceptable in keeping with sanitary ideals. The exterior was 'a great improvement to the North Circular Road' while inside the main building glass roof lights, ventilation ducts and impervious surfaces ensured the introduction of light and air and the easy removal of wastes.[87] The arrangements were calculated to contain slaughter and separate it from the senses and experiences of most Dubliners. Doomed cattle could even travel through a tunnel from the cattle market directly into the abattoir. Within the abattoir, mechanical pulleys and winches moved animal carcasses around. Meat left the abattoir in covered carts. Most important for the Corporation, inspection of animals and meat could take place at a single site, thereby simplifying the process of removing diseased meat from the food chain.

Dublin butchers resisted efforts to force them to use a public abattoir. In a representation to the Corporation in 1882, they argued that they were 'being made the scapegoat for the public health'.[88] They blamed the Corporation, which had revoked licences for insanitary slaughterhouses and thereby increased crowding in the remaining slaughterhouses. The butchers, assembled into the Dublin Victuallers' Association, boycotted the abattoir. Because the abattoir was technically outside of the city boundary, the Corporation could not force them to use it. Throughout the 1880s, the butchers insisted that the Corporation was attacking their rights and freedoms as tradesmen.

In 1888, butchers appealed to the Corporation that the public health committee had injured their trade and prevented improvement by refusing slaughterhouse licences.[89]

Resistance to a public abattoir took on a specific flavour in the politically divided city. In 1889, William Field of the Victuallers' Association complained that the Dublin Sanitary Association (a 'self-elected irresponsible committee') was dictating policy to elected representatives and maligning the good name of butchers.[90] According to Field, by closing private slaughterhouses the Corporation disenfranchised people. Regulations reduced consumer choice and raised prices, while doing nothing to improve public health. Field was a nationalist politician who later became a Member of Parliament.[91] Field continued to view public abattoirs as both an inconvenience and an economic loss to butchers, and he represented their views as president of a federation of butchers associations.[92] Resisting regulation gave butchers control, just as separating from England would give Irish people control of their state.

Daniel J. Tallerman, an Australian meat entrepreneur, proposed what he believed would be a solution to both the local problem of meat production and the national problem of livestock export. Tallerman envisioned a complete alteration in Ireland's cattle trade, one that would convert Dublin into a centre of industrialised meat production. Writing in 1891, he argued 'that the transport of dead meat over live cattle possesses inherent advantages, and yields beneficial results to both producers and consumers, has been conclusively shown in the United States'.[93] Exporting livestock, as the Irish did, resulted in a devaluation of the produce in transit. Even worse, the value of offal, manure, hides and bones was exploited at the destination. This deprived the Irish farmer of income and cheap meat for local consumption. Tallerman proposed that slaughtering should occur at the place of sale and instead of animals, meat should be moved around. He proposed a demonstrating 'railway abattoir' with a series of processing cars to tour the country and promote his system.[94] He also set up a meat factory and by-products processing facility in Dublin, intended to capture the Leinster fat cattle trade and convert it to premium export beef and local cheaper meat products.[95]

Tallerman's ideas were not taken up and the city struggled on to promote the public abattoir and to begin the winding up of private slaughterhouses. The Corporation became increasingly stringent in its enforcement of controls around diseased meat and the cleanliness of slaughterhouses. From the 1890s, they began buying out the slaughterhouse licences and had, by 1900, reduced the number of slaughterhouses to fifty-six from around ninety in the 1860s.[96] By comparison with London, for example, this number of private slaughterhouses was not especially high. Nonetheless Cameron estimated that private slaughterhouses killed around 18,000 cattle per annum.[97]

The public abattoir represented a significant effort to change human–animal relationships in the urban environment according to one vision of urban modernity. Instead of hundreds of widely dispersed individuals who might each buy and kill a few animals a week, the Corporation favoured the consolidation of animal businesses in as few as possible. As we saw in Chapter 3, the Corporation first aimed at regulating the existing businesses rather than eliminating them. Nonetheless, even inspections tended to favour both larger slaughterhouses and larger piggeries, seeing the smaller butchers and individual pig owners as the source of most nuisances and sanitary violations. Keeping large numbers of animals in a few locations, and killing them efficiently and cleanly, was thought to represent the best method of preserving human health. Yet the consequence of this change was more than the disenfranchisement of small traders. The consolidation of slaughtering, as others have recognised, also changed the life experience of animals. They might no longer have to endure filthy conditions in the yards of the city's worst slaughterhouses but it is debatable whether living out their final days or hours in a large pen of strange animals brought together for slaughter represented an improvement.

While slaughterhouses had long been criticised as polluting urban businesses, in Dublin the reforming gaze shifted to the dairy yard by the closing decades of the nineteenth century. The construction of living cattle as a nuisance and an indication of a city in decline was driven by local circumstances. Firstly, the city's high mortality rate was linked to both the unhealthy urban environment and the circulation of disease germs through foods such as milk. Secondly, public health officials such as Cameron pushed for further consolidation and control by government to eliminate the 'small men' who 'never wash their cows by any chance'.[98] According to Cameron, 'the milk trade should fall into the hands of capitalists' because larger and more profitable dairy yards were cleaner dairy yards.[99]

By contrast with Cameron, Dubliners recalled family dairies with fondness. When the Irish revolutionary Tod Andrews was a child, his grandmother ran a dairy in the north inner city. The extended family lived in a Georgian building that had been converted into a number of separate apartments. After his grandmother was widowed the ground floor became a dairy shop. 'The extensive yard and stables became a dairy yard where she kept cows, a horse and a delivery gig and a couple of pigs to dispose of the swill.' Her sons began a milk round and rented summer pasture for the cows. Rather than dirt and disease, Andrews recalled 'abundant food and continuous meals, of laughing and shouting and quarrelling, of horses, cattle, dogs and cats. Life was abundant and improvident.' Andrews was allowed to ride the horses and cows and spent much of his time hanging around the milk maids and boys.[100]

The Dublin dairy economy was dominated by 'small men' who kept a few cows in a shed in the yard. London, according to Cameron, had around thirty-five yards compared with Dublin's 250 serving a population only one tenth the size.[101] Despite regulations requiring the shed to be a minimum distance from human habitations and to contain at least 600 square feet, dairy cattle and their accompanying wastes might be found almost anywhere in the city. No licensing procedure prevented them from being opened 'next to the Bank of Ireland, College Green, formerly the Parliament House'.[102] Between 1880 and 1900 this situation became increasingly intolerable to the Dublin Corporation's public health committee and to reformers concerned with the city's high death rate.

One of the most important factors in changing attitudes towards living cattle, especially dairy cattle, was the discovery of bovine tuberculosis. In 1883, Robert Koch identified a bacterium that appeared to cause the same disease in humans and other animals.[103] Cattle, meat and milk appeared a potent source of danger.[104] As the parliamentary commission on tuberculosis suggested, the disease 'is detected far more frequently in the carcases of cows than in those of any other animal slaughtered for sale'.[105] Germs could spread between people within and beyond the city. One could not separate Ballymuckbeg and all its filth from Dublin or Dublin from the rest of the United Kingdom. Dirty Dublin dairy yards were a threat not just to Dubliners but to the food supply and health of the United Kingdom.

Despite the progress of germ theories of disease within medical communities in the second half of the nineteenth century, both the Corporation and non-governmental promoters of public health in Dublin continued to focus on environmental issues. As we have seen in the previous two chapters, the elimination of slaughterhouses and home piggeries was based more on issues of disgust than on a proven link between the presence of animals or animal wastes and disease. This situates Dublin well within the bounds of what was normal across cities of the United Kingdom and the United States.[106] Ideas about germs were added to existing sanitary concerns rather than replacing them. A continued fixation on decay and dirt was also related to the idea that circulation brought health.

The way in which cattle were viewed as threats to health was tied up in notions of urban improvement and modernity. In the model of environmental health promoted by Edwin Chadwick from the 1830s, cattle produced smells and 'all smell is disease'. Thus improvements would remove bad smells and their sources, producing a cleaner and more modern urban environment. From the 1860s onward, germ theories of disease (alluded to in Chapter 3) had begun to suggest the potential for the transfer of a wider range of diseases between animals and humans.[107] Yet these new ideas tended to reinforce existing perceptions about which animals were appropriate urban residents. The very real risk of glanders led no one to suggest the removal of horses to the urban periphery, for example. Medical discoveries around human and bovine tuberculosis in the 1880s, however, prompted the expansion of efforts to control the impact of cattle on the city. Reformers still sought a cleaner and more modern urban environment, but cleaner was now defined as fewer germs.

In Dublin the impact of changing ideas about disease is evident between the first and second public health inquiries. As already discussed, the first inquiry (published in 1880) was intended as an investigation into sewerage and drainage with the aim of reducing the nuisance from the River Liffey. The inquiry expanded well beyond this remit to include a wide range of potential environmental and health hazards. The second inquiry (published in 1900) was established to investigate the causes of Dublin's high death rate. During both inquiries, cattle were frequently referred to as causes of ill health. However, only in the second inquiry were cattle implicated in the spread of specific diseases.

By 1900, there was much less ambivalence about dairy cows as a clear danger to public health. The report was emphatic about their link to the spread of disease, especially tuberculosis. 'The conditions, also of many cow sheds and dairy yards in the city are such as to favour Tuberculosis among cattle kept in these places', the commissioners wrote. Such conditions 'therefore to give rise to serious risk of disseminating Phthisis and other Tubercular diseases by means of milk'.[108] They considered slaughterhouses a danger of 'less degree'. Cameron agreed that dairy yards were the biggest animal nuisance, especially for their ability to transmit typhoid fever through milk. He considered that the Corporation ought to have even more stringent powers over them than over slaughterhouses.[109] Many witnesses argued that dairy yards were places that generated and disseminated specific contagious diseases, although the diseases and the methods of dissemination varied. Dr Albert Speedy, a medical officer of health in the north city, claimed that dairy cattle were the means of spreading typhoid, tuberculosis and possibly scarlatina and measles.[110] Enteric fever (typhoid) and tuberculosis were the most commonly mentioned diseases passed via milk, in keeping with the medical literature of the time. Yet the witnesses often presented different ideas about how dairy cattle participated in spreading these diseases. For example, Dr Joseph O'Carroll focused on the health of the humans engaged in preparing the milk, arguing that they were the cause of disease: 'I have attended cases of tuberculosis in dairies where several members of the family were tubercular.'[111] Dr D. Edgar Flinn was concerned with dirty hands and manure heaps as a 'breeding ground' for disease germs.[112] Dr E. W. Hope of Liverpool saw tuberculosis in milk as a by-product of overcrowded dairy cows.[113] Figure 5.4, drawn by cartoonist Thomas Fitzpatrick in the early twentieth century, suggests the wide range of disease concerns in a Dublin dairy yard.

Neither old concerns about dirty slaughter nor new concerns about disease germs had much immediate success in removing cattle from the city, but they did set up an infrastructure that could be used with greater rigour in the future. The 1900 public health inquiry noted a reduction in slaughterhouses but a continued prevalence of dairies. The commissioners failed to condemn the latter in the same terms as they had condemned the former. Yet attempts to regulate cattle did modernise the city, at least in bureaucratic terms. By 1886 the Corporation had centralised their control over cattle. They had complete charge of the market and the public abattoir and they oversaw, through inspection and regulation, the private slaughterhouses, butcher shops, dairy yards and most cattle that entered the city. The bye-laws governing these relationships are too numerous to list. They had, by 1900, a sanitary staff of forty-one including twenty-seven co-opted police officers. Five inspectors were allocated to the dairy yards while another specialised in slaughterhouses. If the Corporation

5.4. 'Registered Dairy' from the collection of cartoons drawn by Thomas Fitzpatrick, *c.* 1905. The cow is labelled 'white plague', a reference to both the colour of milk and a name for tuberculosis. The dairy men display poor hygienic practices and are surrounded by numerous diseases emanating from both animals and wastes. Image courtesy of the Royal College of Physicians of Ireland.

of the late nineteenth century did not choose to enforce the bye-laws as stringently as reformers desired, some future Corporation could (and would) use the legal framework to force larger changes.

If there was one idea about how to manage urban animals that embraced both cattle and horses it was that bigger was better. The horse trams moved larger numbers of people about more efficiently than omnibuses or carriages or individuals on horseback. Public abattoirs and large dairy yards could consolidate meat and milk production while allowing efficient sanitary inspection.

Cameron, for example, saw the large dairy yards of 'capitalists' as models of good practice. He told the public health inquiry in 1900 that 'we have a few of that kind round Dublin, and it is a pleasure to go into their dairy yards and see the cleanliness of their animals. They are groomed just like horses instead of having, as is the case in the smaller dairies, thick masses of cow dung all over their bodies and the udders dirty.'[114] For Cameron, these large dairy yards were an improvement over the scattered and small businesses in the same way that the public abattoir was an improvement over the many small private slaughterhouses. Bigger businesses kept things cleaner and tidier and they moved more animals out of the way of ordinary people. Although the horse was not banished from the city, the tramways had begun to edge him out by 1900. Certainly between trams and carriages there were almost no solitary riders on horses anymore. Mrs O'Donoghue lamented as early as 1881 that 'nobody who has any regard for life and limb now rides through Dublin. All wise persons gave it up when pavement and tram-lines made the city what it is. Consequently, the park is deserted, and only a solitary horse-man is seen in Stephen's Green.'[115] Suburban houses rarely included stables as families no longer needed to keep horses, and inner-city stables often became human habitations. Few of the middle classes experienced individual relationships with horses: they hired them to pull a carriage or saw them at the front of a tram. For many wealthy Dubliners, riding became a leisure activity for the countryside. In the city only working-class drivers continued to have relationships with individual horses. If a Dubliner decided to hire a horse he might quickly find himself looking ridiculous, such as when a writer in *The Diamond* chose one from 'a job establishment'. While he was consider-ing the question of 'do I look noble on horseback?' the horse stumbled and threw him. The writer resolved to always take the tram.[116]

Rather than banishing animals from the city, by the end of the nineteenth century they were increasingly lumped together in larger groups. They did not lose their importance, but many Dubliners, espe-cially middle-class Dubliners, probably lost sight of their individuality.

For sanitary reformers such as Cameron, the triumph of the modern city would be to disentangle the lives of humans from the messy busi-ness of keeping the animals needed to feed them. Consolidating those businesses into larger concerns was the first step towards separating human and animal spheres and a way to ensure that Ballymuckbeg did not come to pass. Cattle and pigs could become an undifferenti-ated herd as they were grouped into larger and larger businesses; there would be no sentiment for 'muck beg', the little pig. For tram promoters, the efficient harnessing of horse power and then mechani-cal power would slowly replace the chaotic assemblage of street vehi-cles. The horse was no longer the familiar animal in the stable, it was the stranger passing on the street.

Notes

1 W. Ridley Thacker [pseud. Edwin Hamilton], *Ballymuckbeg: A Tale of Eighty Years Hence* (Dublin: William McGee, 1884), p. 15.

2 Thacker, *Ballymuckbeg*, pp. 5, 8.

3 *Report of the Royal Commissioners Appointed to Inquire into the Sewerage and Drainage of the City of Dublin and Other Matters Connected Therewith, Together with Minutes of Evidence, Appendix, Index &c.* [C 2605] HC 1880, xxx, 1, minutes of evidence, 119 [Hereafter *Sewerage and Drainage Inquiry*].

4 *Municipal Boundaries Commission (Ireland) Part I. Evidence with Appendices. Dublin, Rathmines, Pembroke, Kilmainham, Drumcondra, Clontarf, and also Kingstown, Blackrock, and Dalkey* [C 2725] HC 1880, xxx, 327, p. 1 [Hereafter *Municipal Boundaries Commission*].

5 *A Pictorial and Descriptive Guide to Dublin and the Wicklow Tours* (London: Ward, Lock and Co., Ltd, *c.* 1900, 7th edn), p. ix.

6 See, for example, Royden Loewen, '"Come watch this spider": animals, Mennonites, and indices of modernity', *Canadian Historical Review*, 96:1 (2015), pp. 61–90. See also Paula Young Lee (ed.), *Meat, Modernity, and the Rise of the Slaughterhouse* (Durham: University of New Hampshire Press, 2008); and Anna Mazanik, '"Shiny shoes" for the city: the public abattoir and the reform of meat supply in imperial Moscow', *Urban History*, 45:2 (2017), 214–32.

7 See Clay McShane and Joel A. Tarr, *The Horse in the City: Living Machines in the Nineteenth Century* (Baltimore, MD: Johns Hopkins University Press, 2007), Epilogue.

8 Raghav Kishore, 'Urban "failures": municipal governance, planning and power in urban Delhi, 1863–1910', *Indian Social and Economic History Review*, 52:4 (2015), 439–61.

9 Scott A. Miltenberger, 'Viewing the anthrozootic city: humans, domesticated animals, and the making of early nineteenth-century New York', in Susan Nance (ed.), *The Historical Animal* (Syracuse, NY: Syracuse University Press, 2015), pp. 261–71: 263.

10 Olga Lockley, *Nannie Lambert Power O'Donoghue: A Biography* (Preston: The Bee Press, 2001), p. 50.

11 Mrs Power O'Donoghue, *Ladies on Horseback: Learning Park-riding, and Hunting, with Hints Upon Costume and Numerous Anecdotes* (London: W. H. Allen & Co., 1881), p. 5.

12 O'Donoghue, *Ladies on Horseback*, p. 26.

13 Mrs Power O'Donoghue, *Riding for Ladies: With Hints on the Stable* (London: W. Thacker & Co., 1887), p. 22.

14 O'Donoghue, *Ladies on Horseback*, p. 147.

15 Sandra Swart, *Riding High: Horses, Humans and History in South Africa* (Johannesburg: Wits University Press, 2010), p. 61, 72–6.

16 Joseph Lee, *The Modernisation of Irish Society: 1848 to 1918* (Dublin: Gill and Macmillan, 1973), pp. 38–9.

17 A native, *Recollections of Dublin Castle & of Dublin Society* (London: Chatto & Windus, 1902), p. 167.

18 Peter O'Brien and Georgina O'Brien, *The Reminiscences of the Right Hon. Lord O'Brien (of Kilfenora): Lord Chief Justice of Ireland* (New York: Longmans, 1916), p. 15.

19 O'Brien and O'Brien, *Reminiscences*, pp. 88, 97. See also Patrick Maume, 'O'Brien, Peter', in James McGuire and James Quinn (eds), *Dictionary of Irish Biography* (Cambridge: Cambridge University Press, 2009), https://dib-cambridge-org.dcu.idm.oclc.org/viewReadPage.do? articleId=a6492 (accessed 20 May 2020).

20 A native, *Recollections*, p. 82.

21 Guinness records of horses, GDB/DB02/0101, Ledger book, Forwarding Department, entry 31 March 1883, Guinness Brewery, Dublin [Hereafter Guinness Ledger Book].

22 Guinness Ledger Book; see quarterly accounts for feeding the horses totalling *c.* £1000; A. Barnard, *The Noted Breweries of Great Britain and Ireland* (London: Sir Joseph Causton and Sons, 1889), p. 41.

23 George Moore, *A Drama in Muslin: A Realistic Novel* (London, 1887), pp. 170–1.

24 *Municipal Boundaries Commission*, Minutes of evidence, evidence of Mr Walker, p. 105.

25 McShane and Tarr, *The Horse in the City*, pp. 178–9.

26 H. D. Richardson, *Horses, Their Varieties, Breeding and Management in Health and Disease* (Dublin: James McGlashan, 1848), p. v.

27 'The Horse Show', *Freeman's Journal* (26 August 1902).

28 See Andria Pooley-Ebert, 'Species agency: a comparative study of horse–human relationships in Chicago and rural Illinois', in Susan Nance (ed.), *The Historical Animal* (Syracuse, NY: Syracuse University Press, 2015), pp. 148–65.

29 *A Pictorial and Descriptive Guide*, p. 20.

30 F. M. L. Thompson, 'Nineteenth-century horse sense', *Economic History Review*, 29:1 (1976), 60–81.

31 *The Census of Ireland for the Year 1851. Part I. Showing the Area, Population, and Number of Houses, by Townlands and Electoral Divisions. County and City of Dublin* [1553] HC 1852–3, xli, 25; *Census of Ireland for the Year 1871. Part I., Area, Population and Number of Houses; Occupations, Religion and Education. Volume I. Province of Leinster* [C 662] HC 1872, lxvii, 1; *Census of Ireland, 1891. Part 1. Area, houses, and population: also the ages, civil or conjugal condition, occupations, birthplaces, religion and education of the people. Vol. I. Province of Leinster* [C 6515] HC 1890–1, xcv, 1; *Returns of Agricultural Produce in Ireland, in the Year 1871* [C 762]

HC 1873, lxix, 375; *Returns of Agricultural Produce in Ireland, in the Year 1891* [C 6777] HC 1892, lxxxviii, 285. The agricultural statistics for 1891 only record livestock by Poor Law Union, which encompassed a larger area than Dublin City.

32 McShane and Tarr, *The Horse in the City*.

33 Michael Corcoran, *Through Streets Broad and Narrow: A History of Dublin Trams* (Hersham: Ian Allan, 2008), p. 21.

34 *Report by the Commissioners Appointed to Inquire into the Horse Breeding Industry in Ireland* [C 8651] HC 1898, xxxiii, 261, Minutes of Evidence, Joseph O'Reilly, 21 [Hereafter *Horse Breeding Commission*].

35 *Horse Breeding Commission*, Minutes of Evidence, Joseph O'Reilly, 22.

36 *Horse Breeding Commission*, Minutes of Evidence, R. Hunter Pringle, 28.

37 Jim Cooke, 'John Hutton and Sons, Summerhill, Dublin, Coachbuilders, 1779–1925', *Dublin Historical Record*, 45:1 (1992), 11–27.

38 *Census of Ireland for the Year 1871*; note that 1871 is the only year in which the census categories for all three jurisdictions were the same and therefore the only year where direct comparisons can be made.

39 Ralph Turvey, 'Horse traction in Victorian London', *Journal of Transport History*, 26:2 (2005), 38–59.

40 Patrick J. Hartigan, 'James McKenny, Principal of the Royal Veterinary College Infirmary', *Irish Veterinary Journal*, 53:5 (2000), 251–8.

41 Patrick J. Hartigan, 'The Royal Veterinary College of Ireland: a veterinary school to flourish' in W. J. C. Donnelly and Michael L. Monaghan (eds), *A Veterinary School to Flourish: Veterinary College of Ireland, 1900–2000* (Dublin: Faculty of Veterinary Medicine, University College Dublin, 2001), pp. 18–37. On the development of veterinarians as professionals see Anne Hardy, 'Pioneers in the Victorian provinces: veterinarians, public health, and the urban animal economy', *Urban History*, 29:3 (2002), 372–87.

42 Census of Ireland for 1901. (Accessed online at www.census.national archives.ie, last accessed 15 May 2020).

43 Corcoran, *Through Streets Broad and Narrow*.

44 *Dignam's Dublin Guide with a Handy Map of the City Laid Down for a Stay of One or Four Days* (Dublin: Eason and Son, 1891), p. 7.

45 H. Saint-Thomas, *Paddy's Dream and John Bull's Nightmare: Notes During a 'Passionate Pilgrimage' Through the Sister Country* (trans. Emile Hatzfield) (London: G. Vickers, *c.* 1888), p. 14.

46 McShane and Tarr, *The Horse in the City*, pp. 64–5.

47 William L. Barrington, *Tramways in Dublin: A Letter Addressed to the Citizens* (Dublin: Richard D. Webb and Son, 1871), pp. 9–10.

48 Barrington, *Tramways*, pp. 14–15.

49 *Municipal Boundaries Commission*, Minutes of evidence, Evidence of D. C. Heron, QC for the Corporation, 1.

50 *Municipal Boundaries Commission*, Report, 10.
51 *Eaton's Pocket Railway Guide and Diary* (March 1887).
52 *Eaton's Pocket Railway Guide and Diary* (November 1884).
53 *Dublin United Tramways Time & Fare Tables* (November 1886).
54 See Susan Galavan, *Dublin's Bourgeois Homes: Building the Victorian Suburbs, 1850–1901* (London: Routledge, 2017), pp. 110–23.
55 *Municipal Boundaries Commission*, Report, 15.
56 *No 57 Report of the Paving and Lighting Committee on Reference of Municipal council of 3rd March, 1884, re Dublin, Swords, and Coolock Tramway, Cnclr Dennehy Jp, Chairman* (Dublin: Joseph Dollard, 1884), pp. 391–3.
57 Corcoran, *Through Streets Broad and Narrow*.
58 'Dublin Corporation and Electric Trams', *Irish Times* (4 March 1896).
59 'Speed of Electric Trams', *Irish Times* (20 March 1897); 'Grey Pony for Sale', *Freeman's Journal* (8 August 1898).
60 'Speed of Electric Trams', *Irish Times* (18 March 1897).
61 Pedestrians were run over by horse-drawn trams; see, for example, 'The fatal tramway accident', *Freeman's Journal* (1 November 1872). Electric trams also collided with cyclists and carriages, for example 'Serious accident on the electric tramway', *Freeman's Journal* (19 April 1897); 'Electric car and dray—collision on the Merrion Road', *Freeman's Journal* (26 September 1898).
62 *Report of the Public Health Committee RE Nuisance arising from the Discharge of Sewage into the River Liffey* (Dublin: Corporation of Dublin, 1884), no. 151, 404.
63 *Report of the Superintendent of Cleansing* (Dublin: Corporation of Dublin, 1882), vol. 2, no. 104, 103.
64 *Report of the Superintendent of Cleansing on the Condition of the Back Streets and Lanes of the City, caused by the Deposit of Refuse upon them, 22 February 1884* (Dublin: Corporation of Dublin, 1884).
65 *Sewerage and Drainage Inquiry*, minutes of evidence, George Alexander Stephens, North Dublin Poor Law Board of Guardians, 121.
66 McShane and Tarr, *The Horse in the City*.
67 Juliana Adelman, 'Contagious bovine pleuropneumonia, germs and public health in Dublin, 1862–1882', *Social History of Medicine*, 30:1 (2017), 71–91.
68 *Sewerage and Drainage Inquiry*, minutes of evidence, Charles R. C. Tichborne, chemistry lecturer in Carmichael School of Medicine, 135–6.
69 DC Reports 1900 vol. 1, No. 22 Report of the markets Committee. Recommending the establishment of a Horse Market or Fair in Smithfield, 307.
70 McShane and Tarr, *The Horse in the City*.
71 Frederic Pim, *A Sketch of Sanitary Progress in Dublin: Being an Address*

Delivered at the Annual General Meeting of the Dublin Sanitary Association, 12 March 1891 (Dublin: R. D. Webb & Son, 1891), p. 29.

72 *Returns of Agricultural Produce in Ireland, in the Year 1865* [3929] HC 1867, lxxi, 435; *Returns of Agricultural Produce in Ireland, in the Year 1870* [C 463] HC 1872, lxiii, 299; *Returns of Agricultural Produce in Ireland, in the Year 1875* [C 1568] HC 1876, lxxviii, 413; *Returns of Agricultural Produce in Ireland, in the Year 1880* [C 2932] HC 1881, xciii, 685.

73 *Report of the Committee Appointed for the Local Government Board for Ireland to inquire into the Public Health of the City of Dublin and Minutes of Evidence* [Cd 243] HC 1900, xxxix, 681, 707; Minutes of evidence, 48 [Hereafter *Public Health Inquiry*].

74 Liam Clare, 'The rise and demise of the Dublin cattle market', *Dublin Historical Record*, 55:2 (2002), 166–80.

75 *Sewerage and Drainage Inquiry*, Minutes of evidence, 170.

76 *Public Health Inquiry*, Minutes of evidence, 40.

77 *Sewerage and Drainage Inquiry*, Report, xxviii.

78 *Sewerage and Drainage Inquiry*, Minutes of evidence, Henry Hennessy, 109.

79 *Sewerage and Drainage Inquiry*, Minutes of evidence, 199.

80 *Sewerage and Drainage Inquiry*, Minutes of evidence.

81 Report by the Royal College of Physicians in Ireland and the Royal College of Surgeons in Ireland on excessive mortality, reprinted in *Minutes of the Municipal Council of the City of Dublin, from the 1st January to 31st December 1881* (Dublin: Corporation of Dublin, 1882), 106.

82 Report by the RCPI and RCSI on excessive mortality, 111.

83 C. F. Moore, *The Sanitary Condition of Dublin Dairy Yards* (Dublin, 1886), pp. 10, 12.

84 Moore, *Dublin Dairy Yards*, p. 3.

85 *Bye-laws Made Under the Public Health (Ireland) Act 1878* (Dublin: Corporation of Dublin, 1881), pp. 10–12.

86 Ignatius Rice, *Notes on the Law of Public Health in Dublin* (Dublin: Public Health Committee of the Corporation of Dublin, 1900), p. 30.

87 'The public abattoir', *Freeman's Journal* (12 April 1882).

88 'The Corporation and the victuallers', *Freeman's Journal* (20 June 1882).

89 'Private slaughterhouses and the health of the city', *Freeman's Journal* (16 May 1888).

90 'Sanitary association, franchise, taxation and public health', *Freeman's Journal* (18 March 1889).

91 Patrick Maume, 'Field, William', in McGuire and Quinn (eds), *Dictionary of Irish Biography*, https://dib-cambridge-org.dcu.idm.oclc.org/view ReadPage.do?articleId=a3075 (accessed 20 May 2020).

92 *Report of the Royal Commission Appointed to Inquire into the Administrative*

Procedures for Controlling Danger to Man Through the Use as Food of the Meat and Milk of Tuberculous Animals, Part II. Minutes of Evidence and Appendices [C 8831] HC 1898, xlix, 365, Evidence of W. Field, 18 [Hereafter *Commission on Tuberculous Animals*].

93 Daniel J. Tallerman, *'Railway Abattoirs' and Other Papers Relating to Meat Distribution* (Dublin: Browne and Nolan, 1891), p. 14.
94 Tallerman, *'Railway Abattoirs'*, p. 26.
95 Tallerman, *'Railway Abattoirs'*, p. 11.
96 *Public Health Inquiry*, Minutes of evidence, 27.
97 *Commission on Tuberculous Animals*, Evidence of Charles Cameron, 115.
98 *Commission on Tuberculous Animals*, Evidence of Charles Cameron, 117.
99 *Commission on Tuberculous Animals*, Evidence of Charles Cameron, 117.
100 C. S. Andrews, *Dublin Made Me* (Dublin: Lilliput Press, 2001), pp. 14–17.
101 Tallerman, *'Railway Abattoirs'*, p. 26.
102 *Commission on Tuberculous Animals*, Evidence of Charles Cameron, 116.
103 The predominant strain of bacteria that causes bovine tuberculosis is now recognised to be different than the strain that usually infects human lungs. Nonetheless it can pass between cattle and humans through infected meat and milk and also probably through the air.
104 See, for example, Keir Waddington, *The Bovine Scourge: Meat, Tuberculosis and Public Health, 1850–1914* (Woodbridge: The Boydell Press, 2006).
105 *Report of the Royal Commission Appointed to Inquire into the Administrative Procedures for Controlling Danger to Man Through the Use as Food of the Meat and Milk of Tuberculous Animals, Part I. Report* [C 8824] HC 1898, xlix, 333, report, 5.
106 Michael Worboys, *Spreading Germs: Disease Theories and Medical Practice in Britain, 1865–1900* (Cambridge: Cambridge University Press, 2000), esp. chapter 2; Martin Melosi, *The Sanitary City: Urban Infrastructure in America from Colonial Times to the Present* (Pittsburgh, PA: University of Pittsburgh Press, 2008), esp. chapters 2 and 3.
107 Worboys, *Spreading Germs*, chapter 2.
108 *Public Health Inquiry*, Report, 11.
109 *Public Health Inquiry*, Report, 26, 28, 40.
110 *Public Health Inquiry*, Report, 57–9.
111 *Public Health Inquiry 1900*, Minutes of evidence, p. 84.
112 *Public Health Inquiry 1900*, Minutes of evidence, p. 128–9.
113 *Public Health Inquiry 1900*, Minutes of evidence, p. 147.
114 *Commission on Tuberculous Animals*, Evidence of Charles Cameron, 117.
115 O'Donoghue, *Ladies on Horseback*, p. 215.
116 '"Lightning" and I', *The Diamond*, 4 (24 March 1883), 30–1.

Epilogue

Some people think that you shouldn't be here, that it's not suitable for the city. But if you know nothing else what can you do about it? Raising pigs now in the city is outdated, like keeping chickens and hens. But I spent me life in it. I'm just seeing an old thing out, you know?[1]

In 1991 Jimmy Riley, pig raiser, explained to Kevin C. Kearns that 'the Corporation want piggeries out of Dublin'. From a multigenerational family of pig keepers, Riley recognised that urban pig-keeping had become 'outdated' but he could imagine no other career for himself. Almost 150 years after the Corporation passed the first bye-laws restricting animal-keeping, the city still contained substantial numbers of animals and people such as Riley 'seeing an old thing out'.

This book has shown how ideas about animals and their place in the city changed over the course of the nineteenth century with significant impacts for Dublin's human and animal residents. Each of the chapters explored how Dubliners began to identify some animals as 'not suitable' and some ways of exploiting them as 'outdated'. In particular, middle-class reformers targeted those who kept a small number of animals in circumstances that they increasingly viewed as detrimental to the public's health or challenging to public order. We have seen how ideas about the control of animals, and their proper treatment, were entangled with ideas about class and thus how new regulations often affected social groups differently. The trend during the century was for middle-class reformers to seek fewer food animals within the city boundaries as well as greater restrictions on how all animals were kept and treated, including pets. Dublin Corporation and the Dublin Metropolitan Police helped to implement these new ideas, creating and enforcing rules that changed ordinary life in the city. These regulations affected social and economic geography, especially by keeping undesirable animals and animal businesses confined to particular areas. It should be no surprise that Jimmy Riley's pig yard was in the north inner city, not far from the Dublin Cattle Market.

By the start of the twentieth century a new animal city had emerged in Dublin, one where dogs could not roam the streets without risking imprisonment and death, where pigs could be reared only in large piggeries, where dairy cows and private slaughtermen were being consolidated or pushed to the periphery and where horses were (slowly) being replaced by machines.

This book has shown that human responses to different types of urban animals played an important role in shaping modern urban life including laws, policing, geography, transportation and culture. The stories of entangled human and animal lives in the city show that there was no inevitable progress towards a city devoid of all domestic animals aside from pets. I have also tried to suggest that ideas of improvement were themselves contentious and require scrutiny; they were often linked to increasing the power of particular social groups over others by controlling their ability to exploit animals.

Although I have not explicitly engaged in the debates over animal agency, I believe I have demonstrated one way in which animals should be considered historical actors. Without reference to ethology or the need to imagine the perspective of an animal, it is clear that animals participate in setting some of the parameters of human history. Our control and consumption of animals has provided us with great advantages and also forced us to deal with constraints and consequences.[2] A society that wishes to consume cattle as food or view exotic animal spectacles must operate differently than one that has no such desire. The impact does not end with agriculture and economy; it extends to ideas about health and morality, the social relationships between classes and the development of political ideas. We have truly been civilised by our continued efforts to understand and shape our relationships to beasts.

Dublin by the end of the nineteenth century had its own unique form of what Keith Thomas called 'compromise and concealment' that allowed the city to continue exploiting animals while reducing their visibility and impact for certain groups. The 'old thing' that Riley was seeing out was not animals in the city per se, but specific animals found in particular places. In modern inner-city Dublin, pigs and cattle no longer had a place and the human livelihoods that went with them also disappeared into the countryside. Yet change was slow, difficult and partial. Actually removing animals from the city proved a much more difficult task than thinking new thoughts or writing new bye-laws. In addition to piggeries, Dublin contained at least thirty private slaughterhouses in 1981. Laws created during the nineteenth century actually appeared to prevent the city from removing them.[3] The Dublin Cattle Market remained until 1971, but, as of 2020, only a few horses, abundant pets and the zoo's exotic residents retain any kind of welcome in the city civilised by beasts.

A brief look at the fates of the Dublin Zoological Gardens and the Dublin Cattle Market during the twentieth century can help us to see how efforts to resolve the human dilemma during the nineteenth century have continued to shape the city. Their longevity and, in the case of the cattle market, eventual demise, express eloquently the complexity and 'hybridity' of Dublin and the ways that the exploitation of animals for a variety of purposes has affected urban change.[4]

The Dublin Zoo (as it is now called) remains one of the most popular attractions in the city with over one million visitors per year.[5] During the turbulent years of the Irish Revolution and the early years of Irish independence, the zoo faced the challenge of gaining the support of the emergent state. Given the significant British imperial connections of both the Zoological Society and the Gardens, this was no small task. The stocking of the gardens relied on these imperial connections while the principal sources of income for the zoo included an annual grant by the British parliament and the breeding of lions, symbols of the British Empire.[6] Yet the gardens quickly entwined themselves with the new state. A cash-strapped government continued the grant to the gardens and the Zoological Society proved adept at negotiating the new political situation. Parties and fundraisers helped to keep it going, but mostly the zoo was sustained by the continued enthusiasm of Irish people for visiting it.[7] Hundreds of thousands of visitors passed through the zoo's gates each year, rising to almost half a million by 1970.[8] More than a hundred years after its foundation, people still enjoyed the experience of looking at animals. The zoo's distinctly imperial flavour did not prevent it from becoming a Dublin institution. As many other scholars have discussed, the presentation of what a zoo is for has changed in the recent past alongside conditions for the animals and methods of collecting them. Yet zoos continue to be designed 'for the pleasure of the public'.[9] The zoo's persistence in Dublin represents acceptance of a particular form of animal exploitation. While zoo visitors would probably object to the opening of a slaughterhouse or a cattle market on their street, most are untroubled by the collection and display of 'wild beasts'.

The ways that the Dublin Zoo connected the city to the world are less visible but no less persistent. The zoo could not exist without an international network of zoos that help to supply animals as well as expertise. The zoo is a destination for international tourists and locals alike. Thousands of Irish children have their first encounter with exotic beasts there every year. Yet the impact for Dubliners over the centuries has been less than for the zoo's animal residents, many of whom have lived their entire lives in captivity. In the zoo we continue to display our acceptance of a certain variety of human ascendancy over animals by paying an entrance fee to see 'wild' animals exhibited in enclosures that, although better than cages, still have humans keeping the doors closed.

Whitley Stokes would probably be delighted to see the thriving success of his zoological project. The Dublin Cattle Market met a different fate to the zoo and has also had, perhaps, a more significant impact on ordinary city life. Despite its economic importance, the cattle market projected an image of Dublin that fewer people endorsed as the twentieth century wore on. While the leaders of the Free State and the Irish Republic may have viewed rural Ireland as 'real' Ireland, they did have ideas about urban modernity and a considerable amount of attention was paid to transforming Dublin into a suitable capital. New civic buildings, new housing developments and new streets expressed optimism (and sometimes nothing much more tangible than that) about the future of the state and its ability to care for its people.[10] Groups with different views about urban space debated the legacy and future of the city's Georgian squares, with some arguing that their association with the Anglo-Irish Protestant Ascendancy meant they should be destroyed.[11] For a while, the Dublin Cattle Market retained its place in this changing urban landscape just as the livestock trade retained its place at the heart of the Irish economy.

Irish political independence did not prevent most of Ireland's exported livestock from travelling to Britain.[12] Export of animals and animal products continues to be an important branch of Irish economic activity, but new ways of selling in 'marts' outside the city took over the trade from the middle of the twentieth century. In the end, the market collapsed not because of public health concerns (although those were significant, alongside outbreaks of animal disease) or because people no longer wanted to see a cattle market in an urban environment (although many did not). The market collapsed because people began buying their cattle elsewhere. The 'new' Dublin Cattle Market went into decline during the 1950s and closed in 1971, ending an ancient tradition of the city as an important sales point for livestock.[13] One way in which Dubliners experienced rural Ireland and the country's dependence upon agriculture has disappeared.

Yet the cattle market and the specific form of animal exploitation that it represents had an enormous impact on the city. Acts of compromise and concealment begun in the nineteenth century have left permanent marks. Jimmy Riley was still rearing pigs at least in part because the Corporation had decided in the 1860s to retain the Dublin Cattle Market within the city. This enmeshed Dublin in Ireland's economic dependence upon the export of live cattle, a dependence that continued into the twentieth century. The cattle and pigs of Arran Quay Ward represented enough wealth, power and opportunity to outweigh their potential threats to public health. Cattlemen and pig keepers were voters and beneficiaries of the political power of the shopocracy and its advocacy for non-interference in private business.[14] Nonetheless, the framework through which Jimmy Riley and his pigs would vanish from urban life had slowly and painfully been put together during the nineteenth century. Laws, practices, daily lives all began to shift towards new ideas about what a civilised, modern city should be.

When the market closed in 1971 the public abattoir swiftly followed and both sites were redeveloped as large tracts of public housing. The old cattle market in Smithfield Square has not been so successfully erased. In 1997, architects vied for the contract to transform the square. Perhaps they were sympathetic to the square's legacy or perhaps they could not see beyond its existing form, but the redevelopment left a large cobbled rectangle while changing the buildings that surround it. Apartments, offices, shops, restaurants, a hotel and a cinema flank a marketless square that now looks as anachronistic as Jimmy Riley's urban pig yard.

Yet Smithfield Square is still a place where human–animal relationships are negotiated. The biannual horse fair is often presented as a clash between tradition and urban modernisation. Many residents of the regenerated area view the horse fair as a dirty, smelly, violent, unregulated throng. Despite police presence, a shooting at the fair in 2011 reinforced the image of the fair as violent, while the Dublin Society for the Prevention of Cruelty to Animals has accused traders of cruelty. The Dublin City Council complains of the cost of cleaning up horse manure. Supporters of the fair say they are preserving 'one of the last few bits of culture we have left'. For visitors, the horse fair provides 'a glimpse of the older piebald Ireland fast receding into myth'. The line between tradition and modernisation, between a city with animals and one without, is also a line between classes. Some city councillors have accused their colleagues of using the fair to crack down on working-class culture. By trying to close the fair, one writer argued, the city council sought to replace authentic Dublin with 'a generic modern European city'.[15]

Whitley Stokes may have told a historical fantasy about the origins of urban life when he claimed that man had been civilised by efforts to evade beasts, but he expressed at least a partial truth about what many humans in the Western world expect from cities. The Dublin Zoo, marketless Smithfield and the public housing that covers the site of the Dublin Cattle Market all remind us of the continued importance of the city as a place where people try to erect walls between human and animal and to define culture as a sphere separated from nature.

* * *

Has something been lost in this reimagining of city space? Reformers of nineteenth-century Dublin such as John Aldridge and Charles Cameron might rejoice if they saw the improvements to human lives that urban change has brought. Dublin's streets are largely free of animal manure, there is no sign of a slaughterhouse and our own wastes from eating meat are flushed away in a hidden network of sewers we take for granted. However, not everyone is convinced that the system of agriculture sustaining our cities has been an improvement for either people or animals. According to Juliet Clutton-Brock,

> it is inevitable that once the number of animals owned becomes large, say in the thousands, their individual identities are lost. This has been the inevitable result of industrial farming in the modern world where the vast numbers of domestic animals, required to feed the

ever-increasing human population, are treated as inanimate vegetables, all bred to look identical and reared in rows of cages, to be
harvested when required. Considering the cruelty this inflicts on the
animals, it is ironic that in western societies we seem to be on a parallel
course, incarcerating ourselves in batteries of small clean buildings,
protected from physical threats, and with a greatly reduced perception
of the living world and its other inhabitants.[16]

Aldridge and Cameron had devoted their lives to creating a city of
humans living in 'small clean buildings', separated from the animals
required to feed them. Reformers of the nineteenth century held that
large, consolidated animal businesses would make them better and
safer for humans. Have we now bleakly arrived at a place where the
city is imitating the battery chicken farm? This is certainly not what
Stokes had in mind when he suggested we had been civilised by beasts.

I am less pessimistic for our future than Clutton-Brock, but if
humans are to survive the next century we must be reminded of our
reliance on 'the living world and its other inhabitants'. The idea of
human ascendancy over animals that Stokes and his contemporaries
felt to be so obvious has occasioned ever greater doubt and debate. We
have not resolved the human dilemma; we continue to exploit animals
and to shy away from experiencing either the process or the effects of
that exploitation. We haven't seen an 'old thing' out; we have moved it
to another location where we don't have to see it at all. Nonetheless, I
hope this book has provided a reminder of our reliance on animals by
showing how important they have been to shaping even those places
that seem at first glimpse to be man-made.

Notes

1 Kevin C. Kearns, *Dublin Street Life and Lore* (Dun Laoghaire: Glendale,
   1991), pp. 61–2.
2 A similar approach, rooted in Bruno Latour's work, is advocated by
   Thomas Almeroth-Williams, *City of Beasts: How Animals Shaped Georgian
   London* (Manchester: Manchester University Press, 2019), p. 9.
3 For complaints arising after the closure of the abattoir, see, for example,
   Tony Hennigan, 'The slaughter that sickens city residents', *Irish
   Independent* (24 July 1981).
4 David Dickson, *Dublin: The Making of a Capital City* (London: Profile Books,
   2014), p. x.
5 As estimated on their website. See https://www.dublinzoo.ie/about/
   (accessed 15 May 2020).

6 Juliana Adelman, 'Second city of science? Dublin *c.* 1880–1900', in Oliver Hochadel and Augustí Nieto-Galan (eds), *Urban Histories of Science* (London: Routledge, 2019), pp. 122–40.

7 See Catherine De Courcy, *Dublin Zoo: An Illustrated History* (Cork: The Collins Press, 2009), pp. 119–25, 161–3.

8 'Dublin Zoo', *Irish Independent* (2 February 1970).

9 On the contemporary zoo and its many meanings see David Hancocks, 'Zoo animals as entertainment exhibitions', in Randy Malamud (ed.), *A Cultural History of Animals in the Modern Age* (Oxford: Berg, 2007), pp. 95–118; Nigel Rothfels, 'Immersed with animals', in Nigel Rothfels (ed.), *Representing Animals* (Indianapolis: Indiana University Press, 2002), pp. 199–224.

10 Yvonne Whelan, *Reinventing Modern Dublin: Streetscapes, Iconography and the Politics of Identity* (Dublin: University College Dublin Press, 2003).

11 Erika Hanna, *Modern Dublin: Urban Change and the Irish Past, 1957–1973* (Oxford: Oxford University Press, 2013).

12 See Paul Rouse, 'The farmers since 1850', in Eugenio F. Biagini and Mary E. Daly (eds), *The Cambridge Social History of Modern Ireland* (Cambridge: Cambridge University Press, 2017), pp. 129–44.

13 Liam Clare, 'The rise and demise of the Dublin cattle market', *Dublin Historical Record*, 55:2 (2002), 166–80.

14 The term 'shopocracy' is Dickson's.

15 Ed O'Loughlin, 'Gentrified Dublin tries to reign in horse fair and 273 years of tradition', *Independent*, 4 June 2002.

16 Juliet Clutton-Brock, 'The unnatural world: behavioural aspects of humans and animals in the process of domestication', in Aubrey Manning and James Serpell (eds), *Animals and Human Society: Changing Perspectives* (London: Routledge, 1994), pp. 25–35: 34.

Bibliography

Manuscripts

Dublin City Library and Archive

C2/A1: Manuscript minute books of the Dublin Corporation, Municipal Council, volumes 14 through 26.
PHC/MINS: Manuscript minute books of the Dublin Corporation 'Committee No. 2' and later 'Public Health Committee', volumes 2 through 10.

Dublin Society for the Prevention of Cruelty to Animals

Manuscript minute books and ephemera, uncatalogued.

Guinness Brewery

GDB/DB02/0101: Ledger book, Forwarding Department.

Irish Traditional Music Archive (online)

18123-BS: 'Dublin Jack of All Trades', traditional ballad, nineteenth century, Lesley Shephard Collection.

National Archives of Ireland

Criminal Index, volume for 1867 to 1870.
CSPS/3/037: Petty Sessions Order Books.

National Gallery of Ireland

Walter Osborne papers: photographs of Dublin, three sketchbooks including drawings of animals.

National Library of Ireland

ETC 118: View of the Post Office and Nelson's Pillar, Samuel Brocas, *c.* 1820.

L CAB 04760: Photograph of trams in Sackville Street from the Lawrence Photographic Collection.

L ROY 08910: Photograph of the Dublin Cattle Market, Lawrence Photographic Collection.

MS 256: 'On the hog and horse', folio 55–6, n.d., *c.* 1840s.

MS 5159: Collection of broadside ballads. (88), 'A new song on the saucy dogs of Ireland'.

MS 7588: Thomas Larcom papers. Misc. newscuttings including those relating to the dog tax bill.

MS 7748: Thomas Larcom papers, newscuttings relating to cattle plague.

MS 11241: Mayo Papers, correspondence with Lord Naas (Richard Bourke, Chief Secretary of Ireland, later Earl of Mayo), on matters related to cattle plague.

MS 21017: John Hutton and Sons, 'Estimate of a new chariot for —— Baker Esq', 17 May 1822.

MS 23573: Lodge Park Stock Book.

MS 32633/1: Anonymous diary of a young man in Dublin, *c.* 1836–37.

MS 32633/2: Anonymous diary of a young woman in Dublin, *c.* 1836–37.

NPA TRAM134: Photograph of trams in front of Trinity College Dublin.

PD 2125 TX 2: Brocas collection, drawing inscribed 'Contrast the poor man's pig', by J. H. Brocas.

PD 3086 TX: Collection of prints, 'Sketches of Irish Character, from life, by Capt Robert Williams', London.

PD 3086 TX 5 (8): Print entitled 'Crinoline in Dublin'/Phoenix Park *c.* 1850, Hanton & Conway.

Royal College of Physicians of Ireland

ACC/2013/6, Thomas Fitzpatrick Cartoons.
TF/2 Cartoon 219, In Loving Memory of Bull Alley.
TF/3 Cartoon 222, Registered Dairy.
TF/4 Cartoon 264, Highest Death Rates in Europe.

Royal Society for the Prevention of Cruelty to Animals, Horsham, England

Manuscript minute books of the RSPCA Council, volumes 1 to 5.
Photostat copies of letters to the Dublin Society for the Prevention of Cruelty to Animals.
Printed reports of the RSPCA.

Trinity College Dublin

MS 5176–84: Philip Crampton Papers, Letters from Philip Crampton to John Crampton.

MS 10608/2: Royal Zoological Society of Ireland, rough minutes 1830 to 1840.

MS 10608/9: Royal Zoological Society of Ireland, transaction books.

MS 10608/24/1: Royal Zoological Society of Ireland, ephemera collection.

MS 10609/16/1: Royal Zoological Society of Ireland, weekly returns book.

MS 10800: Diary of James Christopher Kenny.

Periodicals

British Medical Journal
Dublin Builder
Dublin Literary Journal and Select Family Visitor
Dublin Medical Press
Dublin Mercantile Advertiser
Dublin Penny Journal
Dublin Quarterly Journal of Medical Science
Dublin University Magazine
Duffy's Hibernian Magazine
Freeman's Journal
The Graphic
Irish Builder
Irish Farmer's Gazette
Illustrated London News
Irish Monthly
The Irish Naturalist
Irish Penny Journal
The Irish Sportsman
Irish Times
Journal of the Statistical and Social Inquiry Society of Ireland
The Nation
Paddy Kelly's Budget
The Penny Satirist
Salmagundi
Saunder's Newsletter
Zoz

Other printed primary sources

Anonymous or corporate authors

Anon., A native, *Recollections of Dublin Castle & of Dublin Society* (London: Chatto & Windus, 1902).

Anon., A veterinarian, *The Cattle Keeper's Guide; or, Complete Directory for the Choice Management of Cattle, Including Horses, Oxen, Cows, Calves, Sheep, Lambs, Hogs &c. With a Description of the Symptoms and Most Approved Methods of Curing Every Disorder They are Subject to* (London: Joseph and W. H. Bailey, n.d.).

Anon. [Francis M. Jennings], *The Present and Future of Ireland as the Cattle Farm of England and Her Probable Population* (Dublin: Hodges and Smith, 1865).

A Pictorial and Descriptive Guide to Dublin and the Wicklow Tours (London: Ward, Lock and Co., Ltd, *c.* 1900, 7th edn).

Bye-laws Made Under the Public Health (Ireland) Act 1878 (Dublin: Corporation of Dublin, 1881).

[Central Relief Committee], *Transactions of the Central Relief Committee of the Society of Friends During the Famine in Ireland in 1846 and 1847* (Dublin: Hodges and Smith, 1852).

Dignam's Dublin Guide with a Handy Map of the City Laid Down for a Stay of One or Four Days (Dublin: Eason and Son, 1891).

Dublin Almanac and General Register of Ireland for the Year of Our Lord 1843 (Dublin: Pettigrew and Oulton, 1843).

[Dublin Corporation], 'Corporation of Dublin. Public Health Committee. Annual Return of Sanitary [Dublin Corporation], Operations for the year ending March 31st, 1874', *Reports and Printed Documents of the Corporation of Dublin … 1874* (Dublin: Joseph Pollard, 1875).

[Dublin Corporation], *Reports and Printed Documents of the Corporation of Dublin … 1875*, (Dublin: Joseph Pollard, 1875).

[Dublin Corporation], 'Corporation of Dublin Public Health Committee', *Reports and Printed Documents of the Corporation of Dublin … 1875* (Dublin: Joseph Pollard, 1876).

[Dublin Corporation], *Reports and Printed Documents of the Corporation of Dublin … 1880*, (Dublin: Joseph Pollard, 1880).

[Dublin Corporation], 'Report by the Royal College of Physicians in Ireland and the Royal College of Surgeons in Ireland on excessive mortality', reprinted in *Minutes of the Municipal Council of the City of Dublin, from the 1st January to 31st December 1881* (Dublin: Corporation of Dublin, 1882).

[Dublin Corporation], *Report of the Superintendent of Cleansing* (Dublin: Corporation of Dublin, 1882, vol. 2), no. 104, 103.

[Dublin Corporation], *Minutes of the Municipal Council of the City of Dublin …* *1883* (Dublin: Corporation of Dublin, 1884).

[Dublin Corporation], *Report of the Superintendent of Cleansing on the Condition of the Back Streets and Lanes of the City, Caused by the Deposit of Refuse Upon Them, 22 Feb 1884* (Dublin: Corporation of Dublin, 1884).

[Dublin Corporation], *Report of the Paving and Lighting Committee on Reference of Municipal Council of 3rd March, 1884, re Dublin, Swords, and Coolock Tramway, Cnclr Dennehy Jp, Chairman* (Dublin: Joseph Dollard, 1884).

[Dublin Corporation], *Report of the Public Health Committee RE Nuisance Arising from the Discharge of Sewage into the River Liffey* (Dublin: Corporation of Dublin, 1884), no. 151, 404.

[Dublin Sanatory Association], *Report of the Transactions of the Dublin Sanatory* [sic] *Association, from the 4th June, 1848 to 30th April, 1849* (Dublin: James McGlashan, 1849).

[Dublin Sanatory Association], *Public Health Bill for Ireland: Report of the Dublin Sanatory* [sic] *Association on the Public Health Bill, and on the Nuisance Removal and Disease Prevention Act* (Dublin: James McGlashan, 1850).

[Dublin Sanitary Association], *Report of the Working Committee of the Dublin Sanitary Association to the General Meeting, held June 11th, 1873 …* (Dublin: J. Atkinson & Co., 1873).

The Dublin Songster (Glasgow: John S. Marr, n.d., *c.* 1846).

Dublin United Tramways Time & Fare Tables (November 1886).

Eaton's Pocket Railway Guide and Diary (November 1884).

Eaton's Pocket Railway Guide and Diary (March 1887).

[General Relief Committee], *Report and Proceedings of the General Relief Committee of the Royal Exchange from the 3rd of May to the 3rd of September, 1849* (Dublin: G. O'Shea, 1849).

Instruction Book for Supernumeraries, Kevin-Street Depot (Dublin: Alexander Thom, 1870).

The Irish Comic Song Book (Dublin: J. Harding, n.d.).

[Mendicity Association], *Twenty-ninth Annual Report of the Managing Committee of the Association for the Suppression of Mendicity in Dublin: For the Year 1846* (Dublin: printed for the Mendicity Association, by Shea and Co., 1847).

[Royal Dublin Society], *Classification of Black Cattle, Sheep, Swine, Horses, Poultry, Farm Implements, etc. etc. Entered for Competition at the Cattle Shew* [sic] *to be Held on the Premises of the Royal Dublin Society on Tuesday, the 6th, Wednesday, the 7th, and Thursday, the 8th April, 1847* (Dublin: M.H. Gill, 1847).

[Royal Dublin Society], *Classification of Black Cattle, Sheep, Swine, Horses, Poultry, Farm Implements, etc. etc. Entered for Competition at the Cattle Shew* [sic] *to be Held on the Premises of the Royal Dublin Society on Tuesday, the*

17th, Wednesday, the 18th, and Thursday, the 19th April, 1849 (Dublin: M.H. Gill, 1849).

Royal Society for the Prevention of Cruelty to Animals, 11th Annual Report, with the Proceedings of the Annual General Meeting (London: The Philanthropic Society, 1837).

Royal Zoological Society of Ireland, *Proceedings of the Society as Reported in Saunder's News-letter, The Dublin Evening Post and The Freeman's Journal, 1840–1860* (Dublin: The Council of the Society, 1908).

Thom's Irish Almanac and Official Directory for the Year 1846 (Dublin: Alexander Thom, 1846).

Thom's Irish Almanac and Official Directory for the Year 1865 (Dublin: Alexander Thom, 1865).

Thom's Irish Almanac and Official Directory for the Year 1875 (Dublin: Alexander Thom, 1875).

Thom's Irish Almanac and Official Directory, with the Post Office Dublin City and County Directory, for the Year 1853 (Dublin: Alexander Thom, 1853).

Thom's Irish Almanac and Official Directory, with the Post Office Dublin City and County Directory, for the Year 1855 (Dublin: Alexander Thom, 1855).

Thom's Irish Almanac and Official Directory, with the Post Office Dublin City and County Directory, for the Year 1863 (Dublin: Alexander Thom, 1863).

The Zoological Society of Dublin, List of Members &c. (Dublin: Joshua Porter, 1837).

Individual authors

Aldridge, John, *The Present State of Vegetable Physiology* (Dublin: Hodges and Smith, 1848).

——. *Review of the Sanitary Condition of Dublin* (Dublin: Hodges and Smith, 1847).

Andrews, C. S., *Dublin Made Me* (Dublin: Lilliput Press, 2001).

Antisell, Thomas, *Suggestions Towards the Improvement of the Sanatory [sic] Condition of the Metropolis* (Dublin: James McGlashan, 1847).

Barnard, A., *The Noted Breweries of Great Britain and Ireland* (London: Sir Joseph Causton and Sons, 1889).

Barrington, William L., *Tramways in Dublin: A Letter Address to the Citizens* (Dublin: Richard D. Webb and Son, 1871).

Bradburne, S. Tudor, *City of Dublin Election, July 15th, 1865. Candidates: John Vance Esq., D. L.; Benjamin Lee Guinness, Esq. D. L., L. L. D.; and Jonathan Pim, Esq. List of Electors for the Year 1865, Distinguishing the Names of Those Who Exercised their Franchise at the Above Election, and Showing for Whom they Voted* (Dublin: J. Atkinson, 1865).

Butt, Isaac, *Zoology and Civilization* (Dublin: James McGlashan, 1847).

——. *Irish Life: In the Castle, the Courts, and the Country* (London: How and Parsons, 3 vols, 1840), vol. 1.

Byrne, Patrick, *An Evening in the Green Hills; Or the Complaint of the Dogs on Taxation* (Dublin: J. F. Fowler, 1869).

Cahill, Michael, *Remarks on the Present State of the Cattle Market of Dublin, with Suggestions for the Improvement of Smithfield, and the Erection of a General Abattoir and Carcase Market. With a Map &c.* (Dublin: Hodges, Smith & Co., 1861).

Cameron, Charles, *How the Poor Live* (Dublin: J. Falconer, 1904).

——. *Annual Report of the Medical Officer of Health for the Dublin Corporation ... 1871.*

Carleton, William, *Traits and Stories of the Irish Peasantry, Second Series* (Dublin: William F. Wakeman, 1833), vol. 1.

Carlyle, Thomas, *Reminiscences of My Irish Journey in 1849* (New York: Harper & Brothers, 1882).

Chadwick, Edwin, *Report on the Sanitary Condition of the Labouring Population of Great Britain* (Contained within *Report to Her Majesty's Principal Secretary of State for the Home Department from the Poor Law Commissioners, on an Inquiry into the Sanitary Condition of the Labouring Population of Great Britain, with Appendices* [London: Her Majesty's Stationery Office, 1842]).

Coyne, J. Stirling (drawings by W. H. Bartlett), *The Scenery and Antiquities of Ireland* (London: Mercury Books, 2003 [original publication 1842]).

Cunningham, D. J., *The Origin and Early History of the Royal Zoological Society of Ireland* (Dublin: The Council of the Society, 1901).

Elly, Sandham, *Potatoes, Pigs, and Politics: The Curse of Ireland the Cause of England's Embarrassments* (London: Kent and Richards, 1848).

Foot, Arthur Wynne, *Guide to the Royal Zoological Gardens, Phoenix Park* (Dublin, n.d. [1865], 2nd edn).

Gibson, William, *Rambles in Europe in 1839: With Sketches of Prominent Surgeons, Physicians, Medical Schools, Hospitals, Literary Personages, Scenery &c.* (Philadelphia, PA: Lea and Blanchard, 1841).

Hall, Fanny W., *Rambles in Europe; Or a Tour Through France, Italy, Switzerland, Great Britain and Ireland in 1836* (New York: E. French, 1839, 2 vols), vol. 2.

Hamilton, William Tighe, *A Descriptive Catalogue of the Animals in the Collections of the Zoological Society of Dublin* (Dublin: Hodges and Smith, 1833).

Hancock, William Nielson, *Report on the Importation of Cattle into Ireland: in the Year Ended 16 August 1865* (Dublin: Alexander Thom, 1865).

Hardy, Philip Dixon, *A Visit to the Zoological Gardens, Phoenix Park, Dublin* (Dublin: P. D. Hardy, 1838).

Haughton, Samuel, *Memoir of James Haughton with Extracts from his Private and Published Letters by His Son Samuel Haughton* (Dublin: E. Ponsonby, 1877).

Hogan, William, *The Dependence of National Wealth on the Social and Sanitary Condition of the Labouring Classes: On the Necessity for Model Lodging Houses in Dublin and the Advantages They Would Confer on the Community* (Dublin: Hodges and Smith, 1849).

Inglis, Henry D., *A Journey Throughout Ireland: During the Spring, Summer and Autumn of 1834* (London: Whittaker & Co., 1835).

Lane, Charles Henry, *Dog Shows and Doggy-People* (London: Hutchinson, 1902).

Maberly, Mrs, *The Present State of Ireland and its Remedy* (London: James Ridgway, 1847).

Mapother, Edward Dillon, *The Body and its Health: A Book for Primary Schools* (Dublin: Falconer, 1870).

Milburn, Matthew, *The Cow: Dairy Husbandry and Cattle Breeding* (London: W. S. Orr, 1851).

Moore, C. F., *The Sanitary Condition of Dublin Dairy Yards* (Dublin: Falconer, 1886).

Moore, George, *A Drama in Muslin: A Realistic Novel* (London: Vizetelly & Co., 1886).

O'Brien, Peter and Georgina O'Brien, *The Reminiscences of the Right Hon. Lord O'Brien (of Kilfenora): Lord Chief Justice of Ireland* (New York: Longmans, 1916).

O'Donoghue, Mrs Nannie Power, *Riding for Ladies: With Hints on the Stable* (London: W. Thacker & Co., 1887).

———. *Ladies on Horseback: Learning, Park-riding, and Hunting, with Hints Upon Costume and Numerous Anecdotes* (London: W. H. Allen & Co., 1881).

Pim, Frederic, *A Sketch of Sanitary Progress in Dublin: Being an Address Delivered at the Annual General Meeting of the Dublin Sanitary Association, 12 March 1891* (Dublin: R. D. Webb & Son, 1891).

Porter, Frank Thorpe, *Twenty-Years Recollections of an Irish Police Magistrate* (Dublin: Hodges, Foster, and Figgis, 1880).

Rice, Ignatius, *Notes on the Law of Public Health in Dublin* (Dublin: Public Health Committee of the Corporation of Dublin, 1900).

Richardson, H. D., *The Pig* (Dublin: James McGlashan, 1852).

———. *Horses, Their Varieties, Breeding and Management in Health and Disease* (Dublin: James McGlashan, 1848).

Saint-Thomas, H., *Paddy's Dream and John Bull's Nightmare: Notes During a 'Passionate Pilgrimage' Through the Sister Country* (trans. Emile Hatzfield) (London: G. Vickers, *c.* 1888).

Scharff, Robert, 'On the breeds of dog peculiar to Ireland and their origin (Conclusion)', *Irish Naturalist*, 33:9 (1924), 89–95.

Sidney, Samuel, *The Pig* (London: George Routledge & Sons, 1897).

Stoddart, Rev. George H., *The True Cure for Ireland, the Development of Her Industry; Being a Letter Addressed to the Rt. Hon. Lord John Russell, MP &c&c&c* (London: Trelawney W. Saunders, 1847).

Tallerman, Daniel J., *'Railway Abattoirs' and Other Papers Relating to Meat Distribution* (Dublin: Browne and Nolan, 1891).

Thacker, W. Ridley [pseud. Edwin Hamilton], *Ballymuckbeg: A Tale of Eighty Years Hence* (Dublin: William McGee, 1884).

Urwick, William, *Life and Letters of William Urwick, D.D. of Dublin, Edited by his Son* (London: Hodder and Stoughton, 1870).

Vanston, George T. B., *The Law of Public Health in Ireland: Being the Public Health (Ireland) Act, 1878, and Amending Acts, and Other Statutes Affecting Sanitary Authorities* (Dublin: E. Ponsonby, 1892).

West, Mrs Frederick, *A Summer Visit to Ireland in 1846* (London: Richard Bentley, 1847).

Whately, Richard, *On Instinct: A Lecture* (Dublin: James M'Glashan, 1847).

Whittock, Nathaniel, *A Picturesque Guide Through Dublin* (London: J. Cornish, 1846).

Government publications

Agricultural statistics

Returns of Agricultural Produce in Ireland, in the Year 1847. Part II. Stock [1000] HC 1847–1848, lvii, 109.

Returns of Agricultural Produce in Ireland, in the Year 1848 [1116] HC 1849, xlix, 1.

Returns of Agricultural Produce in Ireland, in the Year 1849 [1245], HC 1850, li, 39.

Returns of Agricultural Produce in Ireland, in the Year 1850 [1404], HC 1851, l, 1.

Returns of Agricultural Produce in Ireland, in the Year 1855 [2174] HC 1857, xv, 81.

Returns of Agricultural Produce in Ireland, in the Year 1860 [2997] HC 1862, lx, 137.

Returns of Agricultural Produce in Ireland, in the Year 1865 [3929] HC 1867, lxxi, 435.

Returns of Agricultural Produce in Ireland, in the Year 1870 [C 463] HC 1872, lxiii, 299.

Returns of Agricultural Produce in Ireland, in the Year 1871 [C 762] HC 1873, lxix, 375.

Returns of Agricultural Produce in Ireland, in the Year 1875 [C 1568] HC 1876, lxxviii, 413.

Returns of Agricultural Produce in Ireland, in the Year 1880 [C 2932] HC 1881, xciii, 685.
Returns of Agricultural Produce in Ireland, in the Year 1891 [C 6777] HC 1892, lxxxviii, 285.

Census

Census of Ireland for the Year 1851. Part I. Showing the Area, Population, and Number of Houses, by Townlands and Electoral Divisions. County and City of Dublin [1553] HC 1852–3, xli, 25.
Census Ireland for the Year 1861. Part IV. Reports and Tables Relating to the Religious Professions, Occupations and Ages of the People. Vol. 1 [C 3204] HC 1863, lix, 1.
Census of Ireland for the Year 1871. Part I., Area, Population and Number of Houses; Occupations, Religion and Education. Volume I. Province of Leinster [C 662] HC 1872, lxvii, 1.
Census of Ireland, 1891. Part 1. Area, houses, and population: also the ages, civil or conjugal condition, occupations, birthplaces, religion and education of the people. Vol. I. Province of Leinster [C 6515] HC 1890–1, xcv, 1.
Census of Ireland for the Year 1901. Accessed via www.census.national archives.ie (accessed 20 May 2020).

Dog licences

Dogs registration (Ireland). Copy of the regulations made by the Lord Lieutenant or the Treasury as to the appropriation in aid of the local county or borough cess of the sums received under the act 28 Vict. c. 50, for the registration of dogs in Ireland; and, return of the gross amount so received, and number of dogs registered in each petty sessional division during the year 1866. HC 1867–1868 (499) lv, 757.
Dogs Regulation (Ireland) Act 1865. Accounts of Receipts and Expenditure Under the Dogs Regulation (Ireland) Act 1865, For the Year Ending 31st December 1868. HC 1868–1869 (350), l, 665.
Dogs Regulation (Ireland) Act 1865. Accounts of Receipts and Expenditure Under the Dogs Regulation (Ireland) Act 1865, For the Year Ending 31st December 1869. HC 1870 (363), lvi, 757.
Dogs Regulation (Ireland) Act 1865. Accounts of Receipts and Expenditure Under the Dogs Regulation (Ireland) Act 1865, For the Year Ending 31st December 1870. HC 1871 (358), lvi, 807.
Dogs Regulation (Ireland) Act 1865. Accounts of Receipts and Expenditure Under the Dogs Regulation (Ireland) Act 1865, For the Year Ending 31st December 1871. HC 1872 (347), xlvii, 769.

Dogs Regulation (Ireland) Act 1865. Accounts of Receipts and Expenditure Under the Dogs Regulation (Ireland) Act 1865, For the Year Ending 31st December 1872. HC 1873 (262), lvi, 311.

Dogs Regulation (Ireland) Act 1865. Accounts of Receipts and Expenditure Under the Dogs Regulation (Ireland) Act 1865, For the Year Ending 31st December 1873. HC 1874 (296), lvi, 873.

Dogs Regulation (Ireland) Act 1865. Accounts of Receipts and Expenditure Under the Dogs Regulation (Ireland) Act 1865, For the Year Ending 31st December 1874. HC 1875 (347), lxiv, 41.

Dogs Regulation (Ireland) Act 1865. Accounts of Receipts and Expenditure Under the Dogs Regulation (Ireland) Act 1865, For the Year Ending 31st December 1875. HC 1876 (314), lxiii, 415.

Dogs Regulation (Ireland) Act 1865. Accounts of Receipts and Expenditure Under the Dogs Regulation (Ireland) Act 1865, For the Year Ending 31st December 1876. HC 1877 (278), lxxii, 391.

Dogs Regulation (Ireland) Act 1865. Accounts of Receipts and Expenditure Under the Dogs Regulation (Ireland) Act 1865, For the Year Ending 31st December 1877. HC 1877 (246), lxv, 151.

Dogs Regulation (Ireland) Act 1865. Accounts of Receipts and Expenditure Under the Dogs Regulation (Ireland) Act 1865, For the Year Ending 31st December 1878. HC 1878–1879 (228), lxi, 181.

Dogs Regulation (Ireland) Act 1865. Accounts of Receipts and Expenditure Under the Dogs Regulation (Ireland) Act 1865, For the Year Ending 31st December 1879. HC 1880 (199), lxii, 203.

Dogs Regulation (Ireland) Act 1865. Accounts of Receipts and Expenditure Under the Dogs Regulation (Ireland) Act 1865, For the Year Ending 31st December 1880. HC 1881 (231), lxxix, 103.

Dogs Regulation (Ireland) Act 1865. Accounts of Receipts and Expenditure Under the Dogs Regulation (Ireland) Act 1865, For the Year Ending 31st December 1896. HC 1897 (249), lxxvi, 781.

Police statistics

Number of persons taken into custody by the Dublin Metropolitan Police, and the results (1838–1840) bound with *Statistical tables of the Dublin Metropolitan Police* (1841–1918). Printed by Alexander Thom for HMSO and found in a single volume in the National Library of Ireland.

Reports of commissions and committees (in chronological order)

Second Report of the Commissioners Appointed to Consider and Recommend a General System of Railways for Ireland, [145], HC 1837–1838, xxxv, 449.

Twenty-eighth Report of the Inspectors-General on the General State of the Prisons of Ireland, 1849. With Appendices, HC 1850 [1229], xxix, 305.

Report from the Select Committee of the House of Lords, appointed to inquire into the best mode of obtaining accurate agricultural statistics from all parts of the United Kingdom; and to report thereon to the House; together with the minutes of evidence, appendix and index (501) HC 1854–55.

Report of the Select Committee on Trade in Animals; together with the proceedings of the committee (427) HC 1866.

Royal Commission on Railways in Ireland. Evidence and Papers Relating to Railways in Ireland [3607], HC 1866, lxiii, 279.

Report on the Transit of Animals from Ireland to Ports in Great Britain with an Appendix [C 2097] HC 1878.

Municipal Boundaries Commission (Ireland) Part I. Evidence with Appendices. Dublin, Rathmines, Pembroke, Kilmainham, Drumcondra, Clontarf, and also Kingstown, Blackrock, and Dalkey [C 2725] HC 1880, xxx, 327.

Report of the Royal Commissioners Appointed to Inquire into the Sewerage and Drainage of the City of Dublin and Other Matters Connected Therewith, Together with Minutes of Evidence, Appendix, Index &c. [C 2605] HC 1880, xxx, 1.

Report of the departmental committee appointed to inquire into pleuro-pneumonia and tuberculosis in the United Kingdom Part I. Report [C 5461] HC 1888, xxxii, 267, 295.

Report of the departmental committee appointed to inquire into pleuro-pneumonia and tuberculosis in the United Kingdom Part II. Minutes of Evidence and Appendix [C 5461-I] HC 1888.

Report by the Commissioners Appointed to Inquire into the Horse Breeding Industry in Ireland [C 8651] HC 1898, xxxiii, 261.

Report of the Royal Commission appointed to inquire into the administrative procedures for controlling danger to man through the use as food of the meat and milk of tuberculous animals, Part II. Minutes of Evidence and Appendices [C 8831] HC 1898, xlix, 365.

Report of the Royal Commission appointed to inquire into the administrative procedures for controlling danger to man through the use as food of the meat and milk of tuberculous animals, Part I. Report [C 8824] HC 1898, xlix, 333.

Report of the Committee Appointed for the Local Government Board for Ireland to inquire into the Public Health of the City of Dublin and Minutes of Evidence [Cd 243] HC 1900, xxxix, 681, 707.

Secondary literature

Adelman, Juliana, 'Second city of science? Dublin c.1880–1900', in Oliver Hochadel and Augustí Nieto-Galan (eds), *Urban Histories of Science* (London: Routledge, 2019), pp. 122–40.

——. 'Contagious bovine pleuropneumonia, germs and public health in Dublin 1862–1882', *Social History of Medicine*, 30:1 (2016), 71–91.

——. 'Animal knowledge: zoology and classification in nineteenth-century Dublin', *Field Day Review*, 5 (2009), 109–22.

——. 'Evolution on display: promoting Irish natural history and Darwinism at the Dublin Science and Art Museum', *British Journal for the History of Science*, 38:4 (2005), 411–36.

Almeroth-Williams, Thomas, *City of Beasts: How Animals Shaped Georgian London* (Manchester: Manchester University Press, 2019).

Anderson, Kay, 'Culture and nature at the Adelaide Zoo: at the frontiers of human geography', *Transactions of the Institute of British Geographers*, 20 (1995), 275–94.

Anderson, Virginia De John, *Creatures of Empire: How Domestic Animals Transformed Early America* (Oxford: Oxford University Press, 2004).

Atkins, P. J., 'London's intra-urban milk supply, circa 1790–1914', Transactions of the Institute of British Geographers, 2:3 (1977), 383–99.

Atkins, Peter (ed.), *Animal Cities: Beastly Urban Histories* (London: Routledge, 2012).

Baics, Gergely and Mikkele Thelle, 'Introduction: meat and the nineteenth-century city', Urban History, 45:2 (2018), 184–92.

Baratay, Eric and Elisabeth Hardouin-Fugier, *Zoo: A History of Zoological Gardens in the West* (London: Reaktion, 2004).

Bayles, Ruth, 'Understanding local science: the Belfast Natural History Society in the mid-nineteenth century', *Science and Irish Culture*, 1 (2004), 139–69.

Bayly, Christopher, *Empire and Information: Intelligence Gathering and Social Communication in India, 1780–1870* (Cambridge: Cambridge University Press, 1999).

Biehler, Dawn, 'Embodied wildlife histories and the urban landscape', *Environmental History*, 16 (2011), 445–50.

Bourke, Eoin, '"Paddy and pig": German travel writers in the "Wild West", 1828–1858', *Journal of the Galway Archaeological and Historical Society*, 53 (2001), 145–55.

——. (ed., trans.), *'Poor Green Erin': German Travel Writers' Narratives on Ireland from Before the 1798 Rising to After the Great Famine* (Oxford: Peter Lang, 2012).

Bradbury, Bettina, 'Pigs, cows, and borders: non-wage forms of survival among Montreal families', *Labour/Le Travail*, 14 (1984), 9–48.

Brady, Joseph and Anngret Simms (eds), *Dublin Through Space and Time* (Dublin: Four Courts Press, 2001).

Brantz, Dorothee, 'Animal bodies, human health, and the reform of slaughter-houses in nineteenth-century Berlin', Food & History, 3:2 (2005), 193–215.

——. (ed.), *Beastly Natures: Animals, Humans, and the Study of History* (Charlottesville: University of Virginia Press, 2010).

Breathnach, Ciara and Brian Gurrin, 'A tale of two cities—infant mortality and cause of infant death in Dublin, 1864–1910', Urban History, 44:4 (2017), 647–77.

Brown, Frederick L., *The City is More Than Human: An Animal History of Seattle* (Seattle: University of Washington Press, 2016).

Butler, Richard and Erika Hanna, 'Irish urban history: an agenda', *Urban History*, 46:1 (2019), 2–9.

Campbell, Hugh, 'The emergence of modern Dublin: reality and representation', Architectural Review Quarterly, 2 (1997), 44–53.

Cantwell, Ian, 'Anthropozoological relationships in late Medieval Dublin', Dublin Historical Record, 54:1 (2001), 73–80.

Carroll, Lydia, In the Fever King's Preserves: Sir Charles Cameron and the Dublin Slums (Dublin: A. & A. Farmar, 2011).

Casey, Christine, *Dublin: The City Within the Grand and Royal Canals and the Circular Road with the Phoenix Park* (New Haven, CT: Yale University Press, 2005).

Clare, Liam, 'The rise and demise of the Dublin cattle market', *Dublin Historical Record*, 55:2 (2002), 166–80.

Clutton-Brock, Juliet, 'The unnatural world: behavioural aspects of humans and animals in the process of domestication', in Aubrey Manning and James Serpell (eds), *Animals and Human Society: Changing Perspectives* (London: Routledge, 1994), pp. 25–35.

Clyde, Tom, *Irish Literary Magazines: An Outline History and Descriptive Bibliography* (Dublin: Irish Academic Press, 2003).

Comeford, R. V., 'Ireland 1850–1870: post-Famine and mid-Victorian', in W. E. Vaughan (ed.), *A New History of Ireland V. Ireland Under the Union 1801–1870* (Oxford: Oxford University Press, 2010 paperback edition), 372–95.

Cooke, Jim, 'John Hutton and Sons, Summerhill, Dublin, Coachbuilders, 1779–1925', *Dublin Historical Record*, 45:1 (1992), 11–27.

Corcoran, Michael, *Through Streets Broad and Narrow: A History of Dublin Trams* (Hersham: Ian Allan, 2008).

Craig, Maurice, *Dublin 1660–1860* (London: The Cressett Press, 1952).

Cronon, William, *Nature's Metropolis: Chicago and the Great West* (New York: W. W. Norton & Co., 1992).

Crosbie, Paddy, *'Your Dinner's Poured Out!'* (Dublin: O'Brien Press, 1981).

Crotty, Raymond, *When Histories Collide: The Development and Impact of Individualistic Capitalism* (Walnut Creek, CA: Alta Mira Press, 2001).

Crowley, John, Mike Murphy and William J. Smyth (eds), *Atlas of the Great Irish Famine, 1845–1852* (Cork: Cork University Press, 2012).

Cruikshank, Ken and Nancy B. Bouchier, 'Blighted areas and obnoxious industries: constructing environmental inequality on an industrial waterfront, Hamilton, Ontario, 1890–1960', Environmental History, 9:3 (2004), 464–96.

Cullen, Clara, 'The Museum of Irish Industry, Robert Kane and education for all in the Dublin of the 1850s and 1860s', *History of Education*, 38:1 (2007), 1–14.

Daly, Mary E., *Dublin, the Deposed Capital: A Social and Economic History, 1860–1914* (Cork: Cork University Press, 1984).

——. Mona Hearn and Peter Pearson, *Dublin's Victorian Houses* (Dublin: A. & A. Farmar, 1998).

D'Arcy, Fergus, 'The Dublin police strike of 1882', *Soathar*, 23 (1998), 33–44.

De Courcy, Catherine, *Dublin Zoo: An Illustrated History* (Cork: The Collins Press, 2009), 24.

Delaney, Enda, *The Great Irish Famine: A History in Four Lives* (Dublin: Gill and Macmillan, 2014).

Dickson, David, *Dublin: The Making of a Capital City* (London: Profile Books, 2014).

——. 'The state of Dublin's history', *Éire-Ireland*, 45:1&2 (2010), 198–212.

Donald, Diana, '"Beastly sights": the treatment of animals as a moral theme in representations of London, *c.* 1820–1850', *Art History*, 22:4 (1999), 514–44.

Donnelly, James S., Jr, 'Landlords and tenants', in W. E. Vaughan (ed.), *A New History of Ireland V: Ireland Under the Union 1801–70* (Oxford: Oxford University Press, paperback edn, 2010), 332–49.

Donnelly, W. J. C. and Michael L. Monaghan (eds), *A Veterinary School to Flourish: Veterinary College of Ireland, 1900–2000* (Dublin: UCD Faculty of Veterinary Medicine, 2001).

Dukova, Anastasia, *A History of the Dublin Metropolitan Police and its Colonial Legacy* (London: Palgrave Macmillan, 2016).

Durbach, Nadja, 'Roast beef, the new Poor Law, and the British nation, 1834–63', *Journal of British Studies*, 52 (2013), 963–89.

Elias, Norbert, *The Civilising Process: Sociogenetic and Psychogenetic Investigations* (trans. Edmund Jephcott) (London: Blackwell, 2000, revised edn).

Erickson, Arvel B., 'The cattle plague in England, 1865–1867', *Agricultural History*, 35 (1961) 94–103.

Evans, Richard J., *The Pursuit of Power: Europe 1815–1914* (London: Allen Lane, 2016).

Foucault, Michel, 'Governmentality', in Paul Rabinow and James D. Faubion (eds), *Power: The Essential Works of Foucault 1954–1984*, vol. 3 (New York: The New Press, 2000), pp. 201–22.

Fudge, Erica, 'A left-handed blow: writing the history of animals', in Nigel Rothfels (ed.), *Representing Animals* (Bloomington: Indiana University Press, 2002).

Galavan, Susan, *Dublin's Bourgeois Homes: Building the Victorian Suburbs, 1850–1901* (London: Routledge, 2017).

Garnham, Neal, 'The survival of popular blood sports in Victorian Ulster', *Proceedings of the Royal Irish Academy, Section C*, 107C (2007), 107–26.

Geier, Ted, *Meat Markets: The Cultural History of Bloody London* (Edinburgh: Edinburgh University Press, 2017).

Gibbons, Luke, *Limits of the Visible: Representing the Great Hunger* (Hamden, CT: Quinnipiac University Press, 2014).

Gilligan, Jim, *Graziers and Grasslands: Portrait of a Rural Meath Community, 1854–1914* (Dublin: Four Courts Press, 1998).

Gregory, James, *Of Victorians and Vegetarians: The Vegetarian Movement in Nineteenth-Century Britain* (London: I. B. Tauris, 2007).

Grew, Raymond, 'More on modernisation', *Journal of Social History*, 14:2 (1980), 179–87.

Grier, Katherine C., *Pets in America: A History* (Orland: Harcourt, Inc., 2006).

Gugliotti, Angela, 'Review essay: nature and policy in the city: environmental history and urban history', *Journal of Urban History*, 35:4 (2009), 561–70.

Guinnane, Timothy W. and Cormac Ó Grada, 'Mortality in the North Dublin Union during the Great Famine', *Economic History Review*, 55:3 (2002), 487–506.

Gunn, Simon, 'From hegemony to governmentality: changing conceptions of power in social history', *Journal of Social History*, 39:3 (2006), 705–20.

Gwynn, Stephen, 'Walter Osborne and Ireland', *Studies*, 32 (1943), 463–6.

Hamlin, Christopher, 'The rise and fall of the city as chemical system and of the chemist as urban environmental professional, 1780–1880', *Journal of Urban History*, 30 (2007), 702–28.

——. *Public Health and Social Justice in the Age of Chadwick: Britain, 1800–1854* (Cambridge: Cambridge University Press, 1998).

Hancocks, David, 'Zoo animals as entertainment exhibitions', in Randy Malamud (ed.), *A Cultural History of Animals in the Modern Age* (Oxford: Berg, 2007), pp. 95–118.

Hanna, Erika, *Modern Dublin: Urban Change and the Irish Past, 1957–1973* (Oxford: Oxford University Press, 2013).

Hardy, Anne, 'Pioneers in the Victorian provinces: veterinarians, public health, and the urban animal economy', *Urban History*, 29:3 (2002), 372–87.

Hartigan, Patrick J., 'The Royal Veterinary College of Ireland: a veterinary school to flourish', in W. J. C. Donnelly and Michael L. Monaghan (eds), *A Veterinary School to Flourish: Veterinary College of Ireland, 1900–2000* (Dublin: Faculty of Veterinary Medicine, University College Dublin, 2001), pp. 18–37.

——. 'James McKenny, principal of the Royal Veterinary College infirmary', *Irish Veterinary Journal*, 53:5 (2000) 251–8.

Howell, Philip, *At Home and Astray: The Domestic Dog in Victorian Britain* (Charlottesville: University of Virginia Press, 2015).

Ito, Takashi, *London Zoo and the Victorians, 1828–1859* (Woodbridge: Boydell and Brewer for the Royal Historical Society, 2014).

Jackson, Alvin, *Ireland, 1798–1998: War, Peace and Beyond* (Oxford: Wiley-Blackwell, 2010).

Jeffrey, Keith (ed.), *'An Irish Empire'? Aspects of Ireland and the British Empire* (Manchester: Manchester University Press, 1996).

Jones, David Seth, *Graziers, Land Reform and Political Conflict in Ireland* (Washington, DC: Catholic University of America Press, 1995).

Jones, Stefanie, 'Dublin reformed: the transformation of the municipal governance of a Victorian city, 1840–1860' (Unpublished PhD dissertation, Department of History, Trinity College Dublin, 2 vols, 2001).

Joyce, Patrick, *The Rule of Freedom: Liberalism and the Modern City* (London: Verso, 2003).

Kean, Hilda, *Animal Rights: Political and Social Change in Britain Since 1800* (London: Reaktion, 1998).

Kearns, Kevin C., *Dublin Street Life and Lore* (Dun Laoghaire: Glendale, 1991).

Kennedy, Liam and Peter Solar, *Irish Agriculture: A Price History from the Mid-Eighteenth Century to the Eve of the First World War* (Dublin: Royal Irish Academy, 2007).

Kete, Kathleen, 'Introduction', in Kathleen Kete (ed.), *A Cultural History of Animals in the Age of Empire* (Oxford: Berg Publishers, 2011), pp. 1–24.

——. 'Animals and ideology: the politics of animal protection in Europe', in Nigel Rothfels (ed.), *Representing Animals* (Bloomington: Indiana University Press, 2002), pp. 19–34.

——. *The Beast in the Boudoir: Pet Keeping in Nineteenth-Century Paris* (Berkeley: University of California Press, 1998).

——. *'La rage* and the bourgeoisie: the cultural context of rabies in the French nineteenth century', *Representations*, 22 (1988), 89–107.

Kinealy, Christine, *This Great Calamity: The Irish Famine, 1845–52* (Dublin: Gill and Macmillan, 1994).

Kishore, Raghav, 'Urban "failures": municipal governance, planning and power in urban Delhi, 1863–1910', *Indian Social and Economic History Review*, 52:4 (2015), 439–61.

Larkin, Felix, '"A great daily organ": the *Freeman's Journal* 1763–1924', *History Ireland*, 14:3 (2006), 44–9.

Latour, Bruno, *Science in Action: How to Follow Scientists and Engineers Through Society* (Cambridge, MA: Harvard University Press, 1987).

Laxton, Paul, '"This nefarious traffic": livestock and public health in mid-Victorian Edinburgh', in Peter Atkins (ed.), *Animal Cities: Beastly Urban Histories* (London: Routledge, 2012), pp. 107–72.

Lee, Joseph, *The Modernisation of Irish Society: 1848 to 1918* (Dublin: Gill and Macmillan, 1973).

Lee, Paula Young 'Hide, seek, slaughter meat: the slaughterhouse as site', Food & History, 3:2 (2005), 241–90.

——. 'The slaughterhouse and the city', Food & History, 3:2 (2005), 7–25.

——. (ed.), *Meat, Modernity, and the Rise of the Slaughterhouse* (Durham: University of New Hampshire Press, 2008).

Lockley, Olga, *Nannie Lambert Power O'Donoghue: A Biography* (Preston: The Bee Press, 2001).

Loewen, Royden, '"Come watch this spider": animals, Mennonites, and indices of modernity', Canadian Historical Review, 96:1 (2015), 61–90.

McCullen, John, *An Illustrated History of the Phoenix Park* (Dublin: Office of Public Works, 2009).

MacDonagh, Oliver, 'The age of O'Connell, 1830–45', in W. E. Vaughan (ed.), *A New History of Ireland V. Ireland Under the Union 1801–1870* (Oxford: Oxford University Press, 2010), pp. 158–68.

McGuire, James and James Quinn (eds), *Dictionary of Irish Biography* (Cambridge: Cambridge University Press), https://dib-cambridge-org.dcu.idm.oclc.org/home.do (accessed 20 May 2020).

MacLachlan, Ian, 'A bloody offal nuisance: the persistence of private slaughter-houses in nineteenth-century London', Urban History, 34:2 (2007), 227–54.

——. '*Coup de grâce*: humane cattle slaughter in nineteenth-century Britain', Food & History, 3:2 (2005), 145–71.

McNeur, Catherine, 'The "swinish multitude": controversies over hogs in antebellum New York City', Journal of Urban History, 37:5 (2011), 639–60.

Marshall, Catherine, *Monuments and Memorials of the Great Famine* (Hamden, CT: Quinnipiac University Press, 2014).

McShane, Clay and Joel A. Tarr, *The Horse in the City: Living Machines in the Nineteenth Century* (Baltimore, MD: Johns Hopkins University Press, 2007).

Mazanik, Anna, '"Shiny shoes" for the city: the public abattoir and the reform of meat supply in imperial Moscow', Urban History, 45:2 (2017), 214–32.

Melosi, Martin, 'Humans, cities and nature: how do cities fit in the material world?', Journal of Urban History, 36:1 (2010), 3–21.

——. *The Sanitary City: Urban Infrastructure in America from Colonial Times to the Present* (Pittsburgh, PA: University of Pittsburgh Press, 2008).

Miele, Kathryn, 'Horse-sense: understanding the working horse in Victorian London', Victorian Literature and Culture, 37:1 (2009), 129–40.

Miller, David and Leonard J. Hochberg, 'Modernisation and inequality in Pre-Famine Ireland: an exploratory spatial analysis', Social Science History, 31:1 (2007), 35–60.

Miller, Ian, *Reforming Food in Post-Famine Ireland: Medicine, Science, and Improvement, 1845–1922* (Manchester: Manchester University Press, 2014).

Miltenberger, Scott A., 'Viewing the anthrozootic city: humans, domesticated animals, and the making of early nineteenth-century New York', in Susan Nance (ed.), *The Historical Animal* (Syracuse, NY: Syracuse University Press, 2015), pp. 261–71.

Mizelle, Brett, *Pig* (London: Reaktion, 2011).

Mokyr, Joe, *Why Ireland Starved: A Quantitative and Analytical History of the Irish Economy, 1800–1850* (London: Allen & Unwin, 1985).

Morris, R. J., 'Voluntary societies and British urban elites, 1780–1850: an analysis', *Historical Journal*, 26 (1983), 95–118.

Mosley, Stephen, 'Common ground: integrating social and environmental history', *Journal of Social History*, 39:3 (2006), 915–33.

Mullan, Bob and Garry Marvin, *Zoo Culture: The Book About Watching People Watch Animals* (Urbana: University of Illinois Press, 1987).

Murphy, James, *Abject Loyalty: Monarchy and Nationalism in Ireland During the Reign of Queen Victoria* (Cork: Cork University Press, 2001).

Nance, Susan, *Animal Modernity: Jumbo the Elephant and the Human Dilemma* (London: Palgrave Macmillan, 2015).

——. (ed.), *The Historical Animal* (Syracuse, NY: Syracuse University Press, 2015).

Nash, Linda, 'Purity and danger: historical reflections on the regulation of environmental pollutants', *Environmental History*, 13:4 (2008), 651–8.

Nugent, Joseph, 'The human snout: pigs, priests and peasants in the parlor', *Senses & Society*, 4:3 (2009), 283–302.

O'Brien, Joseph V., *Dear, Dirty, Dublin: A City in Distress, 1899–1916* (Berkeley: University of California Press, 1982).

O'Connell, Helen, 'Animal welfare in post-Union Ireland', *New Hibernia Review*, 19:1 (2015), 34–52.

O'Donovan, John, *The Economic History of Livestock in Ireland* (Cork: Cork University Press, 1940).

Ó Grada, Cormac, *Eating People is Wrong, and Other Essays on Famine, its Past, and its Future* (Princeton, NJ: Princeton University Press, 2015).

——. *Black '47 and Beyond: The Great Irish Famine in History, Economy and Memory* (Princeton, NJ: Princeton University Press, 2000).

——. *Ireland Before and After the Famine: Explorations in Economic History, 1800–1925* (Manchester: Manchester University Press, 1988).

——. and Timothy Guinnane, 'Mortality in the North Dublin Union during the Great Famine', in Cormac Ó Grada (ed.), *Ireland's Great Famine: Interdisciplinary Perspectives* (Dublin: University College Dublin Press, 2006), pp. 86–105.

Oksala, Johanna, 'From biopower to governmentality', in Christopher Falzon, Timothy O'Leary and Jana Sawicki (eds), *A Companion to Foucault* (London: Blackwell, 2013), pp. 320–36.

Ó Maitiú, Séamus, *The Humours of Donnybrook* (Dublin: Four Courts Press, 1993).

O'Neill, Ciaran, 'Bourgeois Ireland, or, on the benefits of keeping one's hands clean', in James Kelly (ed.), *The Cambridge History of Ireland*. *Volume III 1730–1880* (Cambridge: Cambridge University Press, 2018), pp. 517–41.

O'Sullivan, Tanya, *Geographies of City Science: Urban Lives and Origin Debates in Late Victorian Dublin* (Pittsburgh, PA: University of Pittsburgh Press, 2019).

——. 'The perception of place and the "origins of handedness" debate: towards a cognitive cartography of science in nineteenth-century Dublin', *Endeavour*, 39:3–4 (2015), 139–46.

Otter, Chris, 'The vital city: public analysis, dairies and slaughterhouses in nineteenth-century Britain', *Cultural Geographies*, 13:4 (2006), 517–37.

Pearson, Chris, 'Stray dogs and the making of modern Paris', *Past and Present*, 234 (2017), 137–72.

Pemberton, Neil and Michael Worboys, *Mad Dogs and Englishmen: Rabies in Britain, 1850–2000* (London: Palgrave, 2007).

Perren, Richard, *The Meat Trade in Britain 1840–1914* (London: Routledge and Kegan Paul, 1978).

Pooley-Ebert, Andria, 'Species agency: a comparative study of horse-human relationships in Chicago and rural Illinois', in Susan Nance (ed.), *The Historical Animal* (Syracuse, NY: Syracuse University Press, 2015), pp. 148–65.

Prunty, Jacinta, *Dublin Slums 1800–1925: A Study in Urban Geography* (Dublin: Irish Academic Press, 1998).

Rains, Stephanie, *Commodity Culture and Social Class in Dublin, 1850–1916* (Dublin: Irish Academic Press, 2010).

Raymond, Raymond J., 'Dublin: The Great Famine, 1845–1860', *Dublin Historical Record*, 33:3 (1980), 98–105.

Ritvo, Harriet, *Noble Cows and Hybrid Zebras: Essays on Animals & History* (Charlottesville: University of Virginia Press, 2010).

——. 'Pride and pedigree: the evolution of the Victorian dog fancy', *Victorian Studies*, 29:2 (1986), 227–53.

——. *The Animal Estate: The English and Other Creatures in the Victorian Age* (Cambridge, MA: Harvard University Press, 1984).

Robichaud, Andrew, 'Trail of blood', Stanford University Spatial History Project (visualisations co-created with Erik Steiner). (2010) www.stanford.edu/group/spatialhistory/cgi-bin/site/pub.php?id=31 (accessed 20 May 2020).

Romano, Terrie M., 'The cattle plague of 1865 and the reception of "the germ theory" in mid-Victorian Britain', *Journal of the History of Medicine*, 52 (1997), 51–80.

Rouse, Paul, 'The farmers since 1850', in Eugenio F. Biagini and Mary E. Daly (eds), *The Cambridge Social History of Modern Ireland* (Cambridge: Cambridge University Press, 2017), pp. 129–44.

Ross, Dorothy, 'AHR Roundtable: American modernities, past and present', *American Historical Review*, 116:3 (2011), 702–14.

Rothfels, Nigel, 'Immersed with animals', in Nigel Rothfels (ed.), *Representing Animals* (Indianapolis: Indiana University Press, 2002), pp. 199–224.

Santoyo, Antonio, 'De cerdos y de civilidad urbana. La descalificación de las atividades de la explotación porcina en la ciudad de Mexico durante el último tercio del siglo xix', *Historia Mexicana*, 47:1 (1997), 69–102.

Scola, Richard, *Feeding the Victorian City: The Food Supply of Manchester, 1770–1870* (Manchester: Manchester University Press, 1992).

Sheehy, Jeanne, *Walter Osborne* (Ballycotton: Gifford and Craven, 1974).

Smyth, William J., 'The province of Leinster and the Great Famine', in John Crowley, William J. Smyth and Mike Cronin (eds), *Atlas of the Great Irish Famine* (Cork: Cork University Press, 2012), 325–33.

Solar, Peter, 'Shipping and economic development in nineteenth-century Ireland', *Economic History Review*, 59:4 (2006), 717–42.

Stearns, Peter N., 'Modernisation and social history some suggestions and a muted cheer', *Journal of Social History*, 14:2 (1980), 189–209.

Stephenson, Bruce, 'Review essay: urban environmental history: the essence of a contradiction', *Journal of Urban History*, 31:6 (2005), 887–98.

Strickland, Walter G., *A Dictionary of Irish Artists* (Dublin: Maunsel and Company, 1913).

Swart, Sandra, *Riding High: Horses, Humans and History in South Africa* (Johannesburg: Wits University Press, 2010).

Tague, Ingrid, *Animal Companions: Pets and Social Change in Eighteenth-Century Britain* (State College: Pennsylvania State University Press, 2005).

Takagami, Shin-Ichi, 'The Fenian Rising in Dublin, March 1867', *Irish Historical Studies*, 29:115 (1995), 340–62.

Thomas, Keith, *Man and the Natural World: Changing Attitudes in England 1500–1800* (London: Penguin, 1984).

Thompson, F. M. L., 'Nineteenth-century horse sense', *Economic History Review*, 29:1 (1976), 60–81.

Tilley, Elizabeth, 'Trading in knowledge: the *Irish Builder* and nineteenth-century journalism', *Revue LISA/LISA e-journal*, 3:1 (2005), 110–20.

Turvey, Ralph, 'Horse traction in Victorian London', *Journal of Transport History*, 26:2 (2005), 38–59.

Vaughan, W. E., 'Ireland c. 1870', in W. E. Vaughan (ed.), *A New History of Ireland V. Ireland Under the Union 1801–1870* (Oxford: Oxford University Press, 2010), pp. 726–800.

Velten, Hannah, *Beastly London: A History of Animals in the City* (London: Reaktion, 2013).

Waddington, Keir, *The Bovine Scourge: Meat, Tuberculosis and Public Health, 1850–1914* (Woodbridge: The Boydell Press, 2006).

Wallace, Ciaran, 'Civil society in search of a state: Dublin 1898–1912', *Urban History*, 45:3 (2018), 426–52.

Whelan, Yvonne, *Reinventing Modern Dublin: Streetscapes, Iconography and the Politics of Identity* (Dublin: University College Dublin Press, 2003).

Woodham-Smith, Cecil, *The Great Hunger: Ireland 1845–1849* (London: Hamish Hamilton, 1962).

Worboys, Michael, *Spreading Germs: Disease Theories and Medical Practice in Britain, 1865–1900* (Cambridge: Cambridge University Press, 2000).

Index

Note: all street names refer to Dublin unless otherwise specified. Illustrations indicated by italics.

Abell, Joshua 49
Act of Union 26, 50, 137, 139
Act to Consolidate and Amend the Several Laws Relating to Cruel and Improper Treatment of Animals (1835) 40, 46
Aldridge, John 69–76, 204–5
Almeroth-Williams, Thomas 5, 8
America 113, 128, 174
    cities in 5, 13, 131, 148, 181
Amiens Street (Connolly) Station 109
Andrews, Tod 187–8
Annesley Bridge 40
Antisell, Thomas 75–6
Apothecaries Hall 70
Ardee Street 149
Arran Quay Ward 105, 112–14, 116, 203
Association for Promoting Rational Humanity Towards the Animal Creation 40
Association for the Suppression of Mendicity of Dublin 69
Athlone 109, 112
Atkins, Peter 5
Aughrim Street 113–116, *115*

bacon-curing 4, 16, 80, 102, 129, 143, 146
Ballinasloe Market 104

Barrington, William 177–8
Battersea Dog's Home 144–5
Belfast 35, 37, 48–9, 109, 137, 175
Birmingham 109, 130
Blackhall Place 102
Borough, Sir Edward 73
Boston 174
Boyle, James 154, 156, 182
Branagan, Charles 96
Brantz, Dorothee 2
Britain 13, 26, 28, 50, 84, 104–5, 109, 118, 137, 139, 143, 147, 153, 159, 168, 202
British Empire 28, 201
Broadstone Station 109
Brocas, Samuel 2, 16, *81*
Brown, Frederick L. 5, 7, 8
Bull Alley 11
Burton, Decimus 31–2
Butt, Isaac 33–4, 42

Cabra 40, 96
Camden Street 101
Cameron, Charles 99, 100, 155, 180, 185, 187, 188, 190–2, 204–5
Carleton, William 65, 80
Carlyle, Thomas 52, 64
Carman, Thomas 40
Catholic Emancipation 14, 26, 27

cattle
cruelty to 26, 38–41, 49, 51,
100
dairy 188–91
manure of 77, 83, 95, 100, 116,
182–4, 186, 190
market 11, 14–16, 41, 110–12
'new' Dublin market (1863) 91,
100–7, *105*, 113–19, 170,
182, 185, 200–4
plague 100, 116–18
railway transport of 66, 109–12
shows 71–2
Chadwick, Edwin 73, 189
Chamber Street 146
Chicago 5, 113
Circular Road 15, 104, 114, 115,
185
city analyst 98, 99, 147, 153, 155,
185
City of Dublin Steam Packet
Company 66, 109
Clanbrassil Street 154
Clarendon Street 102
Clontarf 176
Clutton-Brock, Juliet 204–5
Cole's Lane 98, 103
College Green 22, 46, 103, 188
Collins, Anna Maria 141–3
Commissioners of Police 43–4, 155
Connacht 51, 106, 108 (table)
Coolock 179
Cork 109
corporations (municipal) 14, 26, 28,
73, 92
Crampton, Philip 33, 42, 47–8,
135
Cronon, William 5
Cross-Guns Road 41
Cullen, Paul (Archbishop of Dublin)
117

dairy yards 11–12, 77–8, 117, 170,
181–92
Daly, Mary E. 6
de Beauvoir, Sir John 40, 43–4, 49
Dickson, David 6

dogs
butchers' 95, 137
cruelty to 28, 39–40, 48, 50–1
hunting with 47–8
licensing of 137–42, 158
shows of 129–36
Dolphin's Barn 41
Donnybrook Fair 34, 40–3, *45*, 47
Dorset Street 36
Doyle, Denis 93–9, 101–2, 104
Drumcondra 40, 176
Dublin Castle 118, 127, 172
Dublin Corporation 6, 11, 47, 73,
74, 76–7, 82, 92–6, 98, 99,
101–5, 112, 116, 118,
143–57, 168–9, 178, 180,
181, 184–9, 199, 200, 203
Dublin Improvement Act (1849) 14,
92, 93, 95, 111, 151
Dublin Metropolitan Police 10, 14,
44, 47, 74, 82, 93, 94, 96, 99,
119, 127–9, 136, 142, 144,
145, 147, 151–2, 155–9, 200
Dublin Penny Journal 30–2, 34–5
Dublin Sanatory Association
(founded 1848) 73, 82, 150
Dublin Sanitary Association
(founded 1872) 149, 150–1,
182, 186
Dublin Society for the Prevention
of Cruelty to Animals (DSPCA)
10, 22–8, 33, 38–9, 40–9, 51,
144, 204
Dublin Statistical and Social Inquiry
Society 73
Dublin University Magazine 31, 33–4,
36, 135
Dublin Victuallers' Association
185–6

Elly, Sandham 72, 79
Engels, Friedrich 148
England
early modern 3, 63
Victorian 5, 8, 25, 39, 49, 50–1,
66, 72–3, 76, 104, 106,
117–18, 129, 139, 143–4, 186

English Kennel Club 132
Ennis, John (MP) 112

Fenians 139, 159
Field, William 186
Fitzpatrick, Thomas 168, *169*, 170, 190, *191*
Fitzwilliam Square 150
Food and Drug Act (1862) 100
Foucault, Michel 9, 92
Freeman's Journal 33, 35, 65, 69, 71–2, 97, 102, 118, 130, 132–3, 136, 141, 143, 149
Fudge, Erica 9

Galavan, Susan 6
Galway 39, 109, 168
Garryowen (red setter) 133–4
Glasnevin 40, 52, 176
Grattan, Henry 139
Gray, John 103
Great Britain Street (Parnell Street) 96
Great Famine (1845–50) 10, 14, 52, 62–84, 91–2, 95, 105–6, 112, 117, 149
    Dublin General Relief Committee 65
Green Hills 139, 159
Grimshaw, Thomas Wrigley 149
Guinness, Arthur E. 149
Guinness Brewery 172
Guinness, Robert 48

Hall, Fanny 82
Hamilton, Edwin, [W. Ridley Thacker] 168, 170–1
    Ballymuckbeg 168, 182, 189, 192
Hamilton, William Tighe 34
Hammond Lane 40
Hardy, Philip Dixon 34
Hart, John 101
Haughton, James 70–1
Haughton, Samuel 9
Hemans, George Willoughby 111
Hennessy, Henry 183
Hogan, William 76

Holyhead 109, 116
Home Rule 33, 168
horses
    cruelty to 22–3, 25, 27–9, 38–47, *44, 45*
    manure of 77, 83, 181, 184
    portraits of 134
    riding of 171–3, 192
    showing of 147, 173
    use as food 71, 78
    use in street scavenging 180–1
    see also trams
Hutton, John 24, 174

India 68
Inglis, Henry 42, 44, 71
Inn's Quay Ward 16
Irish Farmer's Gazette 67, 72, 146
Irish Harness Horse Society 174
Irish Kennel Club 134
Irish Sportsman 25, 133
Irish Times 130, 133, 142

Jameson, John 116
James's Street 149
Jervis Street 40

Kearns, Kevin C. 199
Kete, Kathleen 48
Kingsbridge (Heuston) Station 109
Kingstown 24, 66, 137
Knox, Harry Blake 132–3, 145
Koch, Robert 188

Leeds 130
Leinster 45, 104–9, 108 (table) 113, 118–19, 174, 186
The Lepracaun 168, *169*
Liffey (river) 15–16, 110, 113, 183, 189
Liverpool 31, 62, 66, 104, 109, 116, 131, 174–5, 190
London 5, 8, 14, 26–7, 31, 37, 39–42, 45, 48–9, 95, 105, 117, 127, 129, 130–1, 143–4, 148–9, 158, 172, 174, 175, 176, 187–8

Lord Lieutenant of Ireland 23, 29,
    95, 118, 124, 130
Lord Mayor
    Mansion house 27, 49
    of Dublin 29, 47, 71, 93, 113,
       118, 179

Maberly, Catherine 64
Maclean's Lane 149
McShane, Clay 5
Manchester 109, 130, 176
Mapother, Dr Edward 100
Marsh, Dr Henry 172
Martin, Richard 27, 39, 48
Mary's Lane, 149
Meath (county) 104, 113
Meath Hospital 141
medical officers of health 100, 153,
    155, 185, 190
Merrion Square 135
Moore, Dr Frederick 183–4
Moore, George 172
Moore, Major William 40, 45–9
Moore Street 16
Mosley, Stephen 4
Munster 106, 108 (table)
Murray, Rev Dr Daniel 49

Nance, Susan 7
The Nation 65–8, 72, 117
nationalism 6, 10, 14, 23, 27–8, 33,
    39, 49, 51, 65, 72, 79, 103,
    117–18, 139, 159, 170, 179,
    186
Neville, Park 179
New York City 77, 127, 129, 148,
    158
Nicholas Street 41
North Circular Road 104, 114, *115*,
    185
North Earl Street 93–4
North Frederick Street 41
North Wall 66, 104, 110–13,
    116
Nugent, James 65, 116
nuisances 76, 82, 92, 94, 96, 189
    dog 127–8, 143–5

inspection of 74, 92, 99, 149,
    154, 156, 187
pig 77, 82–3, 147, 149, 151–4,
    157
slaughterhouse 94, 96, 100, 102,
    119
Nuisances Removal and Disease
    Prevention Act (1848) 74

O'Brien, Peter 172
O'Connell, Daniel 26, 28, 33, 47–9,
    70, *79*
O'Connell, Helen 27
O'Connell, Maurice J. 48
O'Connell Street: *see* Sackville Street
O'Donoghue, Mrs. Nannie Lambert
    Power 171, 173, 192
omnibuses 16, 41, 129, 130,
    175–7, 191
O'Neill, Ciaran 159
Ordnance Survey of Ireland 114,
    115
Ormond Market 16
Ormond Quay 103
Osborne, Walter *97*, 134
Otway, Caesar 38–9

Paddy Kelly's Budget 35–6
Paris 5, 37, 52, 127, 129, 143, 158,
    176
Paving and Lighting Board 73, 92
Paving and Lighting Committee 180
Peel, Sir Robert (1822–95) 128,
    142
Pembroke 137, 176
Phoenix Park 29, 40, 42, *43*, 176
pigs
    compared to poor humans 62–8,
       72, 78–9
    keeping of 74, 77–83, 111,
       128–9, 145–59, 181–4,
       187–9, 192, 199–203
    market 157–8, 181
    meat of 101–2
    personality of 79–80, 168–9, 171
    railway transport of 112
Pim, Frederic 182

Pipe Water Board 92
Poor Law 26, 46–7, 67, 69, 151,
    155, 184–5
  Boards of Guardians 47, 74
  North Dublin Union 117
Practical Agricultural Association
    75
Prospect Street 41
Prunty, Jacinta 6
Prussia Street 105, 113–16, *115*
Public Health Act
    (1874) 14, 151
    (1878) 14, 151, 153, 182, 184
Public Health Committee 151, 153

Quakers 49, 69
Queen Victoria 24, 28, 48, 174

railways 4, 14, 66, 104, 109–13,
    142, 168, 174, 176, 178, 186
  commissions on 109, 112
  Dublin and Drogheda Railway
    109
  Great Southern & Western
    Railway 109
  Midland & Great Western Railway
    Company 66, 109, 112
Rathgar 141
Rathmines 40, 137, 141, 176
Red Cow Lane 41
Repeal, movement for 26, 47–51
  Loyal National Repeal Association
    49
Reynolds, John 103, 110
Reynolds, Lawrence 116
Richardson, H. D. 80
Riley, Jimmy 199, 200–1, 203
Ritvo, Harriet 5, 7, 28
Rothe, Mr. (of the SPCA) 40–1, 45
Rotunda Hospital 130
Royal Agricultural Improvement
    Society 130, 147
Royal Barracks 73
Royal College of Physicians of
    Ireland 183
Royal College of Surgeons of Ireland
    48, 100, 183

Royal Dublin Society 70–2, 78, 132,
    147, 173
Royal Society for the Prevention
    of Cruelty to Animals
    (RSPCA) 26–7, 39, 40, 43,
    48–9
Russell, Lord John (Prime Minister)
    68, 118

Sackville (O'Connell) Street 2, 15,
    16, 24, 29, 41, 130, 176
St Stephen's Green 192
sanitation 4, 72–4, 76–7, 80–3,
    94, 96, 99, 119, 127, 129,
    145–59, 170, 181–92
Sanitary Act (Ireland) 1866 147,
    151, 154
Scharff, Robert 132
Scotland 104, 143
Sheil, Richard Lalor 26
Ship Street 40
Smithfield Market 11, *13*, 96, 103,
    105, 110–14, 146, 157–8,
    181, 203–4
South City Ward 16
Soyer, Alexis 68–9
Speedy, Dr Albert 183, 190
steam shipping 41, 66, 104–6, 109,
    111, 113
Stokes, Whitley 1–2, 4, 9, 202,
    204–5
Stokes, William 149
Stoneybatter 11
Sullivan, William K. 91

Tallerman, Daniel J. 186
Tarr, Joel 5
Thacker, W. Ridley: *see* Hamilton,
    Edwin
Thomas, Keith 3, 7–8, 63, 200
Thomas Street 41, 102
Thompson, Frances Maria 39–40,
    43–4, 47
Townsend Street 16, 82
trams
  Dublin United Tramways 178
  electric 173

trams (*cont.*)
  horse 4, 10, 14, 16, 129, 142,
    174–80, *176*, 191–2
  South Dublin Street Tramways
    179
  steam 173, 178–9
Trinity College 82, *177*
Trinity Ward 101
tuberculosis 37, 188–91

Ulster 106, 108 (table) 174
unionism 23, 27–8, 33
United Kingdom 14, 23, 27, 73,
    104, 118, 129, 181, 188–9
Urwick, Rev Dr William 48–9

Velten, Hannah 5

Watling Street 16
West, Mrs Frederick 43–4

Westmoreland Street 15
Whatley, Richard 78
Wide Streets Commissioners 73, 92
William Street 73
workhouse 46, 62–3, 67
  North Dublin Union 69

zoological gardens
  Dublin 11, 22–41, 52, 69, 137,
    201–2, 204
  Liverpool 31
  London 27, 31, 37
  Paris 37
zoological society
  Dublin 1, 3, 10, 13, 22–3, 26–39,
    43, 47–8, 51–2, 71, 73, 78,
    201
  London 27, 31
Zoz 134, *138*